THE CONDITIONS
OF LEARNING

THE CONDITIONS
OF LEARNING

Robert M. Gagné
Director of Research
American Institute for Research

HOLT, RINEHART AND WINSTON, INC.
NEW YORK   CHICAGO   SAN FRANCISCO   TORONTO   LONDON

90123 40 9

Copyright © 1965 by Holt, Rinehart and Winston, Inc.
All Rights Reserved
Library of Congress Catalog Card Number: 65-12799

2502854

Printed in the United States of America

PREFACE

ON A NUMBER OF OCCASIONS during a considerable period of years, various professional people interested in educational improvement have asked me what is known about the process of learning that can be put to use in designing better education. I have given them various answers. While these were certainly not entirely consistent in terminology, I hope they were somewhat congruent in their main themes. This book is simply a latest attempt to answer the question in a fairly comprehensive fashion.

It will be evident that I do not think learning is a phenomenon which can be explained by simple theories, despite the admitted intellectual appeal that such theories have. Although many people, including me, have tried for years to account for actual instances of learning in terms of a small number of principles, I am currently convinced that it cannot be done. To the person who is interested in knowing what principles of learning apply to education, my reply is: The question must be asked and answered with consideration of what kind of capability is being learned. The answer is different depending on the particular class of performance change that is the focus of interest. There are no "general" rules of learning known at present that can be used as guides in designing instruction.

There are, however, a number of useful generalizations that can be made about several distinguishable classes of performance change (learning), of which I think there are at least eight. These principles are described in this book as the conditions of learning.

Psychologists of the experimental persuasion will doubtless

note that I have tried to cite the results of experiments on learning when these are relevant. At the same time, it will be quite evident that the point of view adopted for the purposes of this book is not one of interpreting the findings of learning studies. Quite the reverse is true, for I have instead asked the question, What are the dimensions of learning phenomena which need to be studied experimentally?

In general, the descriptions of learning conditions are derived from observations, either my own or those of other investigators. Some are undoubtedly more reliable than others, depending on how often they have been repeated under comparable conditions. As for theory, the book says little about it. If the outlines of a theory are identifiable, surely the latter must consist of the idea that complex forms of learning require simpler forms of behavior as prerequisites. As a generalization, this is certainly not novel. Perhaps, though, an articulate theory of learning might someday be based upon it.

Robert M. Gagné

Pittsburgh, Pennsylvania
November, 1964

CONTENTS

THE CONDITIONS
OF LEARNING

INTRODUCTION | 1

FEW THINGS are so intriguing to wonder about as the development of human behavior. The adult human being becomes a marvelously adaptable, competently functioning person within a complex society. How he progresses to this point from a beginning as a highly dependent, relatively noncapable, newborn infant is a question of great intellectual interest and importance. One part of the answer to this question, to be sure, lies in an understanding of the processes of growth and development, characteristic properties shared by all living things. The other part, relating to a different set of circumstances in the life of the individual, is learning. The human skills, appreciations, and reasonings in all their great variety, as well as human hopes, aspirations, attitudes, and values, are generally recognized to depend for their development largely on the events called learning.

One may, if one wishes, cease to wonder about learning at this point, having confirmed to one's own satisfaction that human development in all its manifestations must depend on the twin factors of growth and learning and their interactions with each other. One can say about a child, "He'll learn," just as one says "He'll grow into it (or out of it)," and such a statement is difficult to deny. But to equate learning and growth as natural events is to overlook the one most important difference between them. The factors that influence growth are to a very large extent genetically determined, whereas the factors that influence learning are chiefly determined by events in the individual's living environment. Once the individual's genetic stock has been chosen at the moment of conception, his growth cannot be altered very much, except by rather extreme measures. But members of the human society, which itself is responsible for the care of a developing person, have a tremendous degree of control over those events that affect his learning. Experience, we are told, is the great teacher. This means that the events the developing individual lives through—in his home, in his geographical environment, in school, and in his various social environments—will determine what he learns and therefore to a large extent what kind of person he becomes.

This enormous dependence of learning on environmental circumstances implies a great responsibility for all members of human society. The situations in which the developing child is placed, whether deliberately or otherwise, are going to have great effects on him. In fact, there is not a very clear understanding at present of what the limits of these effects may be. Are the situations in which the growing person is nowadays customarily placed the sort that will encourage the development of disciplined thinkers, of great artists and scientists? Or are they such as will discourage such development and inhibit the full exploitation of human thought and intellect?

The realization that learning is largely dependent on events in the environment with which the individual interacts makes it possible to view learning as an occurrence that can be examined more closely and understood more profoundly. Learning is not simply an event that happens naturally; it is also an event that happens under certain observable conditions. Furthermore, these conditions can be altered and controlled; and this leads to the possibility of examining the occurrence of learning by means of the methods of science. It becomes possible to observe the conditions under which learning takes place, and to describe them in objective language. It is possible to detect relationships between these conditions and the changes in human behavior that occur in learning, and thus to make inferences about what has been learned. It is also possible to construct scientific models and theories to account for the changes observed, just as it is with other types of natural events.

LEARNING AND ITS CONDITIONS

This book is about the *conditions of learning*. It attempts to consider the sets of circumstances that obtain when learning occurs, that is, when certain observable changes in human behavior take place that justify the inference of learning. It will deal with a number of varieties of these changes, and accordingly with a number of relationships between them and the situations in which they occur. It will stop short of a theory of learning, although the raw materials from which one or more theories may be constructed will hopefully become apparent. Its major concern is to find a reasonable answer to the question, What is learning? This answer is to be phrased mainly in terms of an objective description of the conditions under which learning takes place. These conditions will be identified, first of all, by reference to the situations of ordinary life, including those of the school, in which learning occurs. Their identification will also be aided in certain instances by reference to experiments from the psychological laboratory.

Learning is a change in human disposition or capability, which can be retained, and which is not simply ascribable to the process of growth. The kind of change called learning exhibits itself as a change in behavior, and the inference of learning is made by comparing what behavior was possible before the individual was placed in a "learning situation" and what behavior can be exhibited after such treatment. The change may be, and often is, an increased capability for some type of performance. It may also be an altered disposition of the sort called "attitude," or "interest," or "value." The change must have more than momentary permanence; it must be capable of being retained over some period of time. Finally, it must be distinguishable from the kind of change that is attributable to growth, such as a change in height or the development of muscles through exercise.

THE ELEMENTS OF THE LEARNING EVENT

On one and the same day, a child may learn to tie his shoelaces and may also learn to call the mailman by his name, "Mr. Wells." Somehow, the events in the child's environment, whether deliberately arranged or not, conspire to bring about these changes in his performance. The changes are also in his capabilities, as shown by the fact that he can now tie his shoelaces or call the mailman "Mr. Wells" any time he is asked to. What are the elements in either or both situations that can be abstracted as having to do with learning?

1. First, there is a *learner*, who is a human being. (It would be possible for the learner to be an animal, but that is another story.) For the events considered here the most important parts of the learner are his senses, his central nervous system, and his muscles. Events in his environment affect the learner's senses, and start chains of nervous impulses that are organized by his central nervous system, specifically, by his brain. This nervous activity occurs in certain sequences and patterns that alter the nature of the organizing process itself, and this effect is exhibited as learning. Finally, the nervous activity is translated into action that may be observed as the movement of muscles in executing responses of various sorts.

2. The events that stimulate the learner's senses are spoken of collectively as the *stimulus situation*. When a single event is being distinguished, it is often called a *stimulus*.

3. The action that results from stimulation and subsequent nervous activity is called a *response*. Responses may be described more or less specifically; for example, one can speak of the movement of a particular muscle, or of the action of the whole body in walking. For this reason and others, responses are often described in terms of their effects rather than in terms of their appearances. When so classified, they are called *performances*. For example, a response might be "moving the finger rhythmically over a small area of the scalp." But it may often be more useful to refer to the performance of "scratching the head."

A learning event, then, takes place when the *stimulus situation* affects the learner in such a way that his *performance* changes from a time *before* being in that situation to a time *after* being in it. The *change in performance* is what leads to the conclusion that learning has occurred.

At the level of general description, the child's learning to tie his shoelaces came about in the following way. Before the learning, his performance was such that he could not tie his shoelaces. (Perhaps he could do certain parts of this performance, but not the whole thing.) Then a stimulus situation was introduced, which may have included a parent who used verbal communication to get the child to make certain responses. Still another kind of stimulus that may have been employed is a picture or drawing. At any rate, a sequence of stimulus events was made to occur. At the end of this sequence, the child succeeded in producing a tied shoelace (much to his satisfaction, no doubt). The parent then verified to himself, and to the child, that learning had taken place by asking the child to tie the lace on his other shoe. The performance was again exhibited successfully, and the inference was made that learning had taken place. It had produced in the child a new *capability*.

Learning to call the mailman "Mr. Wells" likewise involves these same elements. The child's initial performance indicates that he does not say "Mr. Wells" when he sees the mailman, but perhaps calls him "man," or simply points to him. Assuming that the child has a certain verbal facility by this age, the stimulus situation might be as simple as the statement by a parent "That's Mr. Wells." The child then makes the response "Mr. Wells." When the mailman is next seen again, the child once more exhibits the performance, saying "Mr. Wells." At this point, one concludes that the child has learned; his performance has undergone a change; he has acquired a new capability.

Each of these examples is somewhat oversimplified, of course. But the framework for the events of learning exhibits a constant set of elements. As our discussion of the *conditions* of learning proceeds, there will be many occasions that call for reference to these elements of the learning event.

What is the nature of new capabilities established by learning? It should be recognized that there are as many different kinds of capabilities as there are performances. But there are also different levels of complexity of these capabilities. With the simplest kind of learning that can be observed or even imagined, there is an unvarying relation between the stimulus and the response. The learning change is from:

$$\text{Stimulus} \rightarrow (\text{nothing})$$
$$\text{to}$$
$$\text{Stimulus} \rightarrow \text{Response.}$$

This basic kind of learned capability is called an *association*. Suppose a child of suitable maturity does not originally respond when the parent says "Smile!" Following a suitable learning situation, he now *does* smile invariably to the same spoken stimulus. One can say he has acquired an association. If an adult who previously could not supply the English word "horse" for the French word "cheval" now does so, it is similarly appropriate to call this newly learned capability an association. There will be many references to learned associations in the following pages. It will also be seen that the learning of *single* associations is a rare event. Most investigators of learning, however, are of the opinion that the association is the simplest form of learned capability, and also that it constitutes a fundamental "building block" for other more complex performances. This trend of thinking can clearly be seen in the development of ideas about learning in American psychology.

LEARNING IN AMERICAN PSYCHOLOGY

How people learn, and the conditions under which they learn, are questions that have been investigated by several generations of American psychologists, as well as by those in other parts of the world. But learning has always been a favorite problem for American writers and researchers, partly no doubt because of a philosophical tradition that tended to place great emphasis on experience as a determiner of knowledge. It is of some value, therefore, to spend a little time in describing what these historically important ideas about the nature of learning have been, since they will point the way to the influences that have shaped current learning theory, and that will undoubtedly affect future developments as well.

Research on learning has generated several typical "models," or *prototypes*, which are frequently referred to by writers on the subject. There are the conditioned response, trial-and-error learning, insight, and others, which are often used to communicate basic similarities and contrasts among situations in which learning occurs. It is important for an understanding of the varieties of learning, as discussed in subsequent chapters, to become acquainted with these prototypes of learning and the situations in which they have typically been observed.

THE ASSOCIATIONIST TRADITION

One of the oldest lines of thinking about learning in American psychology derives from the British associationist psychologists, who formulated a number of theories about how ideas are associated. These theorists were primarily concerned with the question of how complex ideas like "flower" or "number" are constructed in the human mind from elementary sense impressions. In other words, they were interested in the question of how such "complex ideas" were learned in the first place. On this latter point, they were generally agreed that acquiring a new idea necessitated (1) *contiguity* of the sense impressions or simple ideas that were to be combined to form the new idea, and (2) *repetition* of these contiguous events. Some of these psychologists also discussed "mental concentration" (which is now usually called attention) as an important condition for the learning of new ideas by association (Mill, 1869).

American psychologists like William James and John Dewey added some distinctly new interpretations to this associationist tradition. The ideas of Darwin concerning the functions of living phenomena in adaptation exerted a considerable influence on these American scholars. Accordingly, they sought to discover the *functions* of behavioral events like learning and thinking, rather than simply the composition of these events. A most important characteristic of learning was considered to be its function in the life of the organism. This view led them to place the *nervous system,* rather than "the mind" in a position of central importance to an understanding of how sense impressions get connected with behavior. And perhaps most significant of all, they assigned a critical role to *action* as a factor in learning. Action did not simply follow ideas, as the British associationists had proposed, but became an essential feature of the process of behavioral organization called learning.

ANIMAL TRIAL AND ERROR

Another direction taken by American psychology in its treatment of learning established perhaps the most important trend of all. This was the use of animals for the performance of experiments on learning. Edward L. Thorndike (1898) was a pioneer in these efforts to understand the learning of animals by performing experiments rather than by collecting anecdotes about animal behavior. From his controlled observations of cats, dogs, and chickens escaping from problem boxes, he concluded that many previous accounts of animal thought were erroneous in that they attributed greater power to animal intelligence than actually existed. His investigations suggested the possibility that all that was necessary to explain animal learning were specific bonds between "sense impressions" and "impulses to action." These associations he considered to be stamped in by the consequences resulting from the completed act (such as escape from the problem box). Thorndike believed that associations of this sort also made up a large part, although not all, of what human beings learned and remembered.

A hungry animal, such as a cat, is placed in a box with slatted sides and a door that can be opened by pressing a wooden lever to release a latch, allowing the animal to reach food placed within his view outside the box. At first, the cat is observed to engage in a variety of acts, including scratching at the sides and door of the box. Sooner or later, these various activities lead by chance to the depression of the latch that opens the door. The animal then immediately leaves the box and eats the bit of food. When placed in the box again, the animal's behavior is obviously changed. He spends less time scratching at the sides of the box, and more time making movements in the region of the latch. On this second trial, it takes him much less time to release the latch and get to the food. Subsequent trials reduce the time still more, until he is releasing the latch only a few seconds after he is placed in the box.

The view of learning that is represented by this prototype situation may be described briefly as follows. When confronted with a novel situation, the motivated learner engages in various "tries" to attain satisfaction. Sooner or later, largely by chance, he makes a set of responses that lead to motive satisfaction. The particular responses that are immediately followed by motive satisfaction (eating the food, in this case) become "stronger" in relation to others. Thus, when the animal is placed in the box a second time, the latch-pressing responses occur sooner, whereas the other responses (like scratching the floor of the box) tend to be shorter in duration or entirely absent. On subsequent trials in the box, these "errors" progressively weaken and disappear. The correct responses, in contrast, are progressively strengthened by being followed immediately by motive satisfaction. This generalization was called the "law of effect" by Thorndike. The learning situation does not differ in basic characteristics from that of the rat pressing a lever, employed later by Skinner (1938). "Reinforcement" is the term Skinner uses to identify the events that Thorndike called the law of effect.

Is the animal trial-and-error prototype representative of human learning? The answer is clearly in the negative. It is, in fact, rather difficult to relate it to the learning that might occur in a human being. If a person is put in a problem box, we know that he is likely to adopt a strategy of searching for a way out. He recognizes latches, knobs, or other devices as having certain functions. He "thinks out" the consequences of his actions before he takes them, and chooses the most likely alternative. Once he finds his way out, he will under most circumstances remember it, and there will be no gradual error reduction on subsequent trials. How can such behavior be in any sense comparable to "trial-and-error"? The strategies, the recalling, the recognizing, the thinking, the choosing are all there in his behavior; they can readily be observed if the proper experimental conditions are provided.

By searching hard, one can probably find some degree of

comparability between the trial-and-error prototype and the acquisition of a motor skill by young children, such as balancing blocks, making a simple knot, or learning language sounds. Insofar as the prototype helps us to understand such learning, it is useful. But this is, of course, an extremely circumscribed usefulness for the field of learning in general.

A number of more modern learning theorists have made the individual association, as seen in animal behavior, the basis of their ideas on learning. Among these are Edwin R. Guthrie (1935), Clark L. Hull (1943), and B. F. Skinner (1938), each of whom has proposed somewhat different interpretations of the basic idea that the *association*, as observed in animal learning of simple acts, is the typical form of learning. Other investigators of animal learning opposed this tradition, however. Chief among these was Edward C. Tolman (1932), whose experiments convinced him that Thorndike and those who followed him were wrong in asserting that nothing but an "association" existed between a situation and the response that followed it. Tolman's theory maintains that association is an internal matter, between a representation (within the animal's nervous system) of the stimulus situation, and a representation of the alternatives of action to be taken. He thus attempted to restore to animal behavior the "ideas" (although this was not his term) that had been considered unnecessary by Thorndike.

THE CONDITIONED RESPONSE

I. P. Pavlov (1927) found that when a signal such as a buzzer was sounded at the time food was shown to a hungry dog, and this set of events was repeated several times, the dog came to salivate at the sound of the buzzer alone. Whereas the salivation at the sight of food could be considered a natural (or unconditioned) response, salivation to a buzzer had to be acquired as a conditioned response. This learning occurred when the new signal (the buzzer) was presented together with the food in a number of trials. A new signal-response connection was thereby established.

John B. Watson (1919) championed the view of learning suggested by the work of Pavlov in his studies of conditioning in dogs. In Watson's writings, learning was viewed as a matter of establishing individual associations (conditioned responses) firmly based in the nervous system. More complex human acts were considered to be chains of conditioned responses.

Most investigators of Pavlovian conditioning now believe it to be a very special kind of learning, representative of the establishment of *involuntary*, "anticipatory" responses such as the startled eyeblinking that may follow a threatening gesture (Kimble, 1961). It is likely, of course, that human beings acquire many conditioned responses of this sort in the course of their lives. One may find oneself, for example, waking with a start at the slight click the alarm clock makes before it actually rings. Hearing an automobile horn from an unexpected direction may evoke a tensing of muscles in the hands on the wheel and in the foot on the brake. In the schoolroom, the teacher's pointing to an object to be described may become a conditioned signal for students to be alert for other stimuli to come from that direction. It is even possible that learned anticipatory responses may be largely what is meant by "paying attention" to something. Conditioned emotional reactions of an involuntary sort may be involved in reactions to snakes, spiders, or other events that are accompanied by unexpected signals. Perhaps they also play a part in the determination of attitudes.

Despite the widespread occurrence of conditioned responses in our lives, they remain unrepresentative of most of the events we mean by the word "learning." Voluntary acts can be conditioned only with difficulty, if at all. If a child wants to learn to ride a bicycle, he will get no help in this activity by arranging the pairing of a conditioned and unconditioned stimulus, because voluntary control of his actions is not acquired in this way. The same is true, needless to say, for most other kinds of things he must learn, beginning with reading, writing, and arithmetic. There can be little doubt that Watson's idea that most forms of human learning could be accounted for as chains of conditioned responses is wildly incorrect; and this has been pretty generally conceded for many years.

THE LEARNING OF VERBAL ASSOCIATES

Hermann Ebbinghaus (1913) carried out an ingenious set of experimental studies of learning and memorization. He used himself as an experimental subject, and as materials, series of nonsense syllables of the sort NOF-VIB-JEX, and so on. These constructed syllables were employed in the attempt to gain control over the unwanted variable of previous practice, since it was immediately apparent to Ebbinghaus that an association like BOY-MAN was already more or less well learned. In committing to memory these series of nonsense syllables, he was able to study the effects of such variables as length of series, order of presentation, and many others. Later investigators saw in the nonsense syllable a versatile tool for the study of *verbal association*.

An important and productive line of investigation of the learning of nonsense syllables and other verbal units was carried on by Robinson (1932), McGeoch (1942), and down into the present day by Melton (1940, 1964), Underwood (1964), Postman (1964), and many others. Generally speaking, investigators in this tradition have championed empirical research rather than the development of comprehensive theory.

For a period of some years, investigators of verbal associate learning apparently believed that their findings could account for the learning of *single* associations. But even Ebbinghaus's results showed that committing one syllable to memory was strongly influenced by the presence of other syllables. During the many years of research following Ebbinghaus, the number of factors that have been found to affect the learning of nonsense lists has constantly increased, and the difficulty of experimental control has similarly become greater. The learning of any single association in a sequence has been shown to be markedly affected by the *interference* of other associations both within the list and outside it. A great many of the characteristics previously thought to describe the learning of single associates are now attributed to the effects of interference.

The verbal associate prototype must also be considered to represent a very limited range of actual learning situations. The differences in learning and retaining logically connected prose and poetry, as opposed to nonsense lists, have been apparent for many years (see Ausubel, 1963), and it is doubtful whether the interference that occurs within these two types of material follows the same laws. There may be a limited number of instances in which human beings engage in the learning of material whose members are arbitrarily related, as in learning the alphabet, or π to ten places. But the vast majority of verbal learning that occurs must be affected strongly by its meaningfulness, as experiments on verbal associates have themselves demonstrated.

INSIGHT

Opposed to these associationist trends in studies of learning has been the *Gestalt* tradition, reflected in the writings of Max Wertheimer (1945), Wolfgang Köhler (1929), and Kurt Koffka (1929). As conceived by these writers, learning typically takes the form of an *insight,* which is a suddenly occurring reorganization of the field of experience, as when one "has a new idea" or "discovers a solution to a problem."

Köhler used a variety of problem situations to study insightful learning in chimpanzees (1927). For example, a banana was suspended from the top of the animal's cage, out of his reach. Several wooden boxes were available within the cage, but the animal could not reach the banana by standing on any one of them. A great variety of restlessness and trial and error was exhibited. On occasion, however, an animal was observed to act suddenly, as though he were carrying out a plan, by placing one box on top of another, then immediately climbing on this structure to reach the banana. As another example, one chimpanzee was observed, again after much trial and error, to put together two jointed sticks, which he then used as a single long stick to reach a banana placed outside his cage. Köhler called such learning *insight,* and emphasized the discontinuity it had with the previous trial-and-error behavior. The total successful act was put together and exhibited suddenly, without error and as if by plan. Köhler's interpretation was that insight involved a "seeing" of relationships, a putting together of events that were internally represented.

This form of learning by human beings has also been described by other Gestalt writers like Wertheimer (1945) and Katona (1940). For example, Wertheimer describes solutions to a geometric problem by children, insightful and otherwise. Children who knew the "formula" for the area of a rectangle as $h \times b$ were asked to derive a means of finding the area of a parallelogram. Some proceeded in a "rote" fashion to multiply the length of the base times the length of the side, which, of course, is incorrect. Others were able to see the correct solution by cutting a right triangle from one side of the parallelogram, and attaching it to the other side, thus reconstructing a known figure, the rectangle. Still others were able to see the problem as one of dividing up the entire parallelogram into little squares (a very sophisticated solution). Although a child may have tried several wrong approaches, a "good" solution was arrived at, according to Wertheimer, when the child could see the essential structure of the problem situation.

The most frequent criticism of the "insight" explanation of these learning events is, however, a very serious one. This is to the effect that animals and children solve these problems by *transfer from previous learning*. The chimpanzee is able to pile boxes one upon another because he has previously learned to do this, although not necessarily in this particular situation. The child is able to identify the triangles as similar because he has previously done this with other right triangles. It cannot be said that such an explanation is not true, because in fact in these Gestalt examples the factor of prior learning has not been controlled. Despite the neatness of a theory that accounts for insight on the basis of the structure of the observed situation, the phenomena of insight have in one instance after another been shown to be affected by previous learning.

One of the most impressive modern evidences of the effects of prior learning on insightful behavior occurs in Harlow's studies of *learning set* (1949). Harlow trained monkeys to solve problems in which the correct choice among three objects was the "odd" one, the object dissimilar to the others. By trial-and-error learning, monkeys learned to choose the odd one of three objects when they were consistently rewarded for doing so. In the next problem, three new objects were presented, including an odd one, and the monkeys again learned to choose the odd one, somewhat faster this time. A third problem, again with a new set of objects, was solved faster than the second. After solving a few more oddity problems of this sort, the animal was able to solve oddity problems (involving objects he had not previously encountered) at once, without any hesitation. He had acquired, Harlow said, a learning set that enabled him to solve oddity problems correctly without trial and error.

This evidence implies that previous learning, acquired through a number of encounters with similar problems, can establish a kind of internal capability that makes the animal quite different from naïve monkeys of the same age and strain. He becomes an "oddity-problem solver" monkey, who displays insight when given an oddity problem to solve. Obviously, this capability for insight did not arise because of a "structuring of the situation." It came, rather, from accumulated experience based on many individual trials of previous learning.

What can be said about the representativeness of insight as a prototype of learning? On the one hand, it does appear to represent some common learning occurrences that are rather easy to identify. When children are led to "see" relationships, such as those between addition and multiplication or between weight and the "pull" of gravity, they often display insight. On the other hand, it is difficult to find insight in the learning of a great variety of other things. A child cannot learn the names of plants or stars in an insightful manner. He cannot learn to read by insight, nor to speak a foreign language. A student of biology does not learn the structures and functions of animals by insight. In short, insight cannot be a prototype for a vast amount of learning that human beings ordinarily undertake. Perhaps it occurs when we learn by "solving problems," but we also learn many, many things that are not problems at all. They may simply be facts, or propositions, or principles.

THE SIGNIFICANCE OF LEARNING PROTOTYPES

Thus we see that learning in American psychology has usually been considered a problem of understanding the *association*. To the British associationists, the association of interest was between sense impressions and ideas, or between simple and complex ideas. Following James and Dewey, Watson, Thorndike and others set out to study the association between sense impressions and impulses to action, or, in more modern terms, between stimulus and response (S and R). Tolman believed that the essential kind of association in learning was an internal event connecting "significates" and "expectations." And then there have been those who, all along, have denied that association is a central event in learning at all.

Throughout the period of scientific investigation of learning, there has been frequent recourse to certain typical experimental situations to serve as *prototypes* for learning. Most prominently, these have been derived from animal learning studies, the conditioned response, the learning of verbal associates, or insight studies. Actually, the choice of these prototypes has had considerable influence on the course of learning research. When contrasting predictions are made by theories, it is these prototypes that are appealed to as concrete ways of settling the issue. And it is from these prototypes that experiments are designed to test theoretical predictions. They have become, in other words, the concrete models that investigators of learning think about when they set out to study learning experimentally.

As examples, the prototypes themselves represent a variety of kinds of learning. It has not been found possible to "reduce" one variety to another, although many attempts have been made. In addition, there are many instances of learning that these prototypes apparently do *not* represent. There seem, in fact, to be a number of varieties of learning that are not considered at all by these standard examples; their representativeness of all the varieties of actual learning phenomena is not at all comprehensive.

These learning prototypes all have a similar history in this respect: each of them started to be a representative of a particular variety of learning situation. Thorndike wanted to study animal association. Pavlov was studying reflexes. Ebbinghaus studied the memorization of verbal lists. Köhler was studying the solving of problems by animals. By some peculiar semantic process, these examples became prototypes of learning, and thus were considered to represent the domain of learning as a whole, or at least in large part. Somehow, they came to be placed in opposition to each other: either all learning was insight or all learning was conditioned response. Such controversies have continued for years, and have been relatively unproductive in advancing our understanding of learning as an event.

THE VIEW OF LEARNING PRESENTED IN THIS BOOK

How can one determine what learning is? The plan to be followed in this volume is to classify some everyday observations about learning, and thus to identify and distinguish some varieties of situations in which learning occurs. Once these varieties of learning have been identified, an account can be given of the *conditions* that govern the learning occurrences. This will lead to a description of the factors that determine learning, derived insofar as possible from available evidence in controlled experimentation. By this means it will be possible to differentiate several kinds of learning, each requiring a different set of conditions for its occurrence.

From this naturalistic viewpoint, it will be possible to show that there are eight kinds of learning, not just one or two. The traditional prototypes described in the previous section are considered to represent only parts of the situations in which learning occurs, and therefore to depict the generation of mere fragments of the human capabilities that are acquired. The kinds of questions to be raised and answered by subsequent chapters are suggested by the following set of contrasted ideas:

1. The conditioned response prototype is used to account for the fast alerting reaction of an automobile driver to a flashing red light. What about the subsequent actions requiring skilled control of the car?

2. An infant's first words may be acquired as simple associations. Is it possible also to understand how the child learns to construct meaningful sentences?

3. A traditional prototype may be used to represent learning the name of a particular dog. Can one also account for the differentiation of dogs from cats?

4. Learning the names of the numerals 7, 8, and 9 can be represented by a simple learning prototype. How does an individual learn to use these numerals as numbers to express quantity?

5. Verbal association can represent the memorizing of a particular expression of Newton's first law. Is it possible to understand how an individual learns to apply this law to an actual situation involving the motion of bodies?

6. Insight is often used as a prototype for the solution of a mathematical puzzle. How does a learner acquire knowledge of the structure of mathematics?

All these human activities are learned. To suppose that there is one set of conditions that govern their occurrence is to ignore the facts of common observation. A serious attempt to describe learning must take all these varieties into account. Naturally, it must make differentiations among them, and classifications of them, if these are possible. But to begin with the premise that "all learning is the same" would be quite unjustifiable.

THE CONDITIONS OF LEARNING

The occurrence of learning is inferred from a difference in a human being's performance as exhibited before and after being placed in a "learning situation." One may, for example, think of designing some conditions of learning to teach a child how to form the plurals of nouns. The child could then be placed in the learning situation, and following this, his performance in making plural nouns could be observed. But it would be embarrassing to discover that his performance in making plurals was no better than that of a child of equivalent age and ability who had *not* been placed in the same learning situation. The presence of the performance does not make it possible to conclude that learning has occurred. It is necessary to show that there has been a *change in performance.* The incapability for exhibiting the performance *before* learning must be taken into account as well as the capability that exists after learning.

It is in fact the existence of prior capabilities that is slighted or even ignored by most of the traditional learning prototypes. And it is these prior capabilities that are of crucial importance in drawing distinctions among the varieties of conditions needed for learning, as will be seen in later chapters. The child who is learning to tie his shoelaces does not begin this learning "from scratch"; he already knows how to hold the laces, how to loop one over the other, how to tighten a loop, and so on. The child who learns to call the mailman "Mr. Wells" also does not begin without some prior capabilities: he already knows how to imitate the words "mister" and "Wells," among other things. The theme is the same with more complex learning. The student who learns to multiply natural numbers has already acquired many capabilities, including adding and counting and recognizing numerals and drawing them with a pencil. The student who is learning how to write clear descriptive paragraphs already knows how to write sentences and to choose words.

The initial capabilities of the learner play an important part in determining the conditions required for subsequent learning. If one has determined that a child does not have the capability of saying the words "mister" and "Wells," obviously the conditions of learning represented by a parent saying "That's Mr. Wells" will not succeed in teaching the child the mailman's name. One must, instead, begin this learning with quite a different set of conditions. For an individual who has one kind of prior capability, the printed sentence "When glucose sugar ferments, alcohol is formed, and carbon dioxide is given off" may serve to bring about in that individual the learning of a principle, at least as readily as the child learns to name the mailman. But for another individual without the prerequisite capabilities, such a printed statement is likely to accomplish nothing at all.

The set of initial capabilities possessed by the learner may be spoken of as conditions *internal* to the learner. But there is also a second category of learning conditions that are *external* to the learner, and that are independent in their action. Let us suppose an individual possesses all the prerequisite capabilities needed for learning the English equivalents of ten foreign words. Another individual possesses all the prior capabilities for learning how to multiply two negative numbers. Ignoring the differences in content, there is no particular reason to suppose that the external conditions needed for learning in one case are the same as the external conditions needed for learning in the other. In the first case, common observation would lead us to expect that the pairs of words would need to be repeated a number of times in order for learning to occur. But in the second case it is not at all apparent that similar amounts of repetition would work very well. The differences between these two sets of external conditions, among others, will be discussed more completely in the chapters to follow. At this point, the important thing to note is that the conditions are not the same. Two different kinds of capabilities are being learned. They require not only different prior capabilities, but also different external conditions for learning.

The point of view to be expanded on in this book will probably be apparent from previous paragraphs. In brief, it is this: There are as many varieties of learning as there are distinguishable conditions for learning. These varieties may be differentiated by means of descriptions of the factors that comprise the learning conditions in each case. In searching for and identifying these, one must look, first, at the capabilities internal to the learner, and second, at the stimulus situation outside the learner. Each type of learning starts from a different "point" of internal capability, and is likely also to demand a different external situation in order to take place effectively. The useful prototypes of learning are those delineated by these descriptions of learning conditions.

EDUCATIONAL IMPLICATIONS

The identification of varieties of learning in terms of the conditions that produce them obviously has some definite implications for education and educational practices. Some of these may be immediately evident to the reader as he becomes acquainted with the conditions of learning for each variety. Others, however, need to be separately specified and more extensively discussed, since they are so fundamentally related to educational procedure.

It will be apparent from the discussion of educational problems in later chapters that the fewest possible assumptions are made about the mechanics (or "logistics") of education. None of these logistic elements is assumed as a "given." Quite to the contrary, the point of view is presented that these features of the educational process should be determined by the requirements of getting students to learn efficiently. In discussing implications, therefore, it is not assumed that a school building is necessarily needed, nor a set of books, nor desks, nor blackboards, nor even a teacher. Insofar as these components of the educational system are shown to be necessary because of the requirements of learning, well and good. The only thing that must be assumed is the existence of a student who is capable of learning. This is the starting point.

LIMITATIONS OF LEARNING IMPLICATIONS

The reader needs to be made aware, also, that there are some problems of great importance to education which *cannot* be solved by applying a knowledge of the principles of learning as they are here described. For example, there are many aspects of the personal interaction between a teacher and his students that do not pertain, in a strict sense, to the acquisition of skills and knowledges that typically form the content of a curriculum. These varieties of interaction include those of motivating, persuading, and the establishment of attitudes and values. The development of such human dispositions as these is of tremendous importance to education as a system of modern society. In the most comprehensive sense of the word "learning," motivations and attitudes must surely be considered to be learned. But the present treatment does not attempt to deal with such learnings, except in a tangential sense. Its scope is restricted to what may be termed the intellectual, or "subject matter" content that leads to improvement in human performances having ultimate usefulness in the pursuit of the individual's vocation or profession.

Another kind of limitation needs to be mentioned. Regardless of how much may be known about how to *begin* the process of establishing competence through learning, it is clear that no one knows very much at present about how to *continue* the process to its highest levels. It does not seem possible at present to specify all the conditions necessary to attain the highest and most complex varieties of human performance such as those displayed in invention or esthetic creativity. How does one produce an Albert Einstein or a Leonardo da Vinci? Certainly there are distinct limits to currently available knowledge bearing on such questions. The most that can be said here is that the production of genius is not based on "tricks," but on the learning of vast amounts of knowledge.

To understand how learning operates in everyday situations of the school is a most valuable kind of understanding. But it does not unlock all the mysteries of education. What it can do is to illuminate some of the activities of the curriculum planner, the course designer, and the instructor. Specifically, an understanding of the conditions of learning is of value in the kinds of activities mentioned in the following paragraphs, which are to be discussed more extensively in the later chapters of this book.

PLANNING FOR LEARNING

One important implication of the identification of learning conditions is that these conditions must be carefully planned *before* the learning situation itself is entered into by the student. In particular, there needs to be planning in terms of the student's capabilities both before and after any learning enterprise. From where does the student begin; and where is he going? What are the specific prerequisites for learning, and what will he be able to learn next? The needed specificity of such planning is suggested by the following: What is meant by "prerequisite" is not that "fourth-grade" Social Studies must precede "fifth-grade" Social Studies. Rather, the meaning is that learning to pronounce foreign words must precede learning to use them in sentences; or that learning to count numerically must precede learning to add numbers.

The planning that precedes effective design for learning is a matter of specifying with some care what may be called the *learning structure* of any subject to be acquired. In order to determine what comes before what, the subject must be analyzed in terms of the types of learning involved in it. The acquisition of knowledge is a process in which every new capability builds on a foundation established by previously learned capabilities. The convenient escape mechanism that the student is not "mature" enough to learn any particular content needs to be studiously avoided, since it is valid for only the very earliest years of life. A student is ready to learn something new when he has mastered the prerequisites; that is, when he has acquired the necessary capabilities through preceding learning. Planning for learning is a matter of specifying and ordering the prerequisite capabilities within a topic to be learned, and later perhaps among the topics that make up a "subject."

MANAGING LEARNING

The learning conditions to be described also have implications for the management of learning. How can the student be motivated to begin and to continue learning? How should the direction of his interest and effort be guided? What can be done to assess the outcomes of learning? These are questions that pertain to the *management* of learning and the learning situation. They are questions which are general, in the sense that their answers are independent of both the content to be learned and the particular conditions of learning required for that content.

Clearly, these functions are among the most important that a teacher performs. A student cannot ordinarily do these things by himself (although, to be sure, he tends to improve constantly as he gains experience in taking over these functions). Getting the student interested in what he is doing, in the capabilities he is going to acquire, is a task that takes great skill and persuasiveness by a person, usually a teacher, who represents the adult world of experience and wisdom. Determining and advising on the branches of knowledge, the directions of further learning, the possibilities of additional topics and areas to be explored are important activities of learning management that again demand a great deal of knowledge and broad experience of the sort that may be possessed by a good teacher. Finally, the outcomes of learning, the achievements of the learner, need to be assessed by an agent "external" to the student, in order to ensure that they are objective and unbiased. Such assessment needs to be undertaken for the primary purpose of informing the student of what he has been able to achieve through learning, and is therefore likely to be intimately connected with his motivation.

The needs for these various functions of learning management are clearly implied for any system whose purpose it is to accomplish learning in an effective manner. They are required regardless of what particular conditions of learning may be appropriate at any given time. The proper exercise of these functions in an educational setting by a teacher requires that he understand the conditions of learning. Knowing these conditions makes it possible for the teacher to reach the proper decisions about what achievements the student is being motivated for, and to give suitable guidance concerning the possible directions of future learning that may be available to the student. In addition, the teacher must know the conditions of learning that have entered into any new attainment of the student in order to assess such achievement realistically.

INSTRUCTING

The function of *instructing* derives in a specific sense from a description of the required conditions of learning. Instructing means arranging the conditions of learning that are external to the learner. These conditions need to be constructed in a stage-by-stage fashion, taking due account at each stage of the just previously acquired capabilities of the learner, the requirements for retention of these capabilities, and the specific stimulus situation needed for the next stage of learning. As a consequence, instruction is seen to be a very intricate and demanding activity.

Sometimes instruction is predesigned, as in the case of a well-constructed textbook or workbook, or, more typically, in the programmed instruction of teaching machines. Sometimes it is extemporaneously designed by a teacher. In any case, instruction very often involves communicating verbally with the student for the purposes of informing him of what he is going to achieve, reminding him of what he already knows, directing his attention and actions, and guiding his thinking along certain lines. All these events are instituted for the purpose of establishing the proper external conditions for learning. Assuming that the necessary internal capabilities have been previously learned, a suitable arrangement of instructional events will bring about efficient learning.

Instructing is an activity that is at the heart of the educational process. It is extremely difficult to do well with a group of students. It is easier to accomplish under the rare conditions in which a single teacher communicates with a single student. Alternatively, it can be largely if not wholly predesigned and used in programs of self-instruction. There is reason to suppose that an instructional mode which requires self-instruction may be very efficient, when properly designed, and may also help to establish valuable habits of independent study on the part of the student. Obviously, the mature student (for example, the university graduate student) is a person who has developed his own very efficient habits of self-instruction.

One aspect of instructing, however, deserves special mention because it takes a special form. This pertains to the function of *knowledge generalization* (or *knowledge transfer*), which is to be contrasted to the initial learning of knowledge. Knowledge transfer is frequently emphasized as a purpose of education. It is said that education should be concerned not simply with the acquisition of knowledge, but more importantly with the use and generalization of knowledge in novel situations. First of all, it is evident that knowledge transfer cannot occur if the knowledge itself has not been initially mastered. But beyond this, there is an important question of what conditions of instruction are required to encourage generalization of knowledge. For a number of reasons, the instructional mode of organized *group discussion* is one that appears to be well designed to accomplish this function. When properly led, such discussion not only stimulates the production of new extensions of knowledge by students but also provides a convenient means of critical evaluation and discrimination of these ideas.

SELECTING MEDIA FOR INSTRUCTION

Still another implication that derives from a specification of the conditions of learning concerns the choice of media for instruction. Media are here to be considered in a broad and inclusive sense, including such traditional instructional media as *oral* and *printed verbal communication,* and such relative newcomers as *motion pictures* and *television receivers.*

The required conditions for learning can be put into effect in different ways and to differing degrees by each medium. Some media are much more broadly adaptable for instructional purposes than are others. For example, the concrete objects that may be needed to convey the distinctions among a solid, a liquid, and a gas can obviously not be successfully supplanted by a mere verbal description in print. Conversely, though, examples of a solid, a liquid, and a gas, or even pictures of them, have extremely limited functions in instruction when compared with verbal communication. By themselves, the objects or pictures cannot instruct in the varieties of solids, liquids, and gases, nor in the principles that relate them to each other. There are, then, some positive characteristics and some limitations of each instructional medium that become evident when they are examined in the light of their learning functions.

As has often been said, instructional media constitute the valuable "resources for learning" that an educational system has to draw on. When these resources are put to use, they are usually placed in some particular arrangement called a *mode of instruction.* Some of these, like the lecture, are very widely and frequently used, but others, like the tutoring session, are employed rather infrequently (at least in this country). The various modes of instruction are employed for the purpose of getting the greatest instructional usefulness from media and combinations of media. Thus the choice of modes is also a matter of aiming for optimal functioning in generating the proper conditions for learning. As will be seen in later chapters, it is these conditions that provide the immediate instructional purposes on the basis of which correct decisions can be made about media and modes of instruction.

GENERAL REFERENCES

Learning and Learning Theories

> Deese, J. *The psychology of learning.* (2nd ed.) New York: McGraw-Hill, 1958.

> Hilgard, E. R. *Theories of learning.* (2nd ed.) New York: Appleton-Century-Crofts, 1956.

> Hill, W. F. *Learning: a survey of psychological interpretations.* San Francisco: Chandler, 1963.

> Kimble, G. A. *Hilgard and Marquis' "Conditioning and learning."* New York: Appleton-Century-Crofts, 1961.

> Melton, A. W. (Ed.) *Categories of human learning.* New York: Academic Press, 1964.

Points of View about Learning

> Hull, C. L. *Principles of behavior.* New York: Appleton-Century-Crofts, 1943.

> Keller, F. A., and Schoenfeld, W. N. *Principles of psychology.* New York: Appleton-Century-Crofts, 1950.

> McGeoch, J. A., and Irion, A. L. *The psychology of human learning.* New York: McKay, 1952.

> Pavlov, I. P. *Conditioned reflexes.* (Transl. by G. V. Anrep.) London: Oxford University Press, 1927. (Also available in paperback; New York: Dover.)

> Skinner, B. F. *The behavior of organisms; an experimental analysis.* New York: Appleton-Century-Crofts, 1938.

> Thorndike, E. L. *Animal intelligence.* New York: Macmillan, 1911.

Thorndike, E. L. *Human learning*. New York: Appleton-Century-Crofts, 1931.

Tolman, E. C. *Purposive behavior in animals and men*. New York: Appleton-Century-Crofts, 1932.

Wertheimer, M. *Productive thinking*. New York: Harper & Row, 1945.

VARIETIES
OF LEARNING

2

THIS CHAPTER CONTAINS brief descriptions of the varieties of learning that are distinguishable from each other in terms of the conditions required to bring them about. There are some old friends here, in new dress, who will be recognized from the previous chapter. There are also some new characters, who should be quite familiar from common experience, but whose names no one, perhaps, has been very confident about.

In discussing the various kinds of learning, it is necessary to refer to the components of the situation that are used to establish its presence, and occasionally also to employ simple diagrams to represent these components. These are a stimulus situation, represented by S, a set of responses, R, and the inferred connection between them, often shown by a set of connecting lines. These are simply convenient descriptive terms, and should not be considered to imply any of the varieties of "S-R theory," or other inferences concerning the mechanisms of behavior. The present consideration of the conditions of learning makes no attempt to evaluate the usefulness of these theories; it does not attempt to deal with them in any systematic fashion.

An observer of learning must deal with an input, an output, and a functioning entity in between. The input is a *stimulus situation (S)*, which includes the varieties of changes in physical energy that reach the learner through his senses. Sometimes these stimuli are described in a shorthand way, for convenience, as when one describes a stimulus situation as "a projected slide image of the letter E," rather than specifying the brightness, size, and shape

31

of this stimulus in physical terms. The stimulus situation is in general (except for the special instance of stimulation from the muscle sense) *outside the learner*, and can be identified and described in the terms of physical science.

The output, R, is also in a real sense outside the learner. It is a response or a set of responses that produces an identifiable product. The R that is the focus of interest here is not muscular movements, although it is well known that these are necessary for it. The output may be something like a "wave of the hand," but strictly speaking, it is not the muscular movements that underlie this event. Rather, it is the external, observable effect of these movements. The learner may produce a spoken output, which may leave no permanent record unless the observer of learning has used a recording machine; speaking the words is what is meant by R. Alternatively, the learner may write some words, and thus incidentally produce a permanent record. But the R is "writing words," as this may be seen by an observer. However, the record of these words may frequently be employed in judging the adequacy of this output.

The nature of the connection between an S and an R cannot be directly observed. Studies of nervous system functioning may some day provide a much greater understanding of these mechanisms than is now available. But in the meantime, it is desirable and necessary to make some immediate inferences (cf. Northrop, 1947) about the kind of transformation that must occur. To speculate about *how* such mechanisms work would be to construct a theory, as Pavlov, Hull, and other investigators have done, and which is not intended here. But simply to describe what the requirements must be in order for an observed transformation between S and R to occur is not constructing a theory, in the strict sense of the word. It may, however, be thought of as a description of what theories of learning have to explain, now or in the future. The kind of immediate inference that is based on observations of learning consists, then, of a statement (or diagram) indicating *what capability of the learner exists following the events of learning that was not there before.*

A simple example may be useful. A *reflex* is the inferred capability one is accustomed to make in describing the transformation between an S of a light shining on the retina, and an R of pupil contraction. In a diagram, such a simple transformation may be represented as a line, as

$$S \underset{\text{light}}{\rule{3cm}{0.4pt}} R_{\text{pupil contraction}}$$

Obviously, the reflex is neither the S of the light nor the R of the contracting pupil; instead, it is the immediate inference we make about the nature of the transformation that occurs, the capability for which resides within the individual. This particular capability is of the sort that some authors have described as a one-to-one correlation; that is, whenever light (of specified brightness) shines on the retina, pupil contraction occurs. Of course, the reflex capability used here as an example is an unlearned one. But there are transformations of similar simplicity that are learned, and can therefore be represented in the same way. Also, as will be seen, there are more complex transformations that occur as a result of learning.

EIGHT TYPES OF LEARNING

Subsequent chapters are devoted to descriptions of eight sets of conditions that distinguish eight types of learning, called *signal learning, stimulus-response learning, chaining, verbal-associate learning, multiple discrimination, concept learning, principle learning,* and *problem solving.* A preview of these varieties is given here in order to set the stage for later discussion.

LEARNING TYPE 1: SIGNAL LEARNING

Learning to respond to a signal is a kind of learning quite familiar to everyone. Guthrie (1935, p. 48) gives this example of it:

Two small country boys who lived before the day of the rural use of motor cars had their Friday afternoons made dreary by the regular visit of their pastor, whose horse they were supposed to unharness, groom, feed and water and then harness again on the departure. Their gloom was lightened finally by a course of action which one of them conceived. They took to spending the afternoon of the visit re-training the horse. One of them stood behind the horse with a hay-fork and periodically shouted "Whoa" and followed this with a sharp jab with the fork. Unfortunately no exact records of this experiment were preserved save that the boys were quite satisfied with the results.

This is, of course, a description of a set of conditions appropriate for the establishment of a *conditioned response*. It is customary to represent what has been learned here in the following way:

$$S \underset{\text{"Whoa!"}}{\makebox[2cm]{\hrulefill}} R_{\text{pain response}}$$

In other words, a capability has been acquired by the horse that was not previously present: making a response typical of that to pain (including struggling, shying, running) to the sound of "Whoa!" It is as if the horse had learned to anticipate the painful stimulus; the verbal command has become a *signal* for pain. Some authors, notably Mowrer (1960a), propose that the response signaled in such situations as this is one of fear.

The conditions for establishment of this form of signal learning seem fairly clear. There must be nearly simultaneous presentation of two forms of stimulation: (1) the stimulus producing a generalized reaction of the sort one is interested in establishing, and (2) the stimulus providing the signal. If the "whoa" comes after the painful stimulus by a fraction of a second, it cannot become a signal; if it comes too many seconds before the painful stimulus, it also fails to produce the desired learning. The number of times this pairing of stimuli must occur is a question that has no single answer. There are many instances of signal learning of this type that have occurred in one trial, and there are many others that seem to require several pairings of the proper stimuli.

Obviously, such learning represents a somewhat specialized type, although it is not exactly rare in the occurrences of everyday existence. People who have peeled onions may feel tears at the sight of one. The young child may learn that a shout by one of his parents signals pain-to-come. The military command "Attention!" is designed to signal a condition of alertness. Involuntary fears of many sorts, such as fear of the water and fear of heights, may be engendered in individuals as children when these signals have been accompanied by painful or frightening stimulation. Presumably, pleasant emotions may also be involved in signal learning. The sight of the mother's face may become a learned signal to the infant for various pleasurable events associated with the presence of his mother. The sight of one's old high school after many years of absence may evoke pleasant feelings of nostalgia that are quite independent of the recall of any specific events.

All these examples, however, merely serve to emphasize one important characteristic of this type of signal learning (that is, the Pavlovian conditioned response): *the responses are general, diffuse, emotional ones.* This is learning that has a truly "involuntary" character, and applies to responses that are not typically under voluntary control (cf. Kimble, 1961, pp. 44–108). A fear response, involving general, diffuse activity including speeded heartbeat, con- striction of blood vessels, and other internal involuntary behavior may readily acquire a connection with a signal under the condi- tions we have described. But precise voluntary responses, such as kicking a football or writing one's name, cannot be acquired in this way.

LEARNING TYPE 2: STIMULUS-RESPONSE LEARNING

Another type of learning to respond to a signal is probably much more important than the classical type we have just de- scribed. This is a kind of learning that involves making very pre- cise movements of the skeletal muscles in response to very specific stimuli or combinations of stimuli. In the human being, we often speak of "voluntary responses" as constituting the observed output. In other words, this kind of learning makes it possible for an in- dividual to perform an action when he wants to; so far as we know, the same is probably true of animals also.

A simple and well-known example of such learning occurs when a dog learns to "shake hands" in response to a vocal stimulus supplied by his master, or by another friendly person. The events that take place in such learning, as Mowrer (1960a, p. 215) describes them, are somewhat as follows: While playing with the puppy, the master says, "Shake hands!" At the same time, he gently raises the dog's paw and shakes it, then pats the dog's head, or gives him a piece of dog biscuit. He then repeats this entire procedure on several subsequent occasions, perhaps using progressively lighter force to raise the paw. After several occasions of this sort, the dog raises his own paw when his master says, "Shake hands," and is patted or fed as usual. Eventually, the dog comes to perform this act promptly and more or less precisely whenever the proper signal is given. It can then be said that the dog has learned what may be called a *stimulus-response* capability.

Obviously, this kind of learning is distinguishable from *signal learning* in terms of its outcome. The response acquired by this means is a fairly precise, circumscribed, skeletal muscular act, far different from the generalized emotional responding that characterizes the Pavlovian kind of signal-responding. In fact, as Kimble points out (1961), attempts to establish the latter type of learning by means of a sequence of events similar to that described for stimulus-response learning have generally been quite unsuccessful.

Returning to stimulus-response learning itself, it is important to take note of certain other conditions that attend the acquisition of this kind of capability. First, there appears to be a typical gradualness to the learning of this act. The dog does not suddenly shake hands, all at once; at least a few occasions of repetition appear to be necessary. Second, the response that the dog makes becomes more and more sure and precise throughout these several occasions. (The response is said by Ferster and Skinner (1957) to undergo "shaping.") Third, the controlling stimulus also becomes more and more precise—whereas initially the dog may respond to other commands than "Shake hands!" these other vocalizations eventually lose their control over the outcome. And finally, a point that many learning theorists would consider of utmost importance, there is *reward* or *reinforcement*. The dog is rewarded for responses that are "correct" or that approach being so in his master's view, and he is not rewarded for those that are incorrect.

The capability that has been acquired in this kind of situation ought to suggest this *differential* characteristic of the learning, by implying that a particular S-R is established, and at the same time other S-R's, equally probable at the beginning of learning, are disestablished. We can show this by using an arrow rather than the line between the S and the R, as $S \rightarrow R$, to emphasize that a *process of discrimination* is an integral part of this kind of learning. A degree of precision has been established in the response, which can easily be distinguished from similar although "wrong" responses. In like manner, there is precision in the stimulus, which is a particular complex of stimulation differing from other stimuli that may be present at the time the response is made.

Still another characteristic of stimulus-response learning must be noted before the description is complete. Every uncomplicated example of $S \rightarrow R$ learning indicates that it is *motor learning*. The implication of this statement is not simply to the effect that muscular movements are involved in the outcome, because this may be true of other varieties, including signal learning (as when an animal learns to struggle or run at a signal originally paired with shock). In $S \rightarrow R$ learning, though, an important component of the *stimulus itself* is generated by muscular movements. While the act is being established, the external stimulus "Shake hands!" is accompanied by proprioceptive stimulation from the muscles that raise the dog's paw. Even when the act is fully learned, some parts of this stimulation are still present. For example, the dog often raises his paw "as if voluntarily," even when no one has said "Shake hands." He may now "invite" his master to shake hands! Presumably, this portion of the total stimulation plays an important role in the learning process, as Mowrer (1960a) has emphasized. As will be seen, it is a very essential part of the capability that is learned.

This kind of learning can accordingly be represented in complete fashion as follows:

$$Ss \longrightarrow R$$

where the S refers to an external signal, s the accompanying internal proprioceptive stimulation, and R the response. The arrow, rather than a line, is used to indicate the precise, discriminated nature of the capability; other potential $Ss \rightarrow R$'s are disestablished (or *extinguished*) by the events of learning.

In the descriptive language used by Skinner (1938), this capability is called a *discriminated operant*. A common example from the animal-learning laboratory is the rat learning to press a lever in the presence of a light (the external S), and at the same time extinguishing this response when the external S is darkness. The conditions for establishment are essentially the same as those we have described: (1) the lever is initially baited with food so that the rat will press it, and thus the presence of a proprioceptive s is ensured; (2) correct lever-pressing responses are reinforced by delivery of bits of food, while incorrect responses including those made in the absence of the light go unrewarded; (3) several repetitions are required to establish the capability.

This form of learning appears to govern the acquisition of a new vocalization habit by a young child and *can* be employed to teach an adult the pronunciation of an unfamiliar foreign word. The young child, being petted by the admiring parent, receives reinforcement for many of the responses he makes, including such things as smiling, gurgling, cooing, and vocalizing. The process of discrimination has already begun because some kinds of responses (such as crossing his eyes) are not likely to be rewarded. The parent may frequently introduce the desired signal, such as, "Say mama," and eventually the child does say, "Mama," more or less by chance, immediately following this signal. Suitable reinforcement follows, and the learning of this new capability is then well launched. It is noteworthy that nothing exactly comparable to lifting the dog's paw for him occurs here; the parent cannot directly manipulate the child's vocal cords. But the parent comes as close to this as he can by cleverly choosing the occasions for the stimulus "Say mama" to correspond with those times when the child is making (or about to make) movements of opening and shutting his mouth while breathing out and vocalizing. The learning conditions for this particular example are therefore somewhat inefficiently arranged, and the parent must make up for this by his astuteness in *selecting* the occasions when an appropriate internal s will occur.

Of course, teaching an adult to pronounce a new foreign word is a somewhat easier process, although much the same set of events is involved. The adult, though, begins with an *approximate* capability already established. When the signal is given, "Say *femme*," he can immediately say something that is almost correct. Subsequent trials in his case, therefore, are largely a matter of bringing about discrimination. He must receive reinforcement for responding to a narrow range of correct external sounds of *femme*, and also for a narrow range of internal stimuli from his muscles in pronouncing the word. The adult learner also reinforces himself, by recognizing a match between his vocalization of *femme* and that of his French teacher. If he is going to do this effectively, he must, of course, have previously adopted a suitably precise set of matching criteria.

LEARNING TYPE 3: CHAINING

Another extremely simple and widely occurring learning situation is called *chaining*. In brief terms, it is a matter of connecting together in a sequence two (or more) previously learned $Ss \rightarrow R$'s. Our language is filled with such chains of verbal sequences, as is well known to students of linguistics, and is also revealed by studies of word association. "Horse and buggy," "boy meets girl," "never again" are three of the hundreds of examples that could be given in which the first member of the sequence seems firmly tied to the second.

It is relatively easy to arrange a set of conditions in which a dog who has learned to shake hands offers his paw after he barks, or, alternatively, offers his paw and then barks. But perhaps one of the simplest human examples is that of a child learning to ask for a specific object by name.

Many a fond parent has attempted to teach his infant to call for an object, say a doll, by its name. After a number of parental tries at presenting the doll and saying "doll," distributed perhaps over several months, the child eventually achieves success. In fact, he appears to acquire such a capability "suddenly," and without there being an entirely clear relationship between his calling for a doll and the events that have gone before. Of course, growth factors are at work during this period: one cannot expect the nervous system of a newborn child to be ready to learn such a chain. But there are other aspects of readiness that are even more relevant to our present discussion, and probably also more important for an understanding of this kind of learned behavior.

Obviously, if the child is going to learn to ask for a doll, he must first know how to make this verbal response. This is a matter of stimulus-response learning (type 2), as we have seen. The sight and feel of the doll accompanied by the spoken word "doll" becomes the stimulus situation that is connected by learning with the child's saying "Doll." Thus there is established the stimulus-response sequence:

$$Ss \xrightarrow[\text{doll}]{} R_{\text{"doll"}}$$

Another $Ss \rightarrow R$ connection has also been learned, perhaps even earlier. The child has picked up the doll, handled it, hugged it, shaken it, and so on. Thus in a fundamental (and nonverbal) sense he "knows what a doll is." A doll is the particular set of stimuli connected with hugging, and is thus distinguished from other stimuli, like a ball or a wagon, that cannot be hugged. Perhaps the hugging of the doll has been associated particularly with lying in his bed, preparatory to going to sleep. There is, then, some such connection as the following:

$$Ss \xrightarrow[\text{lying down}]{} R_{\text{hugging doll}}$$

If both $Ss \rightarrow R$ connections are present, the chain of asking for the doll is a relatively simple matter to establish. First, the child is placed in his crib. Perhaps he makes the movements of hugging the doll that is not there. But now his mother shows him the doll; perhaps she also says, "Do you want your doll?" These events establish a sequence that sets the occasion for learning that may be depicted as follows:

$$Ss \xrightarrow[\text{lying down}]{} R_{\text{hugging doll}} \sim Ss \xrightarrow[\text{doll}]{} R_{\text{"doll"}}$$

The capability that has been learned is simply this: The child, on lying in his crib and seeing the doll outside the crib, "asks for" it by saying "Doll." He may even come to do so without actually seeing the doll, since the hugging responses he makes may generate internal stimuli (small *s*'s that are a part of the stimulus situation of feeling the doll) that have themselves been previously connected with the vocalization "doll."

In a similar manner, the chain can be extended. Perhaps the child is initially placed in his crib in an upright position. His mother now says, "Lie down," and he has previously learned to respond to this stimulus in an S-R manner. Having lain down, the next connection in the sequence comes into play: he makes the incipient hugging movements toward his absent doll, and this in turn sets off the next link in the chain—he asks for his doll.

Now all these events are likely to occur in a very natural manner in the natural world. They occur so naturally, in fact, that it may not be apparent that any learning has occurred at all. Yet, at one period in time these chains are not there, and in a subsequent period, as if by magic, they *are* there! The magic, though, may be made to happen deliberately if we want it to, as may be true in teaching a child a chain like tying a knot or printing a letter. These are the conditions that appear to be necessary:

1. The individual links in the chain must have been previously established. The child must already have learned to say "Doll," to hug the doll, to lie down when his mother tells him to. (Of course, one *can* attempt to establish all these links at a single time, but that is not an efficient procedure.)

2. There must be *contiguity* of each link with the next following one. The hugging responses must be followed in a brief period by the stimulus leading to the child's vocalization "Doll," or the chain will not be established. Often such contiguity is "built into" the chain of events, as is the case, for example, when the response of lying down (Link 1) is immediately followed by the stimulus situation for Link 2, which is the "lying down" situation.

3. When the two previous conditions are fully met, it appears that the acquisition of a chain is not a gradual process, but one which occurs on a single occasion. (Of course, if these prior condi-

tions are *not* met, the occasion may have to be repeated for the purpose of establishing the links themselves. This would be the case, for example, if the child had not fully learned the $Ss{\rightarrow}R$ connection of saying "Doll.")

LEARNING TYPE 4: VERBAL ASSOCIATION

In view of the amount of attention devoted to the learning of verbal associates and nonsense lists since the time of Ebbinghaus, it would be unusual if we did not find a place for this type in a list of learning varieties. However, verbal association might well be classified as only a subvariety of chaining. There are short chains, such as that of a single pair of associates, like GUK-RIV, and long ones like 10- or 12-syllable lists that have been so extensively studied. But because these chains are verbal, and therefore exploit the remarkable versatility of human processes, verbal association has some unique characteristics. For this reason, it is described here as a fourth form of learning, to be established by a distinguishable set of learning conditions. It should be possible to discern what kind of chaining is involved, and what the links are.

One learns to translate an English word into a foreign one by acquiring a chain. For example, the French word for "match" is "alumette." In order to learn this equivalent most expeditiously, something like the following set of events occurs. One examines the combination "match-alumette" and notices that something already known connects the two: the syllable "lum" which occurs in the word "illuminate." One then runs through the sequence, not necessarily out loud, "a match illuminates; lum: alumette." For many people, the chain is most readily established by means of an image of a match bursting into flame, so that the entire chain would be something like this:

$$Ss \xrightarrow[\text{"match"}]{} r \quad \sim \quad s \quad \longrightarrow \quad r \underset{\text{illuminate}}{\sim} \overset{s}{\text{lum}} \longrightarrow R_{\text{"alumette"}}$$

The internal parts of this chain, denoted by *s*'s and *r*'s, are likely to be highly individualistic, since they depend on the previous learning history of the individual. Thus, if a person doesn't know the word "illuminate," it is obvious that the chain he acquires must be an entirely different one. It may be a longer one, or a shorter one; and it may involve a visual image, or some other kind of internal representation.

The conditions for the learning of verbal chains of this sort would appear to be as follows:

1. An $Ss \rightarrow R$ connection must have been previously learned that associates the word "match" with the image of a burning match (or with whatever other internal response may be employed). In simple terms, the individual must "know what a match is."

2. Another $Ss \rightarrow R$ connection must have been learned that enables the individual to associate the key syllable *lum* with the response "alumette." In other words, response differentiation must have previously taken place. The individual must know how to say the word "alumette" with sufficient accuracy to be considered correct (whether or not he sounds like a native Frenchman).

3. A "coding connection" must also be available, that is, must previously have been learned, if the chain is to be established with ease. In this case, the code is represented by the association of the image of the flaming match and the word "illumination." As we have said, the selection of this code by the individual depends on his own previous history. A highly verbal person may have many codes available, whereas an individual who ranks low in such ability may have very few. Probably, the code we have depicted here would serve adequately for a large portion of the adult population.

4. The chain must be "reeled off" in a sequence, so that each $Ss \rightarrow R$ is contiguous in time with the next; in other words, contiguity is necessary for learning. Under these circumstances, the chain, like other learned behavior chains, is probably acquired on a single occasion.

It is noteworthy that a young child may have few "codes" available to him. Thus he may have considerably greater difficulty in acquiring a verbal chain of this sort. If the words "match" and "alumette" are repeated together frequently enough, the child eventually will find a code that will enable him to learn the chain. If one wants him to learn it rapidly, however, presenting a dis tinctive code (perhaps in a picture) would seem to be an important aspect of the process. The efficacy of using pictures in the learning of foreign word meanings is well known.

What about the nonsense chains that connect the stimulus GUK with the response "riv"? There is no particular reason to believe that these require any different conditions for learning. The optimal conditions may, however, be more difficult to achieve. For example, $Ss \rightarrow R$ learning must be established, both for the stimulus member GUK and for the response member RIV. Then a coding connection must be selected, and there may be only a few available to the individual, depending on the "meaningfulness" (to him) of these syllables. He may have to resort to a somewhat lengthy chain, as would be the case if he said to himself "GUK suggests gook (engine sludge), which may affect the engine when you 'rev' it, or RIV."

LEARNING TYPE 5: MULTIPLE DISCRIMINATION

Considered as isolated acts, the learning of single $Ss \rightarrow R$'s and the learning of chains of $Ss \rightarrow R$'s represent fairly simple events. Each seems easy, and in fact *is* easy, just so long as each instance of learning is carefully distinguished and insulated from other instances that may tend to occur at the same time, or from other instances of a similar sort occurring at different times in the same individual. But we also know that, practically speaking, making a permanent change in behavior by means of learning is not always so easy. The reason at once comes to mind: people readily *forget* what they have learned. The marvelous plasticity that characterizes the nervous system and makes possible these fundamental varieties of modification is counterbalanced by another characteristic: what has been learned and stored is readily weakened or obliterated by other activities.

When an individual acquires a chain that makes it possible for him to say "alumette" to "match," and then goes on to learn to say "fromage" for "cheese," he may by so doing weaken the first chain; he may forget the French word for "match." By experiment, it may also be shown that it is harder for him to remember "fromage" (for "cheese") than it would have been had he not first learned alumette for "match." If he tries to learn four French words at once, rather than two, this will be more than twice as difficult; six at once will be more than three times as difficult; and so on. Obviously, some new kind of process has entered the picture. Short chains are easy to learn but hard to retain. Increasing the number to be learned does not change the basic nature of the learning process, but it highlights the effects of another process—*forgetting*.

Many an American boy undertakes to learn to identify by name all the new models of automobiles produced in this country in any given year. He does not learn this in school, but it is surely as marvelous an accomplishment as many that do take place there. Each year there are new model names, as well as old ones, and these in turn are but subordinate categories of larger classes of names for major automobile manufacturers. Within a few weeks after all the new cars appear, a boy may be able to identify correctly the scores of new models that are adding to road congestion, as well as the ones he learned last year or the year before. His father, in contrast, may never get them straightened out—he has given this up long ago.

What the boy has acquired is a set of *multiple discriminations*. Each single identifying connection he learns is, of course, a chain. As a stimulus, each automobile must be discriminated from other stimuli, like trucks and buses, as the initial $Ss \rightarrow R$ connection in the chain that has as its terminal response the model name. As an individual chain, each is learned rather easily. But then something else is added to the situation. Each individual model, with its distinctive appearance, must be connected with its own model name and *with no other*. How is this ever possible, thinks the adult, when they all look so much alike anyhow? It is possible because they are in fact physically different, and they can be identified when one learns to make different responses to these physical differences. Twin headlights and a vertical grill, with chrome trim around the windshield, may constitute a stimulus combination that can be invariably connected with a single model name. A distinctive body shape may serve to identify another; and so on. In order to acquire multiple discriminations that identify all of them, the individual must first acquire a distinctive set of $Ss \rightarrow R$'s that differentiate the stimuli and set off the chains leading to the responses that are the model names.

But if one starts out to acquire these multiple identifications, it takes longer than one would expect from a simple summing of the occasions for the chaining of each identification. As we have said, the reason is that some get forgotten and have to be reestablished. The new chains *interfere* with the retention of those previously learned, and vice versa. The phenomenon of *interference*, which presumably is the basic mechanism for forgetting, is therefore a prominent characteristic of the learning of multiple discriminations. In fact, it may be said that the question of how to arrange the conditions for the learning of multiple discriminations becomes mainly a matter of reducing or preventing interference.

In brief, then, the conditions for learning multiple discriminations are as follows:

1. Individual chains connecting each distinctive stimulus with each identifying response must be learned. This, of course, implies that the individual $Ss \rightarrow R$'s that differentiate the *stimuli* must have been previously learned, as well as the *response* names themselves. (For American cars, these are usually chosen to be both highly familiar and distinctive.)

2. In order to ensure retention, measures must be taken to reduce interference. A number of methods may be employed, to be described in a later chapter. Generally speaking, they have the purpose of making the stimuli as highly distinctive as possible. (A highly distinctive appearance of a car model virtually ensures that its name will be easily remembered.)

Multiple discrimination is the type of learning the teacher undertakes in order to be able to call each of her pupils by his correct name. It is the type that applies when the student learns to distinguish plants, animals, chemical elements, rocks, and to call them correctly by their individual names. In the young child, it is the kind of learning that happens in learning colors, shapes, common objects, letters and words, numerals and operation symbols. In the student of foreign languages, it occurs in the distinguishing of new words, as the sounds of *fin, femme,* and *faim,* as well as other less confusable ones (less subject to interference). It is, therefore, a kind of learning that is remarkably prevalent in all of formal education.

Is multiple discrimination "rote learning"? Perhaps yes, perhaps no; it depends on what is meant. As we have pointed out, the prominent characteristic of multiple discrimination is not the acquiring of new entities as such, since these are simply chains, each of which is readily acquired in isolation. Insofar as "rote" implies "committed to memory," the emphasis is surely correct: the important factor in multiple discrimination is the interference that must be overcome if retention is to be assured. But if "rote" implies repeated practice as an optimal method of learning, then this is not necessarily the case. A later chapter will deal more extensively with this question.

LEARNING TYPE 6: CONCEPT LEARNING

Attention now turns to a kind of learning that appears to be critically dependent on internal neural processes of *representation* for its very existence. In man, this function is served by language. Although a number of animals have been shown to possess the capacity to make internal representations of their environments, present evidence suggests that this capacity is extremely limited even in the higher apes. Human beings, in contrast, employ this capacity freely and prodigally; they are highly inclined to internalize their environment, to "manipulate" it symbolically, to think about it in endless ways.

Learning a concept means learning to respond to stimuli in terms of abstracted properties like "color," "shape," "position," "number," as opposed to concrete physical properties like specific wavelengths or particular intensities. A child may learn to call a two-inch cube a "block," and also to apply this name to other objects that differ from it somewhat in size and shape. Later, he learns the concept *cube,* and by so doing is able to indentify a class of objects that differ from each other physically in infinite ways. A cube may be represented concretely by objects made of wood, glass, wire, or almost any material; the object may be of any color or texture, and of any size. Considering this great variety of physical stimulation that may correctly be identified as "cubical," perhaps it is not surprising that it takes some very precise language on the part of geometers to define what is meant by "cube." But, of course, a person does not have to understand such a definition in order to identify correctly a cube under most ordinary conditions of his existence. Except for some very special purposes of mathematical theory, an individual identifies a cube "intuitively," that is, on the basis of an internalized representation that does not employ the words of the geometer's definition. Whatever the process may be, there can be little doubt that a concept like cube is learned, and that its possession enables the individual to classify objects of widely differing physical appearance. His behavior comes to be controlled, not by particular stimuli that can be identified in specific physical terms, but by abstract properties of such stimuli.

As an example, we may consider how a child learns the concept *middle*. Initially, he may have been presented with a set of blocks arranged like this: □   □   □ . If previous $Ss \rightarrow R$ learning has enabled him to receive reinforcement for a request such as "Give me a block," he can then readily learn the simple chain of picking up the middle block when his parent says "Give me the *middle* one." Similar chains can then be established with other objects, such as balls arranged in the same configuration ○ ○ ○ , or sticks | | | . One might want to make certain that the chains were generalizable over a range of separations, like | | | and | | . In other words, the deliberate attempt is made to establish a number of chains applicable to a *variety* of specific physical configurations. Continuing this effort, the spoken word "middle" might be applied to various other arrangements of objects, including such situations as these:

By this means, the child comes to respond correctly to middle as a concept meaning "an object between two others." (Other meanings of "middle," such as the "center of an area," are, of course, different, but may be similarly learned.)

How does one know whether the child has in fact learned the concept *middle*? The crucial test is whether he will be able to respond correctly, not by chance, to some new configurations of objects he has not previously used in the course of learning. For example, these might be:

or

If the child can now respond properly when told "Give me the middle one," it may be concluded that he has learned a concept, and that his behavior is *not* controlled by specific stimuli.

Of course, it should be understood that a concept, once acquired, may also be associated by chaining with responses other than lifting. The response may be pointing, or pushing. No new events are involved in such instances; they are simply further examples of chain learning. It may also be noted that an essential part of the chain is the internal response "middle," which is the internal representation that permits discrimination of the correct final response from any incorrect response. This representational $s \rightarrow r$ may be spoken out loud as an overt verbal response "middle," or it may not be. In any case it functions as a word does. The individual must have a name for what he is about to select, even if the "name" is no more than an "ugh!" It is this name that selects and directs the final response, in the face of the varying stimulus situations encountered. A resemblance may also be noted between this naming response and the coding response that occurs in verbal association. Again, a similar function is being served.

The conditions for concept learning that are apparent in the preceding example are as follows:

1. The stimulus portion of the chain, by means of which a *middle block* is differentiated from the two others in the set, must

have been previously learned. Likewise, the internal coding portion of the chain must have been previously acquired, which enables the individual to verbalize the word "middle" (or some other word serving the same function). And the response portion must also be available (saying "Middle," or pointing to it).

2. A *variety* of stimulus situations must be presented incorporating the conceptual property to be learned, in order that this property can become discriminated in its internally represented form.

3. Because of the necessity for this process of discrimination in a variety of different stimulus situations, the learning of a brand-new concept may in some circumstances be a *gradual* process.

One may expect that a child acquires many important concepts by means of this procedure. This is how he first learns what a circle is, or a square, or, for that matter, a cat (the class "cat" as opposed to a particular animal), or a tree. Presumably, he learns concepts like *up* and *down* this way; *near* and *far; right* and *left; larger* and *smaller; outside* and *inside;* and many others. Initially, the mistakes he makes, as in correctly identifying a saucer as circular, but not a dime, result from his having responded to an inadequate variety of stimulus situations. The concept may become more nearly adequate when he has a greater number of experiences in the course of everyday existence. Alternatively, it may become equally comprehensive as a result of a deliberate instructional process carried out over a much shorter period of time.

It is quite important to note, however, that adults do not always, or even frequently, learn new concepts in the manner previously described. Adults can take shortcuts because they have a greater fund of language. If an adult does not happen to know what *middle* means, he can learn it by acquiring a chain linking this word with another concept he already knows, such as *in between.* Suppose an adult were presented with the situation of three cubes in a row: ☐   ☐   ☐ . He is told "Give me the middle one." Now suppose he responds incorrectly. Assume also that he possesses the concept *in between* from previous learning. In order to learn this new and strange concept *middle,* it is simply necessary for another person to say, "Middle means in between." As a result of this communication, the adult acquires a verbal chain (type 4 learning) that becomes a part of the longer chain leading to the correct response.

This example of adult concept acquisition is instructive for two reasons. First, it illustrates how *verbal instruction* can function to remove the necessity for the gradual process of experience with a variety of stimulus situations necessary for concept learning in the child. By means of verbal chaining, an adult can acquire a new concept (at least a fairly adequate one) in a single trial. Second, the example emphasizes the difference between the genuine learning of a truly novel concept, as in a child, and the verbal generalization of an already learned concept, as in an adult. In some experimental studies, the second type of event has been identified as concept learning, whereas it might better be called *concept generalizing* or *concept using,* and distinguished from the concept learning that may be observed most clearly in the child.

LEARNING TYPE 7: PRINCIPLE LEARNING

As an approach is made to a description of the kind of learning that can be identified as most broadly applicable to the content of formal education, the job grows somewhat easier. The most difficult kinds of learning to describe are the simplest kinds, perhaps because it is necessary to be so careful to keep them simple. A kind of learning like *principle learning* has some well-known conditions for its establishment, which all of us employ very frequently. Continuation of the basic theme of the argument—that different varieties of learning can be distinguished by the conditions required to bring them about—leads to the view that principle learning is not only a highly familiar but also a readily understandable kind of learning. As is true with certain other forms, the most important conditions are the prerequisites for learning.

Principle learning may be exemplified by the acquisition of the "idea" contained in such propositions as "gases expand when heated"; "the pronoun *each* takes a singular verb"; "salt is composed of the elements Na and Cl"; "$xa + xb = x(a + b)$"; "the definite article *die* goes with a feminine (German) noun"; and many, many others. Surely there can be little doubt that human beings must learn large numbers of such principles, some interconnected, some not, along the road to attaining the status of being considered educated adults.

Possibly the immediate demurral will be raised, "Why, these are simply verbal facts to be memorized!" Not so; and that is why the word "idea" has been employed to describe these principles, inexact as that word may be. From our previous discussion, it is apparent that each of these statements *can* be learned as a verbal chain. If we want to teach a five-year-old to memorize them in that way, this surely can be done. But the only kind of performance that would be possible following such learning would be something like this: Complete the statement: "The pronoun *each* takes __ _____ ____." Such a performance is by no means what is established when one has learned a principle. In fact, one may learn the principle about "each" and its verb without being able to verbalize such a statement at all. What *is* meant by learning such a principle is this capability: being able to use the singular form of the verb in a variety of sentences or clauses having *each* as a subject. If an individual is able to demonstrate this capability in a number of instances of representative sentences and clauses, one is justified in concluding that he has learned a principle.

In a formal sense, a principle is *a chain of two or more concepts*. Some would say, it is a *relationship* between concepts; but it seems preferable to state the nature of this relationship. The simplest type of principle may usually be cast in the form "If A, then B," as in the example "If a feminine noun, then the article *die*." The principles of chaining are essentially those that have been described for type 3 learning, except, of course, that concepts (internal representations) are being linked rather than simply $Ss \rightarrow R$'s. Accordingly, the conditions for the learning of principles appear to be these:

1. The concepts to be linked must have been previously learned. Thus, for an effective capability to be established in using singular verbs with the pronoun *each*, the relevant concepts should be learned as prerequisites. The learner must have previously

learned to respond to *each* as a concept, that is, as having a particular function in a sentence, and as different from other pronouns such as *they* or *all*. In addition, he must have previously learned *singular verb* as a concept differing from *singular noun*, and from *plural verb*. (Again, it is necessary to emphasize that we do not imply simply the acquiring of verbal chains by such learning, but the true establishment of concepts, as described under type 6 learning, leading to the capability of identifying the concepts correctly in a variety of stimulus examples.) In simple terms, when a principle is to be learned, the individual must already understand the concepts being chained.

2. Assuming that the first condition has been fulfilled, the process of chaining is a very simple matter. Usually, one simply states the principle verbally, as "The pronoun *each* takes a singular verb."

3. Under these circumstances, the learning of a principle takes place on a single occasion.

Some writers have suggested that principles need to be *discovered*, by which is meant that examples of the principle should be presented and the learner left to do his own chaining, without the help of verbal statements. The evidence is not particularly one-sided that this is the better method. After all, one should not forget that man is a verbal animal, and there are marvelous shortcuts in learning to be achieved by the use of language. The chances are that, provided condition 1 has been fully realized, telling the learner the principle verbally is much quicker than any other method, and may well be as effective (cf. Ausubel, 1963). But discovery of principles *can* certainly be made. What happens is that the individual selects his own idiosyncratic representations of the concepts to be chained.

The danger in using verbal statements as a kind of shortcut to learning lies mainly in the possibility that sheer *verbal chains* will be acquired rather than truly *conceptual chains*. All teachers are acquainted with the student who can *say* the principle without being able to *do* it. But this is an example of ineffective instruction. What it implies is that the student really has not previously acquired the concepts (condition 1 above); therefore he reacts to the verbal statement as a verbal chain to be memorized. If one makes certain that the concept *each* is known, and the concept *singular verb*, the statement "*each* takes a singular verb" should in fact represent an optimal condition for learning. Of course, to test this, one must determine whether the learner can use the principle.

LEARNING TYPE 8: PROBLEM SOLVING

Once he has acquired some principles, the human being can use them for many purposes in dealing with and controlling his environment. He can also do something else that is most important: he can think. Basically, this means he is able to combine the principles he has already learned into a great variety of novel higher-order principles. He may do this by stimulating himself, in part, and also by responding to various forms of stimulation from his environment. By means of the process of combining old principles into new ones, he *solves problems* that are new to him, and thus acquires still a greater store of new capabilities. The problems he solves are new to him, but they may not be new at all to other people. Of course, every so often a scientist or other creative person may arrive at a problem solution that is novel to society in general.

Problem solving, by which is meant "thinking out" a new principle that combines previously learned principles, is a process that is very familiar to most adults. There is nothing very "special" about such events, since they are likely to occur with a frequency of ten or twenty times daily in the life of an average man. When a driver maps his route through traffic (as opposed to simply being swept along by it) he is solving a problem. When a man replans his luncheon schedule as a result of a new appointment, he is solving a problem. When a housewife decides to shop selectively for certain items on the basis of differential prices, she is solving a problem. These everyday examples bear a close formal resemblance to the problems that are solved by students in composing reports and themes, in marshaling arguments to present a point of view, in performing laboratory experiments, and in reading a properly written textbook.

Suppose that a student of physics encounters this situation in reading his textbook:

Power is defined as the work done divided by the time during which this work is done. That is,

$$\text{Power} = \frac{\text{Work}}{t}$$

Suppose we have a body doing work on another body, acting with force F and velocity v. Can you show that the power delivered to a body is the product of the force acting on it and its velocity?

The solution of such a problem requires thinking, which might go somewhat as follows. First, the student formulates to himself the fact that he wants an expression relating power to force (F) and velocity (v). He then recalls that work is related to force and the distance through which it moves, that is,

$$\text{Power} = \frac{\text{Work}}{t} = \frac{Fs}{t}$$

and he is therefore able to state that

$$\text{Power} = Fv$$

and to recognize this as the formulation he is seeking. Involved in these steps, of course, is the use of other principles he has previously learned, pertaining to the substitution of equivalent quantities in equations.

When these steps have been accomplished, it is reasonable to suppose that the student has learned something new. He has not learned simply that Power $= Fv$, because he could readily have learned that as a verbal sequence (type 4). Rather, he has learned how to demonstrate in concrete terms the relationship of power to force and velocity, beginning with the definition that power is work done per unit time. In other words, he has learned how to *use* this definition, and how to generalize it to some considerable degree to situations in which a force acts against a body with a known velocity. This act of problem solving, then, has resulted in some very substantial learning. The change in the individual's capability is just as clear and unambiguous as it is in any other variety of learning.

A number of conditions can be identified as apparently essential for this act of learning:

1. The learner must be able to identify the essential features of the response that will be the solution, *before* he arrives at it. (Some writers on problem solving have said that the learner must have a *goal*.) This particular condition appears to be important because of the lengthy chains involved, and the steplike character of the problem-solving act. In the present example, the student knows he needs an equation relating power, force, and velocity. Presumably, the function of this identification is to provide directedness to thinking. By checking his successive responses against those of this simple chain, each step of the way, the learner is able to "keep on the track," and also to "know when to stop."

2. Relevant principles, which have previously been learned, are recalled. In the example given, the learner recalls specifically the principles (1) Work $= F \cdot s$, and (2) $v = s/t$, as well as mathematical principles such as $(ab)/c = a(b/c)$, and if $a = b$ and $b = c$, then $a = c$. (It should be noted that in all probability, these mathematical principles would be highly recallable for the usual student of physics, because they have already been so frequently used.)

3. The recalled principles are combined so that a new principle emerges and is learned. It must be admitted here that little is known about the nature of this "combining" event, and it cannot now be described with any degree of completeness. Simply writing down in a sequence the "logical steps" followed in the thinking does not answer this question. These steps are the intermediate responses made by the learner, that is, they are the *outcomes* of his thinking. But they provide few clues as to the nature of the combining process itself.

4. The individual steps involved in problem solving may be many, and therefore the entire act may take some time. Nevertheless, it seems evident that the solution is arrived at "suddenly," in a "flash of insight." Repetition has little to do with it. Nor is repetition a very powerful factor in the prevention of interference, or forgetting, as is the case with multiple discrimination learning. A "higher-order" principle resulting from an act of thinking appears to be remarkably resistant to forgetting.

Problem solving results in the acquisition of new ideas that multiply the applicability of principles previously learned. As is the case with other forms of learning, its occurrence is founded on these previously learned capabilities; it does not take place "in a vacuum," devoid of content knowledge. The major condition for encouraging the learner to think is to be sure he already has something to think about. Learning by problem solving leads to new capabilities for further thinking. Included among these are not only the "higher-order" principles we have emphasized here, but also "sets" and "strategies" that serve to determine the direction of thinking and therefore its productiveness. More will be said about these capabilities in a later chapter.

LEARNING TYPES AND LEARNING THEORY

Eight different classes of situation in which human beings learn have been distinguished—eight sets of conditions under which changes in capabilities of the human learner are brought about. The implication is that there are eight corresponding kinds of changes in the nervous system which need to be identified and ultimately accounted for. Each of these may involve different initial states or different structures, or both. But from the standpoint of the outside of the human organism, they seem to be clearly distinguishable one from another in terms of the conditions that must prevail for each to occur. Might there actually be seven, nine, or ten, rather than eight? Of course. It is possible that as research is continued it will become necessary to make new formulations of these conditions, to separate some, or—what appears less likely—

to collapse some. The distinctions made here are simply those that appear to be consistent with present evidence, much of it based on simple observation.

In brief, the varieties of learning that can currently be distinguished are as follows:

TYPE 1: SIGNAL LEARNING · The individual learns to make a general, diffuse response to a signal. This is the classical conditioned response of Pavlov (1927).

TYPE 2: STIMULUS-RESPONSE LEARNING · The learner acquires a precise response to a discriminated stimulus. What is learned is a connection (Thorndike, 1898) or a discriminated operant (Skinner, 1938), sometimes called an instrumental response (Kimble, 1961).

TYPE 3: CHAINING · What is acquired is a chain of two or more stimulus-response connections. The conditions for such learning have been described by Skinner (1938) and others, notably Gilbert (1962).

TYPE 4: VERBAL ASSOCIATION · Verbal association is the learning of chains that are verbal. Basically, the conditions resemble those for other (motor) chains. However, the presence of language in the human being makes this a special type because internal links may be selected from the individual's previously learned repertoire of language (cf. Underwood, 1964).

TYPE 5: MULTIPLE DISCRIMINATION · The individual learns to make n different identifying responses to as many different stimuli, which may resemble each other in physical appearance to a greater or lesser degree. Although the learning of each stimulus-response connection is a simple type 2 occurrence, the connections tend to interfere with each other's retention (cf. Postman, 1961).

TYPE 6: CONCEPT LEARNING · The learner acquires a capability of making a common response to a class of stimuli that may differ from each other widely in physical appearance. He is able to make a response that identifies an entire class of objects or events (cf. Kendler, 1964).

TYPE 7: PRINCIPLE LEARNING · In simplest terms, a principle is a chain of two or more concepts. It functions to control behavior in the manner suggested by a verbalized rule of the form "If A, then B," where A and B are concepts. However, it must be carefully distinguished from the mere verbal sequence "If A, then B," which, of course, may also be learned as type 4.

TYPE 8: PROBLEM SOLVING · Problem solving is a kind of learning that requires the internal events usually called thinking. Two or more previously acquired principles are somehow combined to produce a new capability that can be shown to depend on a "higher-order" principle.

To distinguish a number of varieties of learning is not, of course, a completely novel idea. Learning types have been distinguished by many other writers. One of the most widely accepted distinctions is that between the classical conditioned response (here called type 1) and trial-and-error learning (type 2). Thorndike believed that this was a valid distinction, and Skinner (1938) considers it a basic and essential one. Hull (1934) considered the distinction between these two learning types to be one of different experimental conditions, rather than of different underlying mechanisms. Several learning theorists have further distinguished chaining (type 3) as a separately identifiable form of learning; these include Skinner (1938), and also Hull (1943) in his treatment of habit-family hierarchies. Some investigators of learning describe a number of different types of distinctive learnings; Tolman (1949) distinguished six kinds; Woodworth (1958), five. Modern writers have tended to pay increasing attention to the more complex forms of learning. For example, Mowrer (1960b) discusses multiple discriminations (type 5) and concept learning (type 6), as well as the simpler varieties. Harlow (1959) has studied the acquisition of concepts in comparison with simpler discriminations in monkeys. A detailed analysis would reveal many ideas within the present volume that are derivative from these writers.

PREREQUISITES TO LEARNING

Throughout many years of experimental investigation of learning, there have been those who have contended that *all learning is basically the same*. Thorndike (1931, p. 160), for example, says essentially this, and there have been many others who have espoused this view, explicitly or implicitly. It should be perfectly

clear from the present chapter that it is this viewpoint about learning which is categorically rejected. The attempt is made to show
that each variety of learning described here begins with a *different
state of the organism* and ends with a *different capability for performance.* It is believed, therefore, that the differences among these
varieties of learning far outweigh their similarities. Furthermore,
great confusion can arise—and has arisen—through believing that
they are somehow alike. To equate the responding of an animal to
a warning signal with the learning of a child asking for a doll, or
the learning of a student to identify a chromosome or the learning
to predict inheritance with the laws of genetics is considered to be
a matter of gross disregard for some obvious and simple observations.

The most important class of condition that distinguishes one
form of learning from another is its initial state; in other words, its
prerequisites. The conditions for chaining, for example, require that
the individual have previously learned stimulus-response connections available to him, so that they *can* be chained. If this condition is not met, one finds oneself dealing with conditions for
establishing these prerequisite $Ss \rightarrow R$'s, and thus likely to draw
incorrect conclusions about chaining itself. This generalization, applied to the varieties of learning we have discussed, may be briefly
stated as follows:

Problem solving (type 8)
    requires as prerequisites:
Principles (type 7),
    which require as prerequisites:
Concepts (type 6),
    which require as prerequisites:
Multiple discriminations (type 5),
    which require as prerequisites:
Verbal associations (type 4) or other chains (type 3),
    which require as prerequisites:
Stimulus-response connections (type 2).

It is tempting to agree with Mowrer (1960a) that S-R connections
(type 2) require signal learning (type 1) as a prerequisite. This

may be true, but it does not seem possible to draw this conclusion with complete confidence from presently available evidence; it remains as a proposition to be further illuminated by experimental research.

GENERAL REFERENCES

Varieties of Learning

Ausubel, D. P. *The psychology of meaningful verbal learning.* New York: Grune & Stratton, 1963.

Cofer, C. N. (Ed.) *Verbal learning and verbal behavior.* New York: McGraw-Hill, 1961.

Melton, A. W. (Ed.) *Categories of human learning.* New York: Academic Press, 1964.

Mowrer, O. H. (a) *Learning theory and behavior;* (b) *Learning theory and the symbolic processes.* New York: Wiley, 1960.

Woodworth, R. S. *Dynamics of behavior.* New York: Holt, Rinehart and Winston, 1958. Chaps. 9–12.

Theories of Learning

See General References to Chapter 1.

BASIC FORMS OF LEARNING | 3

SOME FORMS OF LEARNING are more basic than others. They are basic in two senses of the term. First, the conditions that control their occurrence are relatively simple to establish. And second, the prerequisite states of the learning organism are more largely a matter of innate neural organization than is the case with other forms of learning. These characteristics apply to signal learning and to stimulus-response learning, the two varieties to be described in this chapter. For each of these types, the intention is to discuss the conditions that lead to their occurrence, the nature of the changes that take place in learning, and some of the other characteristics they possess. A number of kinds of life situations in which such learning may naturally occur will also be pointed out.

SIGNAL LEARNING (Type 1)

There is a wide acquaintance with signal learning, whether in common domestic animals or in other human beings. Most people have observed one or more instances of signal learning in household pets; for example, the cat or dog may run to the kitchen when he hears his food dish placed on the floor. The cat may run from the driveway when he hears a car approaching. George Bernard Shaw (1959) thought that these things were completely obvious, and he couldn't see why Pavlov had to "discover" them. Of course, in a real sense, Pavlov did not discover them; but like the true scientist that he was, he attempted to measure them under carefully controlled conditions. And in so doing, he gave us an account of these conditions and characteristics of signal learning that is as valuable today as it ever was.

THE PHENOMENON OF SIGNAL LEARNING

The learning of Pavlov's dog to salivate in response to a signaling buzzer is, in basic outline, a familiar example to most educated adults. Although it is a good example, it will not be used here. Instead, a signal learning situation is chosen that has been extensively studied in human beings, namely, the eyeblink. There are many precise data on the learning of this sort of connection, and these results are particularly instructive concerning the question of what is learned.

When a small puff of air is delivered to the cornea of a person's eye, the eye blinks rapidly. This is the connection Pavlov called the *unconditioned reflex*, meaning that it is there to begin with, not conditional on any previous learning. Now if a click is sounded about a half second before the puff of air reaches the cornea, we have one of the important conditions for the establishment of a learned connection. The click (or other "neutral" stimulus) is called the *conditioned stimulus* (the "signal"). When this sequence of events—click—puff of air—is repeated a few times, it is usually possible to demonstrate the existence of a newly learned connection, namely,

$$S \xrightarrow[\text{click}]{} R \text{ blink}$$

This is done by presenting the click by itself, without the puff of air, and noting that the blink response occurs.

It is generally thought to be of considerable significance that the conditioned blink is *not* the same as the unconditioned blink. These two blink responses have many times been shown to be different in carefully controlled experiments. The unconditioned blink is a more rapid response; it occurs in 0.05 to 0.10 second, whereas the signaled blink takes 0.25 to 0.50 second. With suitable methods of measurement, the two are clearly distinguishable as responses. Thus it appears that what is learned is what may be called an *anticipatory blink* to a signal. Such a blink does not avoid the puff of air; if it did, this would be an instance of type 2 learning, which we shall discuss next. But the learned blink anticipates the puff of air; it signals puff-of-air-to-come.

How often does the pairing of signal and unconditioned stimulus have to be repeated in order for a conditioned response to be established? Although there is no single answer to this question,

Fig. 1. Learning curves showing the increase in frequency of conditioned eyeblinks in successive blocks of trials, for groups of subjects whose rate of conditioning was found to be slow, intermediate, and fast. (Data of K. W. Spence, *Behavior theory and conditioning.* New Haven: Yale University Press, 1956.)

the evidence suggests that a number of repetitions must be used in order to establish a stable response, at least for the eyeblink. Figure 1 shows the form of curves of learning obtained for three groups of subjects differing with respect to "ease of conditioning." These graphs show the frequency of occurrence of the learned response following various numbers of trials in which the pairing of stimuli was made to occur. Other instances have been reported, however, of signal learning taking place much more rapidly than this, depending particularly on the strength of the unconditioned stimulus. Signal-response connections have been shown to occur in a single trial when the signal accompanies a stimulus arousing a strong emotion. This was the case, for example, when the child Albert learned to fear a rabbit when a sudden loud sound (produced by striking a metal bar) was made behind his head at the time he was reaching toward the rabbit (Watson and Rayner, 1920). Following this single event, the child showed fear whenever the rabbit was brought near to him.

CONDITIONS OF LEARNING

With the help of these examples, it should not be difficult to state the conditions necessary for signal learning to occur. Evidently, one must deal with conditions that need to be present *within the learner*, as well as with those conditions that can be manipulated *in the learning situation.*

CONDITIONS WITHIN THE LEARNER · In order for signal learning to occur, there must be a natural reflex, typically a reflexive emotional response (startle, fear, anger, pleasure), on the part of the learner. It must be clear that an *unconditioned stimulus* can evoke such an *unconditioned response.* Further than this, there is much evidence to indicate that there are marked individual differences in the rapidity with which people acquire signal-response connections. Such differences are not markedly related to intelligence (or facility for academic learning). But they *are* significantly related to the level of *anxiety* with which the individual typically faces life's problems and decisions. Many studies have shown that people who tend to be anxious acquire conditioned responses more rapidly than do nonanxious people (Taylor, 1951).

CONDITIONS IN THE LEARNING SITUATION · The conditions for signal learning that can be externally controlled are those of *contiguity* and *repetition.*

1. The signaling stimulus and the unconditioned stimulus must be presented in close proximity to each other, in the order named. These necessary time relationships have been tested in a variety of

situations involving many kinds of signals and responses. Variations have been found to be very small ones, so that it is reasonable to think that they reflect some stable characteristic of nervous system functioning. Learning occurs dependably when the conditioned stimulus precedes the unconditioned by an interval between 0 and 1.5 seconds, and most readily when the interval is about 0.5 second. Although conditioning has occurred with other timings, such instances may not be true examples of signal learning.

2. As Figure 1 shows, repetition of the paired stimuli is also necessary. The amount required, however, may vary considerably depending on the response involved, and on the intensity with which it is evoked (that is, the intensity of the unconditioned stimulus). But it seems quite unreasonable to suppose from present evidence that signal learning is an all-or-nothing occurrence. Rather, the connection appears to increase in strength (or dependability of occurrence) as the repetitions of paired stimuli increase in number.

Thus the conditions of signal learning are relatively simple to describe and rather readily controlled. Besides the eyeblink used in our example, conditioned responses have been established for many varieties of behavior in the human being, including salivation, changes in skin resistance, respiration changes, nausea, hand withdrawal, and others. Early investigators attempted to establish signal learning with the use of certain simple reflexes like the knee jerk and the pupillary reflex, but these have generally been found to be extremely difficult to condition. Diffuse emotional responses, or components of them, are, in contrast, rather easy to condition. A response falling in this category, for example, is the "galvanic skin reflex," which has been used frequently for the study of signal learning. When an electric shock is applied, say, to the individual's hand, physiological processes are set in motion that alter the resistance of the skin to the passage of a weak electric current. This change in resistance can be easily and rather precisely measured by means of simple electrodes attached to the skin and connected with a circuit including a galvanometer. Thus a means is provided for measuring the acquisition of a signal connection. In practice, the subject is seated in a chair and the electrodes are attached. Then the skin resistance (galvanic skin reflex, or GSR) is noted on the galvanometer until a fairly steady base reading is obtained. Signal learning then begins by the presentation of, say, a tone signal followed about half a second later by the shock, evoking the change in skin resistance. These events are repeated at suitable intervals, and the presence of the newly acquired signal connection is detected by a "trial" of the signal tone not paired with shock. The conditioned response can usually be established in such circumstances after only a few repetitions.

SOME OTHER PHENOMENA OF SIGNAL LEARNING

There are some other events that occur in signal learning situations which have great importance for an understanding of this form of behavior modification, as well as of other more complex forms which depend upon it. For one thing, there is the phenomenon of *extinction*, a kind of unlearning, that results in the disappearance of the previously learned connection. There is also *stimulus generalization*, the occurrence of responses to stimuli that are similar to the signal used to bring about learning. Generalization itself may be reduced in breadth so that a much narrower range of stimuli will evoke the response, and this set of events is given the name of *discrimination*.

EXTINCTION • Suppose that a signal response of blinking the eye to the sound of a bell has been reliably established. How may it be eliminated? The most dependable way to bring this about is by repeated presentation, at suitable intervals, of the signal (the bell) *without* the unconditioned stimulus (the puff of air). When these conditions are put into effect, the signal connection undergoes a progressive weakening, in other words, it appears less and less dependably until it fails to occur at all. The rate at which extinction occurs is illustrated in Figure 2. After an initial period of extinction, upon presentation of the signal, the conditioned response may appear again after an interval. Pavlov called this *spontaneous recovery*. However, the connection is obviously weaker, and may be reextinguished in a few trials in which the signal is presented alone. Ultimately, under the extinction procedure the newly learned connection does disappear completely.

Although the conditions for bringing about extinction are quite straightforward, it is nevertheless a puzzling phenomenon to

Fig. 2. A typical curve of extinction for the conditioned galvanic skin response (GSR), showing the decrease in percent of response in five extinction trials that followed immediately after the signal learning. (Data of C. I. Hovland, 'Inhibition of reinforcement' and phenomena of experimental extinction. *Proc. Nat. Acad. Sci.*, 1936, **22**, 430–433.)

explain. There are many different theories of extinction (Kimble, 1961, pp. 281–327). Perhaps the best known are, briefly, (1) that an active process of *inhibition*, generated by the act of responding, depresses the strength of the learned response; and (2) that extinction is mainly a matter of learning other connections that *interfere* with the initially learned one. Despite the theoretical differences that these and other theories imply, there is general agreement concerning the conditions under which extinction of signal learning occurs, as well as on its importance as a basic behavioral event.

STIMULUS GENERALIZATION • The conditioned response, once

Fig. 3. The stimulus generalization gradient obtained for a conditioned GSR to a tone of 1000 cycles. Decreasing amplitude of response was found as the stimulus tones used to "test" the responses were made decreasingly similar to the original tone. (Data of C. I. Hovland, The generalization of conditioned responses. I. The sensory generalization of conditioned responses with varying frequencies of tone. *J. gen. Psychol.*, 1937, **17**, 125–148.)

established, may be elicited by signals other than the one used to establish it. The closer the physical resemblance between these other signals and the original one, the stronger the response obtained. Suppose that a galvanic skin response has been conditioned to a tone signal of 1000 cycles per second. It may then also be shown to occur, in somewhat reduced strength, to a tone of 1025 cycles or to a tone of 975 cycles. The signal connection, in other words, is not a highly precise one. *Generalization* may be shown to other stimuli that resemble the original stimulus, as measured along some physical dimension. Hovland (1937) obtained the results shown in Figure 3 when he measured the strength of the GSR to stimulus tones differing from the original signal by increasing amounts of "just noticeable difference" (JND). Evidently, the *gradient of generalization*, as curves like this are called, drops off sharply at first and then more gradually as the amount of resemblance between the original stimulus and the "test" stimulus grows less.

DISCRIMINATION · If the connection acquired to a signaling stimulus is somewhat imprecise, as the phenomenon of stimulus generalization implies, its precision may nevertheless be increased. One simply has to make use of the two sets of conditions for learning and for extinction, applied differentially in the presence of the two signals, in order to bring about such an increased precision. Suppose that a response has been conditioned to a tone of 1000 cycles, and exhibits generalization to a tone of 950 cycles. Now, on alternate occasions, the 1000-cycle stimulus is paired with the unconditioned stimulus, whereas the 950-cycle stimulus is presented alone. The latter connection will, of course, undergo extinction, whereas the former will increase its strength as a conditioned response. When this happens, it is said that a *discrimination* has been established. Obviously, this means that the new stimulus generalization gradient surrounding the 1000-cycle tone falls away more sharply than was originally the case.

Naturally, there is a limit to the fineness of discrimination that may be established by means of the contrasting-extinction procedure. This limit is determined by the sensory discrimination capacity of the organism doing the learning. The technique of conditioning and extinction has often been used to determine the discrimination capacity of animals—the limits of color discrimination in the rabbit or the pigeon, for example—since verbal responses are unavailable.

FORGETTING · Another important characteristic of signal learning is its great resistance to forgetting. There appear to be few systematic data tracing the course of forgetting of conditioned responses over an extended interval. Most studies have shown some decrement in the learned connection following an interval of disuse. However, there are several observations that indicate remarkable retention over periods of months and years. For example, Hilgard and Humphreys (1938) found that a conditioned eyeblink could be readily elicited after a period of nineteen months.

The procedure for measuring forgetting, of course, should be carefully distinguished from that used for extinction. In the former case, the learned connection is not tested over the interval concerned, that is, the signal is not presented. In the latter, presentation of the signal alone during a number of trials brings about a disappearance of the learned connection. It is this particular contrast between the two phenomena that emphasizes the active nature of the process of extinction.

STIMULUS-RESPONSE LEARNING (Type 2)

Another fundamental kind of learning, simple to observe and widespread in its occurrence, is here called *stimulus-response learning*. Thorndike called it *trial-and-error learning*, but this is probably not a good descriptive name. It is also called *operant learning*, notably by Skinner (1938). Many writers call it *instrumental learning* (Kimble, 1961), and this name has two advantages: (1) it emphasizes the precise skilled nature of the responses involved, as in "using instruments"; and (2) it implies that the learned connection is instrumental in satisfying some motive. The phrase "stimulus-response learning" is chosen to emphasize two other characteristics: (1) such learning concerns a *single* connection between a stimulus and a response, not multiple or chained connections, which will be dealt with later; and (2) the stimulus and the response appear to become integrally bound together in such learning, in a way that does not happen with signal learning. A bell really never has anything to do with eyeblinking, except as a signal for it. But because of the occurrence of stimulus-response learning, a colored block may become for a child a thing-to-be-picked-up.

It is difficult indeed to find an example of human learning that might represent stimulus-response learning in relatively pure form. Many instances that seem at first glance to be suitable examples of this class turn out on closer inspection to represent the somewhat more complex forms of chaining or verbal association. The reason for this is not far to seek: it is simply that human beings rapidly acquire a background of prerequisite learning which enters into the subsequent acquisition of these more complex varieties. No doubt this is the primary reason why animals such as white rats and pigeons have been so extensively used to study the characteristics of stimulus-response learning. One can assume a less extensive repertoire of previous learning for these animals than is the case with human beings.

This difficulty makes it necessary to turn for an example to the behavior of the very young human infant. Although the amount of systematic experimental evidence is very limited for infant learning, it can nevertheless be assumed with some degree of safety that not much previous learning has occurred. Accordingly, the example to be considered here is the infant's learned response of holding the nursing bottle in the proper position for feeding. Under what conditions does a child learn to perform this act?

At first, of course, there is the stage at which this behavior has not been learned at all. The parent must hold the bottle tilted at the proper angle in order for feeding to be possible. During the course of feeding, however, the infant will often grasp the bottle in his hands, somewhat unsystematically to be sure. Now suppose the parent begins to release his own hold on the bottle, so that greater pressure is exerted against the child's own hands. So long as the child's hands exert a sufficiently firm grasp in a sufficiently raised position, the feeding continues. Should this muscular tension be relaxed somewhat, a point will be reached in the tilt angle of the bottle where no formula reaches the mouth. Then perhaps the parent pushes the bottle upward into position again, and feeding is restored. By gradually "helping" the child hold the bottle properly, and gradually removing the help so that the child's own responses are appropriate, the stimulus-response connection becomes established. Eventually the child, once given the bottle, can reinstate the necessary response. He has then "learned to hold his bottle."

This learning event appears to be not so much a "trial-and-error" procedure as it does a "successive approximation" procedure. The learning that occurs here, as Skinner says, is a matter of *shaping*. A set of stimuli, including the sight and feel of the bottle as well as the proprioceptive stimuli from the child's arm and hand muscles, becomes connected with a correct response of holding the bottle in a position from which the formula can be sucked into the mouth. At the same time, a slightly different set of stimuli, involving a slightly different "feel" (when the bottle is lower), results in no food in the mouth. Thus the learning is really a matter of *discrimination* of correct and incorrect stimulation; of that set of stimuli which produces reward (reinforcement) and that set of stimuli which does not. It is equally true to say that the response of holding the bottle correctly becomes progressively *differentiated*, since the muscles involved in making this response actually provide part of the stimulation which is "correct" or "incorrect."

This form of learning is therefore viewed as a gradual process of discrimination of correct from incorrect stimuli. Because some of the important stimuli are internal (proprioceptive, from the muscles), we represent this form of learning as follows:

$$Ss \rightarrow R$$

The small *s* is understood in this paradigm to stand for internal stimuli arising from kinesthesis. The arrow is used to imply the discriminative nature of what is taking place, in contrast to signal learning.

In Skinner's view, the learning we have described is an *operant*. A *discriminated operant*, in contrast, might be established if we had the infant learn to hold the bottle correctly when an additional stimulus (say, a bright light) was presented, but not to hold it correctly when this light was *not* presented. But there appears to be no formal difference between this situation and the one already described, except that *an additional external stimulus becomes a part of the total stimulation.* Any such stimulus may, of course, be made a part of the discriminative task, if one wishes, or alternatively, a stimulus (such as the sight of the bottle) might be removed from the situation. But these changes do not affect the nature of the learning that takes place in any fundamental

Fig. 4. Learning curves from one of Thorndike's cats escaping from two different problem boxes. Box D was opened by pulling a string; box C, by turning a button. (E. L. Thorndike, Animal intelligence: An experimental study of the associative processes in animals. *Psychol. Rev. Monogr. Suppl.*, 1898, **2**, No. 4 [Whole No. 8].)

sense. Thus stimulus-response $(Ss \rightarrow R)$ learning, as the term is employed here, is equivalent to "discriminated operant learning."

How rapidly does $Ss \rightarrow R$ learning take place? Is it really a gradual process? The answer depends on how "easy" the required discrimination is. For Thorndike's animals, some forms of responses required to get out of the "puzzle box" were relatively easy, whereas others were relatively difficult. What is meant by "easy" and "difficult" in this case probably has something to do with the animal's natural exploratory behavior, that is, the kind of behavior it exhibits that is not learned. Figure 4, for example, compares the behavior of one of Thorndike's cats in problem box D, which could be opened by pulling on a string hanging to the right of the door, and in box C, which could be opened by turning a "button" from vertical to horizontal position. Obviously, the discrimination required for D was an easier one, and consequently the learning is very rapid. In the case of C, in contrast, the $Ss \rightarrow R$ appears to be gradually established (or "shaped").

CONDITIONS OF STIMULUS-RESPONSE LEARNING

It is time now to consider more systematically the nature of the conditions necessary for $Ss \rightarrow R$ learning. As before, it is necessary to take into account those conditions within the learner, and those in the learning situation.

CONDITIONS WITHIN THE LEARNER • First of all, it is evident that there must be a terminating (or consummatory) act which provides satisfaction (or *reinforcement*). In the example given here, it is necessary that the infant suck on the nipple and thereby fill his mouth with food. This produces what Thorndike called a "satisfying state of affairs." (Presumably, some aspects of this particular sucking behavior may themselves have been previously learned, but this is not important for the illustration. Sucking occurs immediately after birth, and for present purposes may be assumed to be innately determined.)

However, it seems clear that a single $Ss \rightarrow R$ may be established when the terminal reinforcing act does not immediately follow the response, as in the sucking example, but instead is more remote. This is the more usual case when one is dealing with human behavior. For example, a correctly performed $Ss \rightarrow R$ may be followed by a word of praise, "Good!" which is in turn connected with a response that ultimately provides a physical satisfaction. Thus, in order for this condition to be met it is not necessary that the terminating act be an innate one. It is simply necessary for it to be a reinforcing one, to provide satisfaction.

For learning to occur, one needs to ensure that there is such a response, terminating in reinforcement, which can be performed by the learner.

CONDITIONS OF THE LEARNING SITUATION • Turning to the conditions outside the learner, as a complementary condition, it is apparent that the terminating response must actually result in *reinforcement.* That is, some object or event must be made to occur which will result in satisfaction to the learner, whether this be the provision of food, praise, or the relief of pain. In the example of the infant and his bottle, the $Ss \rightarrow R$ learning will not occur if the bottle is empty (unless of course some other source of satisfaction is provided). Modern learning theorists call this condition "the empirical law of effect," and its validity is supported by a vast amount of experimental evidence.

Contiguity has an important part to play in the establishment of an $Ss \rightarrow R$ connection. The shorter the time elapsing between the occurrence of the learned response and the occurrence of reinforcement, the more rapidly will learning take place. If the infant had to wait, say, five seconds between the time he tilted the bottle correctly and the time food arrived in his mouth, it would be more difficult for him to learn than is the case when this interval is only a second. This relationship between *ease of learning* and *delay of reinforcement* is well established in laboratory studies of $Ss \rightarrow R$ learning (Kimble, 1961, pp. 140–156).

Repetition of the stimulus situation is also a necessary condition for the occurrence of stimulus-response learning. As Thorndike's findings show (Figure 4), the amount of repetition needed may vary from a single trial to many, depending on the difficulty of the discriminations involved, and the degree to which they conform with responding that is either innately determined or previously learned. The function served by repetition, therefore, appears to be one of *selection* of stimuli to be discriminated, as a number of learning theorists, notably Estes (1959), assume. In successive repetitions of the learning situation, particular samples of the total stimulus situation (including, of course, its kinesthetic components) are associated with particular responses. Some of these are more successful than others in producing reinforcement;

the successful ones therefore become selected and the unsuccessful ones drop out of the picture. The correct behavior is gradually *shaped* by means of this selective process. According to this conception, a total learned connection is really composed of a number of individual $Ss \rightarrow R$'s, and learning is a matter of gradual recruitment of the "bundle" of individual connections that lead to reinforcement, rather than to a strengthening of each individual one. This view of $Ss \rightarrow R$ learning is similar to that originally enunciated by Guthrie (1935).

In general, then, if suitable conditions for reinforcement are present both within and outside the learner, the establishment of stimulus-response learning becomes primarily a matter of arranging conditions for the desired *stimulus discrimination* to occur most readily. Anything that is done to make the selection of a correct stimulus sample easier than it would otherwise be will speed up the learning, and thereby decrease the number of repetitions required. If one is interested in *learning efficiency* for $Ss \rightarrow R$ learning, he will seek to arrange the stimulus situation so as to reduce the amount of repetition required for learning. When a dog is learning to raise his paw to the stimulus "Shake hands!" the discrimination of stimuli (particularly those from his muscles) is made easier when his paw is held in position at the time the command is given. Similarly, the infant's learning to hold the bottle correctly is speeded by "help" from his parent in positioning his arms and hands. The connection *can* be learned without such help, but it will require more repetitions of the situation in order for the correct set of stimuli to be selected.

If a learning task puts its emphasis on external stimuli, rather than on proprioceptive ones, the same principle of ease of discrimination applies. Should the external stimuli be faint, or indistinguishable from background stimulation, the acquiring of an $Ss \rightarrow R$ connection will be accordingly difficult and require many repetitions. If the stimuli are vivid and distinct, learning will be rapid. A dog whistle that emits a high-frequency tone may not even be heard by human beings; but to the dog, this tone constitutes an easily discriminated stimulus, which sets off the response that begins his return to home and supper.

Stimulus-response learning has been extensively studied in animals like white rats, pigeons, monkeys, and others. Quantities of objective data have been published concerning the detailed effects of variations in the basic conditions of type 2 learning on the rapidity of the learning event. For example, Ferster and Skinner (1957) have collected a large amount of evidence about the effects of variations in "schedules of reinforcement" on the learning and execution of $Ss \rightarrow R$ connections. The kinds of responses that have been studied by various investigators are of great variety; some of the best known are the traversing of mazes and runways, the pressing of levers, and (in pigeons and other birds) the pecking of keys or discs. Such a vast amount of work on animal learning should not blind us to the fact that $Ss \rightarrow R$ learning can also generate essential capabilities in human beings.

OTHER PHENOMENA OF STIMULUS-RESPONSE LEARNING

EXTINCTION • Just as there is a phenomenon of "unlearning" for signal learning, there is a comparable event in $Ss \rightarrow R$ learning, also called *extinction*. In both cases, these events result in the disappearance of a previously learned connection, and it is understandable on these grounds that the two forms of unlearning should be given the same name. But the conditions under which they occur are *not* the same, and this sometimes leads to confusion. It can be argued, of course, that the existence of unlearning in both types 1 and 2 learning increases the likelihood that these forms are really a single one, but this argument does not seem a valid one in view of the important differences between them.

Extinction of a learned $Ss \rightarrow R$ occurs when the reinforcement that follows the learned response is omitted. Under these circumstances, the connection gradually decreases its likelihood of occurrence when the stimulus situation is presented, until it dies away altogether. It may be noted that extinction is not a matter of omitting an unconditioned stimulus (like a puff of air to the cornea, in type 1 learning), but is rather the removal of the reinforcing state of affairs. The latter can be done in various ways. For example, extinction of the infant's $Ss \rightarrow R$ connection of holding the bottle may be brought about, as has been said, by omitting the milk. It may also be accomplished by making sure that the infant is not hungry when the bottle is presented to him (as might happen, for example, if he were fed by the parent before being allowed to hold the bottle). Under such circumstances, little or no reinforcement would follow the learned response of bottle holding, and it would undergo extinction.

Presumably, extinction is itself directly involved in the establishment of a total stimulus-response connection, if one assumes that this is really a matter of selecting a correct "bundle" of individual $Ss \rightarrow R$'s from those that are incorrect. In such circumstances, the incorrect $Ss \rightarrow R$'s drop out, after having occurred once, because of extinction. They disappear because they have in fact been unsuccessful in bringing about reinforcement. Those that are reinforced, on the other hand, become selected and remain to appear on the next repetition of the situation.

GENERALIZATION · The generalization of the learned connection to stimuli that resemble the set used in learning is another characteristic that type 2 learning holds in common with type 1. In this case, however, the phenomenon is probably exactly the same one, and not merely an analogous event. Guttman and Kalish (1956) established $Ss \rightarrow R$ learning in which pigeons pecked at a transparent plate transmitting light of a given color. Then the birds were tested with this same color and a range of other colors differing in wavelength from the original color by varying amounts. As expected, the frequency with which pecking occurred to a color decreased regularly as the physical resemblance between it and the original hue decreased. The results showing the gradient of generalization obtained are illustrated in Figure 5.

The connection that is learned, then, has a range of precision relative to the stimulus that is reflected in the gradient of stimulus generalization. How precise it is, and how narrow this gradient is, will depend on the task set for the learner. If one wants an $Ss \rightarrow R$ to be very precise (to either internal or external stimuli, or both), reinforcement must be given accordingly, and considerable repetition may be needed. If the precision desired is not very great, the gradient of generalization will be broader, but the connection may be more rapidly established.

DISCRIMINATION • As the previous discussion has indicated, stimulus-response learning involves the establishment of discrimination. The occurrence of learning is conceived to be the selection of stimuli that are successful in bringing about reinforcement, and the rejection (through extinction) of those that are not.

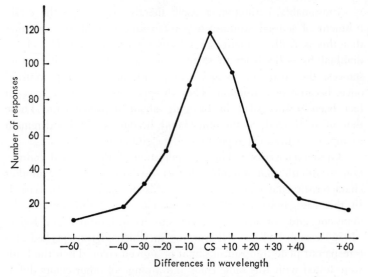

Fig. 5. A stimulus generalization gradient for the stimulus-response connection of pigeons pecking at a plate transmitting colored light. As the color of the test stimulus was altered in wavelength, the frequency of responding decreased. (Data of N. Guttman and H. I. Kalish, Discriminability and stimulus generalization. *J. exp. Psychol.*, 1956, **51**, 79–88.)

It can readily be shown that differential reinforcement is necessary for establishing the discrimination of stimuli in $Ss \rightarrow R$ learning. This was the result of an experiment by Jenkins and Harrison (1960), who trained pigeons to peck at a key in the presence of a tone of 1000 cycles. Under one set of conditions, this tone was continuously present during learning trials, and the pigeons learned to peck at the key with approximately equal frequency when tested with various tones in the range from 300 to 3500 cycles, and also when the tone was entirely absent. In other words, the discrimination learned under these conditions did not include the tone. In another set of conditions, however, the 1000-cycle tone was made a to-be-discriminated stimulus; that is, reinforcement was given for pecking the key when the tone was present but not when it was absent. The pigeons soon acquired the $Ss \rightarrow R$ demanded of them: they learned to peck when the tone was present, but not when it was absent. A typical gradient of generalization appeared, decreasing in amount as the testing tone departed increasingly from 1000 cycles. Differential reinforcement for the 1000-cycle tone vs. no tone brought about the result that this particular tone became an essential part of the stimulus situation controlling the key-pecking response. A similar result could have been obtained, presumably, with almost any other stimulus, whether tone, light, or whatever. Thus it may be seen that discrimination is the basic event in $Ss \rightarrow R$ learning. It occurs whether one deliberately arranges for it or not, and its precision depends on which particular stimuli are differentially reinforced.

RETENTION • Type 2 learning appears to be quite resistant to forgetting. Skinner (1950) reports the retention of a pecking response in pigeons after four years. It is a common experience that "tricks" taught to animals, such as shaking hands or "playing dead" are remembered for many years, sometimes without opportunity for practice. Similarly, the pronunciation of words in a foreign language, if learned correctly in the beginning, tends to be retained for many years without appreciable loss. Some writers have suggested that the retention of such connections, like the retention of more complex motor skills, is as good as it is because they are relatively isolated acts having few activities to exhibit *interference* with them, in contrast with verbal associations, which have many. However, it is true that when single $Ss \rightarrow R$'s are put together with a larger set which *may* interfere with them, considerable forgetting may occur (Leavitt and Schlosberg, 1944).

THE BASIC FORMS OF LEARNING IN EVERYDAY LIFE

The relatively widespread occurrence of types 1 and 2 learning makes these varieties important to a general understanding of human behavior. However, responding to signals and executing simple motor acts are obviously no more than a small portion of the capabilities that human beings can and do learn. To be examined next are some examples of the variety taken by these forms of learning in everyday life and in the school.

SOME EXAMPLES OF SIGNAL LEARNING

Type 1 learning occurs in the lives of all of us. Oftentimes, it happens because of environmental accidents, rather than as a result of planning by parents or teachers. We learn to respond to many kinds of signals, like automobile horns, the bells of alarm clocks, and certain ejaculatory utterances of other people. Generally speaking, we acquire a connection exhibiting a diffuse, imprecise, "emotional" kind of response to such signals, because they are repeated together with other stimuli (unconditioned stimuli) that generate these responses initially and innately.

A number of kinds of children's specific fears are doubtless acquired by means of signal learning. Children may avoid certain locations, animals, or even people, because there has been a pairing (whether adventitious or otherwise) of the stimuli they present with some unconditioned stimulus like a frightening noise. It seems likely that pleasant emotions can also be aroused in essentially the same way, because of previous pairings with particular persons or situations. Possibly the favorite teddy bear or blanket may become a signal for pleasant feelings for the young child, just as may particular scenes or melodies at a somewhat later stage of the individual's development.

Signal learning is sometimes used by teachers to establish a state of alertness on the part of their pupils. A teacher may deliberately use a clap of the hands, for example, as a signal for "paying attention." Such learning might be accomplished initially by making the hand clap a fairly loud and startling stimulus. After a few repetitions, the teacher finds it possible to generate a similar state of alertness by means of a much gentler hand clap. This, of course, is an example of stimulus generalization.

SOME EXAMPLES OF STIMULUS-RESPONSE LEARNING

Type 2 learning has considerable usefulness. It is a kind of learning that characterizes many of the activities displayed by young children, including such things as reaching and grasping for toys or other objects, smiling at the proper people, positioning the body and limbs, and vocalizing particular utterances. As the child acquires a larger and larger repertory of these somewhat isolated $Ss \rightarrow R$'s, they begin to form themselves into longer *chains*, and accordingly it becomes increasingly difficult to isolate "pure" examples of this kind of learning. With adults, finding examples of this kind of learning by itself is a practically impossible task.

Stimulus-response learning is undoubtedly the main variety involved in the initial learning of words by children. An initial utterance like "nha-nha," overheard by a parent, may be "shaped" into a connection that yields the response "ma-ma" by suitable use of the procedure of differential reinforcement. A part of this procedure involves getting the child to respond to the proper external stimulus, which may be "ma-ma" spoken by the parent. Another part requires the discrimination of kinesthetic responses from the child's own vocal and facial muscles. Naturally, deaf children have a difficult time making the required discriminations and so learning the desired $Ss \rightarrow R$. As is well known, language training for deaf children typically takes the form of providing stimuli that such children *can* discriminate. The teacher may, for example, position the child's mouth and tongue so that something approaching the proper articulation will emerge. In addition, the auditory cues available to normal children may be replaced by visual ones, displayed on an oscilloscope. Under such circumstances, it becomes possible for a deaf child to acquire the $Ss \rightarrow R$'s, based on suitably precise discriminations, which produce understandable speech.

Although not a completely pure example, adult learning of the pronunciation of unfamiliar foreign words can also be considered an instance of stimulus-response learning. A German word like *grüss* (as in *grüss Gott*), for example, may be quite unfamiliar to an English-speaking adult because of the pronunciation of the umlaut. In order for him to acquire an $Ss \rightarrow R$ that permits correct pronunciation, discrimination must take place of both aspects of stimulation, external and internal (kinesthetic). The former is provided by discriminating the sound of the word from similar-sounding words, like "groos" and "grease." The latter requires that he imitate the sound of the word, that is, practice saying it, and thus discriminate the "feel" of the word from that of other, incorrect utterances. Several repetitions may be required, involving differential reinforcement, in order for the correct pronunciation of the word to be properly "shaped."

The proper holding of a pencil by a young child is an example of one kind of educational application exhibited by stimulus-response learning. Initially, the pencil may be placed in a correct position in the child's hand by the teacher or parent. This procedure will do for the first two trials or so. But the child must have additional trials in which he himself tries to hold the pencil correctly in writing. Again, the reason for these "trials" is that the proper tactual and kinesthetic stimuli will be selected to be connected with holding the pencil correctly, while others that are incorrect will suffer extinction. With a number of reinforced repetitions, the correct response becomes more and more likely, which is to say that a suitable set of stimuli has been discriminated more and more precisely.

If one were to attempt a generalization, one might reasonably conclude that $Ss \rightarrow R$ learning is almost always involved in the learning of *voluntary motor acts*, including speech utterances. Simple learned acts of the motor sort may be readily identified in young children, and perhaps come as close as any human behavior does to being pure cases of stimulus-response learning.

THE IMPORTANCE OF BASIC FORMS OF LEARNING

These examples of types 1 and 2 learning make it clear that the conditions which bring them about are neither difficult to recognize nor difficult to arrange. These forms of learning have genuine identities; they can be made to happen at will. Yet at the same time it is evident that they have great limitations insofar as the capabilities they can establish are concerned. If these were the only forms of learning, human beings would certainly not get very far. It would be possible, perhaps, to teach children to tend themselves in various life-supporting functions, to make a variety of simple utterances, to use simple tools. But this would be a far cry from the learning required to make it possible for the individual to read, write, and figure.

Are there other reasons why these varieties of learning are of interest? One major additional reason rests on the contention that these varieties are truly fundamental. That is to say, the capabilities established by these forms of learning are prerequisite to other forms, which are yet to be described in detail. One cannot acquire *chains,* or *verbal associates,* unless more basic capabilities have been learned first. It is true, of course, that learning situations can be set up for the learning of these more complex forms *and* the simpler forms all at one time (in fact, many experimental studies of learning appear to have followed such a procedure). But when this is done, the results may reflect a mixture of influences that become difficult to interpret at best. For an understanding of the optimal conditions of learning applicable to the more complex forms, one needs to demonstrate the previous learning of simpler forms (type 1 and particularly type 2). If a verbal association like "two-cyq" is to be learned, the syllable "cyq" must first be acquired in type 2 learning. In commonsense terms, one must learn how to say the individual words before one can learn to say whole phrases.

Mowrer (1960a) contends that type 1 learning is prerequisite to type 2, and this may be so. Mowrer's view is that the individual must first acquire the connection of an emotional response, like "hope" or "fear," to a signal (type 1). Following this, when an increase of hope or a reduction in fear is brought about by a response made by the organism, the reinforcement conditions for stimulus-response learning (type 2) are in effect. The stimuli that have been present at the time of the organism's response, including those arising from his own muscles, become connected with an instrumental response because they bring about a change in emotional state that is the basis of reinforcement.

Whatever may turn out to be the case for type 1 learning as a prerequisite, there is much more extensive evidence of this role for type 2 learning. The large number of simple, isolated motor acts established under the conditions for stimulus-response learning become a vast substructure for all succeeding "higher" forms of learning. The individual truly cannot write before he has learned to hold a pencil; he cannot calculate before he can identify numerals; he cannot read until he has learned to discriminate printed symbols. As the focus of interest shifts to a consideration of other varieties of learning, there will be many reminders of the essentiality of this basic learning type.

GENERAL REFERENCES

Signal Learning (Type 1)

  Kimble, G. A. *Hilgard and Marquis' "Conditioning and learning."* New York: Appleton-Century-Crofts, 1961.

  Mowrer, O. H. *Learning theory and behavior.* New York: Wiley, 1960.

  Pavlov, I. P. *Conditioned reflexes.* (Transl. by G. V. Anrep.) London: Oxford University Press, 1927. (Also in paperback; New York: Dover.)

Stimulus Response Learning (Type 2)

  Keller, F. S. and Schoenfeld, W. N. *Principles of psychology.* New York: Appleton-Century-Crofts, 1950.

  Kimble, G. A. See above.

  Mowrer, O. H. See above.

  Skinner, B. F. *The behavior of organisms; an experimental analysis.* New York: Appleton-Century-Crofts, 1938.

  Thorndike, E. L. *Animal intelligence.* New York: Macmillan, 1911.

General

  Hill, W. F. *Learning: a survey of psychological interpretations.* San Francisco: Chandler, 1963.

  Skinner, B. F. *Walden Two.* New York: Macmillan, 1948.

  Skinner, B. F. *Science and human behavior.* New York: Macmillan, 1953.

CHAINING:
MOTOR AND
VERBAL

4

THE CHAINING OF BEHAVIOR is a frequent and widely occurring event within the sphere of learning. The acquiring of chains typically takes place with some rapidity, and often seems a very simple occurrence. But chains are of varying length; they may be as short as the act involved in pushing a light button, or as long as the recitation of "The Rime of the Ancient Mariner." And so naturally they vary in the rapidity with which they are learned.

By chaining is meant the connection of a set of individual $Ss \rightarrow R$'s in a sequence. There are sequences that are made up of motor responses, like that of turning on a television set or a washing machine. There are also sequences that are entirely verbal, like the greeting "How have you been?" or the pledge of allegiance to the flag. This chapter will deal with both these varieties of chaining, which have much in common with each other. As before, the main emphasis will be one of describing chaining as a phenomenon, and identifying the conditions under which it occurs. For the acquisition of sequences that are nonverbal, the word *chaining* will be used, whereas the subvariety involving verbal behavior will be referred to as acquiring *verbal chains* or *verbal associates.*

CHAINING (TYPE 3)

When one says to a novice driver, "Now start the engine," one is asking for the execution of a learned chain of $Ss \rightarrow R$ connections. If the training has been successful, what will take place

87

is the reinstatement of a sequence something like this: S ("Start the engine") → R (looking forward and to the rear) . . . S (sight of clear road) → R (testing for gear in neutral) . . . S (gear in neutral) → R (turning key to activate starter) . . . S (sound of motor catching) → R (release of key) . . . S (key released) → R (depressing accelerator). Each of the individual acts in the chain is something that the learner knows how to do. The trick is to get them done in the proper order.

Guthrie (1935) tells the story of a young girl who had acquired the habit of dropping her coat on the floor when she entered the house. Being annoyed with this practice, her mother had many times scolded her daughter and required her to go back and pick up the coat. But this was quite ineffective in overcoming the unwanted behavior. The mother, however, discovered an effective procedure: she made the girl go out of the house again with her coat on, then come in and hang it up properly. This illustration shows the importance of correct sequencing of the events in a chain. The original chain that was troubling the mother was: enter house → drop coat → see mother → mother says, "Pick up coat" → pick up coat → hang up coat. But what had to be established was a shorter chain with quite a different sequence, namely: enter house → keep coat on → approach closet → hang up coat. The mother displayed some most useful wisdom when she realized that the second chain could not be learned by simply adding links to the first one. What was necessary was the institution of the desired chain with correct links from start to finish.

THE PHENOMENON OF CHAINING

Unlocking a door with a key provides another simple example of a learned chain that can be used here for analysis. Of course, the assumption needs to be made that such a chain has not yet been learned, as may be true for a child. Descriptively, what must be learned is a sequence like the following: Having the key in his hand, and facing the lock, the child first checks to see that the key is right side up. Then he inserts it into the lock until the stop is reached, turns it until another stop is reached, and pushes the door open. Obviously, each of the individual acts (Ss → R's) of this sequence must be performed correctly, and in the proper order, or the performance of opening the door will be unsuccessful. If the key is not right side up, it cannot be inserted; if the insertion is not complete, it cannot be turned; and so on. The point is, <u>the chain as a chain *cannot be learned unless the individual is capable of performing the individual links.*</u>

Assuming that the individual $Ss \rightarrow R$'s that make up the chain have been previously mastered, it would appear a fairly simple matter to learn the chain. In this example, what is acquired may be represented as follows:

$$Ss_{\text{key}} \longrightarrow R_{\text{positioning}} \quad \sim \quad Ss_{\text{key up}} \longrightarrow R_{\substack{\text{inserting} \\ \text{key}}}$$

$$Ss_{\text{key in}} \longrightarrow R_{\substack{\text{turning} \\ \text{key}}} \quad \sim \quad Ss_{\substack{\text{key} \\ \text{turned}}} \longrightarrow R_{\substack{\text{push} \\ \text{door}}}$$

The opening of the door constitutes a consummatory act, providing reinforcement for the final link and also for the entire chain.

If one were to undertake to set up conditions in which this chain were to be acquired by a human adult who did not know how to do it, it is of interest to note that *verbal instructions* would be used to guide the sequencing. Most probably, one would say something like this: "First hold the key so that the serrated edge points upward, with the point facing the lock. Then push the key into the lock as far as it will go. Now turn the key in the clockwise direction as far as it will go. Now push the door."

What is the function of such instructions? Evidently their most important purpose is to provide *external cues* for the selection of exactly the right links for the chain. Since the learner is capable of inserting the key into the lock in several different ways, an additional external cue may increase the probability that he reinstates the correct response and rejects others. In order to begin the learning, therefore, there must be a situation like this:

$$Ss_{\text{"serrated edge up"}} \qquad Ss_{\text{"push key all the way"}}$$

$$Ss_{\text{key}} \longrightarrow R_{\text{positioning}} \quad \sim \quad Ss_{\text{key up}} \longrightarrow R_{\substack{\text{inserting} \\ \text{key}}} \quad ; \text{and so on}$$

The verbal cues provided by the instructions become, for the verbally competent individual, stimuli that ensure the occurrence of the correct positioning response, or the correct inserting response, rather than an incorrect one. On the second trial they may be quite unnecessary.

Verbal instructions may be self-administered. Some writers have proposed that verbal instructions provided by the individual himself become a part of the chain being learned. This was the suggestion made by William James (1890) in his famous chapter on habit. As James pointed out, if self-generated verbal cues are an initial part of the chain that is acquired, they must later *drop out*, since it is evident that the "reeling off" of a well-established chain leaves no time for these verbal responses to occur. However, it is here proposed that verbal instructions, whatever their origin, are simply accompaniments to the initial establishment of a chain, and not a part of the chain at all. They are provided on an initial trial or two, in order to ensure that the correct links get reinstated. After that they may simply become unnecessary, because the stimuli from one link of the chain provide a suitable stimulus for the occurrence of the next link. One does not have to account for the "dropping out" of self-instructions; it is sufficient to realize that they are not necessary to successful execution of the chain. They are part of the conditions of learning but not a part of what is learned.

But what about learners who may not be able to respond to verbal cues, like animals or very young children? The essential problem is the same: a means must be found of providing external cues during the initial learning trial so that the correct links will be reinstated. If an animal has acquired a set of $Ss \rightarrow R$'s that are to be linked together, this can be done by introducing the external stimuli that have been connected with each link at exactly the proper time in the sequence. Later on, it is possible to eliminate these additional external cues and still have the chain performed satisfactorily. And so too with a very young child. One can imagine "guiding" the production of correct links by suitable cues, even when the individual may not be able to respond properly to such an instruction as "serrated edge." The additional stimuli used for this purpose might include pictures (for example, of a key in the proper position), and gestures (for example, a pushing motion of the instructor's hand). Again, these additional cues would no longer be needed once the chain had been learned.

There are many varieties of chains, and sometimes more than a single trial is required to learn them. This is particularly true when the stimuli of one link are difficult to distinguish from the stimuli of another. Under such circumstances, the learner may tend to reinstate a link out of sequence, and thus be unsuccessful with the chain as a whole. This tends to be the situation in a *maze*, whether one is dealing with animals or with men (using a finger maze). When the learner arrives at a certain point in a maze, it may feel and look almost like some other point, and yet require a different response. Yet when the stimuli controlling each link are made distinctive, such a sequence is not at all difficult to learn. Animals can learn fairly long chains quite rapidly, so long as the stimuli for each new link are readily distinguishable (that is, so long as they have been previously discriminated). Gilbert (1962, p. 16), for example, describes an easily learnable chain for a rat composed of the following acts: pull light cord . . . turn light on → press lever . . . buzzer sounds → approach pan . . . obtain food pellet. Human beings learning a finger maze typically make use of additional external cues, such as self-generated verbal instructions ("First right, then left, then left again," and so on), to increase the distinctiveness of the links.

Much experimental study has been devoted to maze learning in animals. Originally, the maze was chosen because it was "hard enough"; in other words, because it contained difficult link discriminations, and therefore required a number of repetitions for its mastery. The study of maze learning tended to obscure the fact that chains, under optimal conditions, are easy to learn. The learning of mazes appeared to be a gradual process primarily because animals were spending their time learning to discriminate the links that composed them (type 2 learning). Maze learning provides an excellent illustration of the fact that one can, if one wishes, get the learner to undertake two kinds of learning at once, in this case,

$Ss \rightarrow R$ learning and chaining. But the results of such a mixture are not easy to interpret.

THE CONDITIONS FOR CHAINING

The conditions necessary to bring about the variety of learning called chaining can now be described more formally. There are, as usual, some conditions that exist within the learner, and others that may be externally determined.

CONDITIONS WITHIN THE LEARNER • Of utmost importance to the acquiring of chains is the requirement that each individual stimulus-response connection be *previously learned*. One cannot expect a chain like opening a door with a key to be learned in an optimal way unless the learner is already able to carry out the $Ss \rightarrow R$'s that constitute the links. He must be able to (1) identify the key's upright position; (2) insert it into the lock fully; (3) turn it clockwise fully; and (4) push the door open. If a novice (a child, perhaps) complains that he cannot do it after being shown how, one immediately suspects that he has not fully mastered one of these links. Similarly, the chain learned in starting the motor of a car requires the previous learning of the individual links. Failure to learn on a single occasion usually indicates that one or more links have not been previously learned (pressing the accelerator as soon as the motor "takes hold" is an example).

If one could make sure that each individual link were fully learned, the additional external cues required could be reduced to an absolute minimum. But to be *fully* learned each link must have as a portion of its discriminated stimulus some kinesthetic feedback from the just-preceding response. For example, the key is not only seen to be inserted fully, it also "feels" right, and this "feel" becomes a part of the stimulus for the next link in the chain. Because it is difficult to ensure that all the stimulation for each link has been fully discriminated, additional external cues are added. But the fastest learning of chains occurs when the necessity for these additional cues is at a minimum; and this happens when the individual links have been individually well learned.

CONDITIONS IN THE SITUATION • Several conditions in the situation are important to chain learning.

1. Assuming that the links are known, the main condition for the establishment of a chain is getting the learner to *reinstate them* one after the other *in the proper order*. Two different approaches to this sequencing are possible:

    a. One can begin with the terminal act and work backward, as Gilbert (1962) suggests. This ensures that the link one is trying to connect at any given point in the chain will always be introduced in the correct order. Beginning with link 4, one first connects link 3 by waiting for the occurrence of this link and then immediately following it with link 4 (the act leading to reinforcement); then one observes the occurrence of link 2, and follows it with links 3 and 4; and so on. This "progressive part" method, it may be noted, follows the procedure for type 2 learning *for each successive link.*

    b. A *prompting* method may be used, in which additional external cues are employed to ensure the reinstatement of the links in the proper order, beginning from the start of the chain. This is the method illustrated by the example previously given, using verbal instructions as "prompts."

It is evident that both these methods work. Whether or not one is more effective than the other, in some or all circumstances, is a question on which insufficient evidence is currently available.

2. A second condition is the familiar one of *contiguity*. The individual links in the chain must be executed in close time succession if the chain is to be established. The smoothly executed chain pertaining to unlocking a door, for example, requires that the insertion of the key be followed by turning it to the right. Some of the stimuli for the second of these links arise out of the responses made in the first. Should there be a delay between these two links, the stimuli for the second connection will not be like those of the performance aimed for, and under these circumstances the chain may be learned with difficulty. This does not mean, of course, that it is not possible to learn chains that have delays deliberately built into them. Such instances may certainly be ac-

quired; for example, one learns to delay until the coin has dropped fully into a slot machine before operating the lever.

3. A third condition relates to the *repetition* variable. Presumably, if all other conditions were fully met, repetition would be unnecessary. The chain would tend to form itself on the first occasion. Practically speaking, however, it is difficult to ensure that all the conditions are fully met. The individual links may be only partially learned, or the prompting may be not fully effective, or some delays may creep into the execution of the chain. Given these practical circumstances, repetition of the sequence has the function of "smoothing out" the rough spots, and some practice is almost always desirable for this reason.

Another function of repetition is the prevention of forgetting. Since errors do tend to occur, and are more likely the longer the chain, a means must be provided for practicing each link in its proper order. This effect of repetition becomes much more evident in the recall of verbal chains, which are typically subject to greater interference than are motor ones, as will be discussed in a later section of this chapter. To the extent that the links have been forged accurately and are connected precisely in the proper order, the need for practice will be reduced. Practice is used to permit the extinction of residual incorrect connections, rather than to establish new ones.

4. Finally, there is the condition of *reinforcement* present in the learning of chains. The terminal link must lead to a satisfying state of affairs—the food pellet is obtained, the engine starts, the door opens. The occurrence of some terminal satisfaction appears to be essential to the establishment of chains. If the reinforcement is omitted, extinction of the final link occurs, and the chain as a whole then disappears. It has been found that the reinforcement needs to be immediate in order for chain learning to occur most readily. The introduction of a delay in reinforcement markedly increases the difficulty of learning.

OTHER PHENOMENA OF CHAINING

Since chains are made up of stimulus-response connections, it is natural that one can see various phenomena of these $Ss \rightarrow R$'s exhibiting themselves in chain learning.

EXTINCTION · The unlearning of a chain may be brought about in the same manner as that of a stimulus-response connection, namely, by omitting the reinforcement. When this is done, the terminal connection first disappears, followed in short order by the rest of the chain. This method is sometimes employed to remove undesirable habits. For example, the rather elaborate chain connected with smoking cigarettes (removing the pack from pocket, taking out a cigarette, tapping it, inserting in the mouth, striking a match, and so on) may presumably be destroyed if the terminal act of inhaling smoke becomes nonreinforcing, as when a substance generating an unpleasant taste is placed in the tobacco. It has even been suggested that such nonreinforcement might be brought about simply by removing from the smoke its resins, tars, nicotine, and its heat; but this procedure awaits verification.

GENERALIZATION · Any or all of the $Ss \rightarrow R$ links of a chain may exhibit stimulus generalization. The opening of a particular lock with a particular key naturally may be expected to generalize to a stimulus situation that includes a lock and key of somewhat different but similar appearance. Of course, should the second lock look the same but work differently, as in requiring a counterclockwise rather than a clockwise turn, the learner will clearly be in trouble. In order to solve the problem, he will at the very least need to learn two different chains containing two comparable $Ss \rightarrow R$ links that are discriminated from each other, perhaps on the basis of the appearance of the keys. A still higher level of generalizing may be provided by the learning of a concept, in accordance with conditions to be described in a later chapter.

DISCRIMINATION · As has been emphasized throughout this section, the individual $Ss \rightarrow R$'s in a chain are discriminated entities. The more precise this discrimination is, the better they are for the purpose of chaining. Frequently for practical reasons, pains must be taken to establish special discriminations in one or more links, in order that some recurring confusion may be overcome. Such might be the case, for example, with the two different locks just described. The sequence required to start the engine of one automobile is usually different in some respects from that of another automobile. Here again, the individual who operates both cars may need to undertake special discrimination learning for some particular $Ss \rightarrow R$ in the chain (for example, the one that includes the response for releasing the starter switch).

FORGETTING · Motor sequences of the sort described tend to be retained well for long periods of time. Presumably, individual links in chains are subject to differential forgetting. Not a great deal of systematic evidence is available regarding this phenomenon, however. The forgetting of a link in the middle of a chain may, of course, disrupt the entire chain in such a manner that the individual has the impression of having lost the whole. But it is also known that motor chains like those involved in swimming, skating, or bicycling can be recovered in a short time. Once a forgotten link is restored, the entire chain may reappear in its totality. This kind of experience is often reported by instrumentalists who try to reinstate the lengthy chains that make up a long-unpracticed musical exercise.

THE USES OF CHAINS

Although of widespread occurrence among the human being's activities, chains are of essentially humble nature. In the early grades of school, a number of important chainlike skills must be learned. Buttoning, fastening, tying, using a pencil, erasing, using scissors, and many others fall into this category. At a slightly more complex level are the chains involved in printing and writing, which are of considerable importance as components of more elaborate activities to be acquired in the school. Throwing balls, catching balls, kicking balls, and many other fundamental sorts of athletic skills are also acquired as chains in the early years of the individual's life.

In later years of school, there are varieties of additional chains to be learned. Sometimes, these take the form of *procedures*, complex and lengthy chains that often incorporate simpler chains as components. The student may learn in science courses to carry out weighing procedures, liquid-pouring procedures, and many kinds of measurement procedures. Later still, he may learn to adjust and use a variety of scientific instruments, like microscopes, voltmeters, centrifuges—each of them requiring the learning of procedural chains. The vocational student is likely to have to learn a large number of procedures as basic tasks of the occupation he plans to enter. The student of art may learn procedures such as "brush techniques"; the student of music the complex procedures of playing an instrument.

In accordance with the definition used here, chains are nonverbal, although, to be sure, their learning may be facilitated by verbal cues. They cannot therefore be considered to constitute a central part of the school curriculum. But it would obviously be a mistake to call them unimportant as educational objectives. Certain motor skills and procedures are basic to competence as a scholar and even to wholeness as an adjustable adult person. Motor skills, common or uncommon, are an essential part of the process of self-fulfillment, whether they be a part of the activities of golfing, musicianship, artistic creation, or some other human activity.

VERBAL ASSOCIATION (TYPE 4)

If it is true that man is capable of a tremendous variety of performances with the use of his legs, arms, and hands, it is also even more strikingly true that his vocalizations show an enormous versatility. Although the individual sounds he can make are limited in number, the patterns that can be constructed from these sounds are of virtually limitless variety. Such patterns, at least the simplest ones, are learned as chains. But the tremendous variety of these chains as well as the subtlety of resemblances and differences among them make verbal behavior a subject of rather special interest from a learning standpoint. This chapter will deal with only the most elementary kind of verbal behavior, the learning of verbal associations. In later chapters, the roles played by these associations in more complex forms of learning, such as the acquisition of concepts and principles, will be described.

Probably the simplest verbal chains are illustrated in the activity of *naming*. A youngster is told while being shown a three-dimensional object, "This shape is called a tetrahedron." If conditions are otherwise right, the next time he sees this particular object, he will be able to say that it is a tetrahedron. But these other conditions are important. It is fairly easy to identify some conditions which would ensure that the learner would *not* be able to say tetrahedron. To mention two of the most obvious: first, he may not have discriminated the object as a stimulus; and second, he may not have learned its name.

It seems likely that the act of naming a specific object like a tetrahedron is a chain of at least two links. The first of these links is an observing response, an $Ss \rightarrow R$ that connects the appearance of the object with some responses involved in observing the triangular character of its sides, and that at the same time serves to distinguish it from other three-dimensional objects of roughly the same size and color. The second link is the $Ss \rightarrow R$ connection that enables the individual to stimulate himself to say "tetrahedron" (that is, to say it as a voluntary response, in the manner of stimulus-response learning). As a diagram, a simple act of naming is represented by this kind of chain:

$$Ss \xrightarrow[\text{object}]{} R_{\text{observing}} \sim s \xrightarrow[\text{tetrahedron}]{} R_{\text{"tetrahedron"}}$$

The small s in the diagram represents a complex of internal stimulation composed principally of (1) those kinesthetic stimuli that have become discriminated by previous responding with this utterance, coupled with (2) the kinesthetic (or other internal) stimuli arising from the observing response. It is this contiguity of two forms of internal stimulation, presumably, that welds the two links into a chain.

Verbal chains with three links are also of common occurrence. A young child learns not only to name an object "ball," but also to say "that ball" or "my ball."

PAIRED-ASSOCIATE LEARNING

When one learns to read a foreign language, it is not uncommon to acquire a large number of "translation responses," in the manner of give-donner, or buy-acheter. The traditional prototype for such learning is the *paired associate*, sometimes used in nonsense form, as RIV-GEX. A great deal is known about paired-associate learning, but a great deal more remains to be studied (Underwood and Shulz, 1960; Cofer, 1961). In terms of conditions for acquiring verbal associates, and the immediate inferences that seem justified from the evidence about them, these appear to be the most important:

1. Nonsense syllables do not perform the function that Ebbinghaus intended for them, that is, of being equivalently meaningless and unfamiliar. The learning of an association between two verbal elements, whether syllables or words, is markedly affected by *previous* discrimination learning of both the first member and the second (Goss, 1963).

2. Most investigators agree that the efficient learning of a two-element verbal association requires the use of an *intervening link*, having the function of *mediation* or coding. The increased ease of learning resulting from the deliberate use of well-chosen mediation links is striking (Jenkins, 1963). Such links are usually implicit ones, that is, they occur inside the learner and do not appear as overt behavior. In the case of an association like give-donner, an effective coding might be give → donate → donner. Many other mediating links are possible.

3. It is difficult to separate the phenomena of learning *single* associates from those of *multiple* associates. The typical paired-associate learning study, after all, uses ten or twelve pairs like RIV-GEX, not just one. This makes such learning an example of *multiple discrimination*, to be described in the next chapter. But in the present discussion, the attempt must be made to select those conditions that affect only the single verbal association.

The typical three-link chain that constitutes a verbal association, then, is one that involves a previously discriminated verbal element (HAT) which functions as the initial stimulus for the chain. Second, it contains another previously learned connection (FIX) that includes the spoken or written response "fix.' Third, it contains a mediating (or coding) connection that may be supplied either by the learner or by the instructor, and that puts together the other two links. This coding link may be of almost any sort. For ease of learning, the most effective one will be an "association' or "image" that is most highly familiar to the learner. One learner might supply a link taken from a previously learned chain about "Dick's hatband," and so construct the chain: HAT-Dick's-FIX; this is neat because the response "Dick's" rhymes with the response "fix," and thus may make an easily learnable chain. Another may think of a battered hat that needs *fix*ing, by calling up a visual image to serve as a mediating link.

The effectiveness of visual images as mediating links for verbal associates has long been known, and forms a part of some "memory systems." A previously learned chain of words, having some logical order that makes it easy to remember, may be used to form links with a set of words having no easily memorable sequence. Thus, the previously learned word "altar" may be connected with the to-be-remembered word "wolf" by means of a visual image of a "wolf at the altar." But the same set of events may readily occur without the necessity of a formal memory system. For example, a familiar link for the translation connection "le soleil–sun" may be provided by a visual image of a rising "ol' Sol."

Other examples of coding links for certain French words are shown in Figure 6. Verbal links may be formed by choosing English words, already well known to the learner, that bear some similarity to the French word, and some previously learned association with the English associate. On the whole, though, a pictorial link of the sort indicated in the second column of the figure works even better for most people. Still another instructional method, at least equally effective, is to require the learner to generate his own coding link—a word, an image, or anything he thinks of that will link the stimulus word with the response word.

LONGER VERBAL SEQUENCES · Chains of verbal associates may be longer than three links. Relatively brief verbal sequences of previously discriminated words can readily be learned as chains in a single presentation, provided the individual links have been previously well learned. However, even this statement must be made with some reservations, because of the occurrence of *interference* among the links of a chain, which will be discussed more extensively later on in connection with the phenomenon of forgetting.

Obviously, verbal chains may be very long indeed, if we

think of the memorization of digits twenty-eight places beyond the decimal point, or, for that matter, of the verbatim learning of verses of poetry or books of the Bible. Are there some limitations on how long a chain can be to be "taken in" or learned as a single event? So far as the evidence from experiments goes (Miller, 1956; Jensen, 1962), it appears that a chain of about seven links (plus or minus two) represents the limit of what can be learned as a

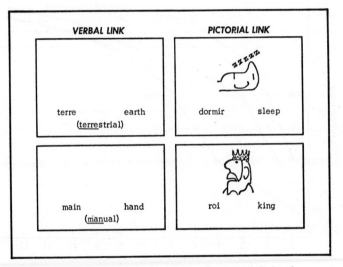

Fig. 6. Some examples of verbal and pictorial links that can become part of verbal chains for French-English associates.

single event. This figure describes the *immediate memory span*. Chains longer than this must be broken up into parts in order for learning to occur most efficiently. However, it may be noted also that the length of the span of immediate memory increases when the material is familiar, and has been organized by previous learning.

If presented with an entire verse of poetry to learn, the learner may "break it up" into various pieces, and put the pieces together in various ways. On the whole, the evidence suggests that under many circumstances the most efficient procedure is what is called the *progressive part* method, in which the learner adds a new part (like a line of the poem) as he continues to rehearse the older parts (McGeoch and Irion, 1952). On the first try, the learner may attempt to say line 1; on the next, lines 1 and 2; on the next, lines 1, 2, and 3; and so on. Such a procedure not only ensures that parts are chosen which are within the span of immediate

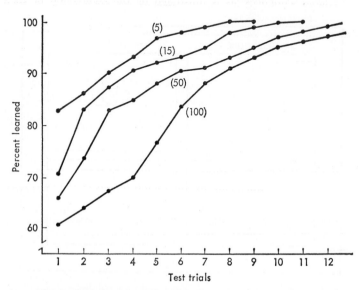

Fig. 7. Learning curves for verbal sequences of 5, 15, 50, and 100 items. (Data of W. C. F. Krueger, Rate of progress as related to difficulty of assignment. *J. educ. Psychol.,* 1946, **37,** 247–249.)

memory, but also allows for the continued practice of earlier learned parts that are subject to forgetting through interference.

Figure 7 shows the rates at which verbal sequences of nonsense syllables were learned, when these were composed of 5, 15, 50, and 100 items. Since these were nonsense syllables, it may be assumed that they were *not* fully discriminated as individual links. Thus, it is quite probable that a sequence of five syllables like BOY ARE HAT TWO RED would have shown close to 100 percent learning after only a single trial. However, the figure does illustrate well the effect of the factor of length of chain on the difficulty of learning.

In the case of lengthy verbal chains, some aspects of the sequence itself may have been previously learned, as well as the individual links. The English language displays some remarkably predictable sequences, as is illustrated by the completion of such phrases as "Boy meets _____," and "Now is the _____." The predictability of such sequences means that the ordering of English words has in many cases been learned previously (see Miller, 1951). Longer chains may be taken in as a "chunk" under such circumstances. Another implication is that the learning of many prose sequences has already been partially accomplished, not only in terms of the discrimination of links, but also in terms of their order.

CONDITIONS OF LEARNING OF VERBAL ASSOCIATES

It should now be possible to state in more formal terms what the important conditions are for the establishment of the capability of reinstating verbal associates and verbal chains.

CONDITIONS WITHIN THE LEARNER · The previous discussion leads to the following summary of the conditions for optimal learning:

1. Each link of the chain to be acquired must have been previously learned as an $Ss \rightarrow R$. This means, of course, that the verbal unit must have been discriminated as a stimulus from other units that may resemble it in a physical sense. It also implies that this unit should be discriminated as the response portion of the connection; in other words, it should be readily pronounceable (Underwood and Shulz, 1960).

2. Mediating connections between each verbal unit and the next must have been previously learned. The greater the learner's available supply of these "coding" connections, the more rapidly will the learning take place. Evidence clearly shows (Noble, 1963) that verbal associates are learned more readily the greater the number of verbal "free associates" there are to the syllables or words being chained. But verbal "codes" are not the only kinds of

mediators usually available. Visual images or auditory images (as in rhymes) may also serve this function extremely well.

CONDITIONS OF THE LEARNING SITUATION · When conditions within the learner are satisfied, the learning of a verbal chain is a fairly simple matter.

1. The verbal units must be presented in the proper sequence. Various methods may be employed to do this, the two most common being presenting the entire chain to be read from left to right, or presenting the units in the chain one after another. This latter method has been extensively used in laboratory studies of verbal sequence learning.

2. The learner must actively make the responses required by the chain. The importance of this condition, as is true for other kinds of chains, is that the responses generate kinesthetic stimuli which become a part of the next succeeding links in each case.

3. As is true for nonverbal chains, learning is aided by the use of external stimuli that furnish cues for order. This kind of extra cue is provided, for example, by mnemonic devices that may have been previously learned. Students of neuroanatomy sometimes learn the names of the cranial nerves in order by learning a rhyme like "On old Olympus' towering top . . . ," the first letters of which cue the order of the nerves "olfactory, optic, oculomotor," and so on. Pronounced poetic meter serves such a function for chains of medium length, as in "When cur'few tolls' the knell' of par'ting day'." Other kinds of "prompting" stimuli may, of course, be used.

4. For words that have not previously been learned in a sequence, it appears that the limit of verbal chain length that can be apprehended as a single event (for previously unchained material) is seven plus or minus two. In other words, the individual's *span of immediate memory* determines the length of chain that can be learned all at once. There is no limit, apparently, to the length of verbal chain that can be learned part by part, for people have memorized entire books verbatim. For long chains, the *progressive part* method has usually been shown to be a most efficient one.

5. There must be provision for *confirmation of correct responses* in the learning situation. This is often provided by exhibiting to the learner a printed form of the entire verbal chain immediately after he has tried to reproduce it, or of each link of the chain following each response. In the learning of sequences of nonsense syllables, the *anticipation method* is often employed, in which the learner attempts to make each response in the chain within a limited time period (for example, two seconds), and then the printed representation of that response is exposed to him. If he has responded correctly, this exposure enables him to confirm the link by matching what he has just said with what he now sees. Many learning theorists consider such an occasion one of reinforcement; presumably, the satisfaction is obtained from knowing that the response is correct.

THE EFFECTS OF INTERFERENCE

One of the most important phenomena that occurs in connection with the learning of verbal associates and sequences is *interference*. Many experimental studies of such learning have led to the inference that the linking of one verbal unit with another (1) tends to reduce the retention of another such linking that has *preceded* it in time, and (2) reduces the probability that a *subsequent* linking will be retained (Underwood, 1964a). In the first case, the interference works "backward" on something previously learned, and so is called *retroactive*; in the second, the interference works forward on something yet to be learned, and is termed *proactive*.

Suppose that one is to learn a verbal chain of six links, such as CAT RED SIT LAM TIN ROW, each one of these links having been well learned as an individual word. If one were to require the learning of chains involving two words at a time, such as CAT-RED, or RED-SIT, it is obvious that each such chain could be learned immediately on a single occasion. Yet when the six words are put together as a six-link chain, and exposed one after another, they probably cannot be learned with perfect accuracy on a single occasion. Why is this so? The most probable explanation is that in the process of connecting up a particular link, because of interference, other links (both previous and subsequent ones) become *harder to remember*.

In the chain CAT   RED   SIT   LAM   TIN   ROW, when one has learned CAT   RED   SIT, these links of the chain will be available in memory when one is later trying to recall TIN (as a later part of the chain), and the recall of TIN will to some extent be made less likely. Similarly, having learned TIN, it will be available in memory when CAT, RED, or SIT are being recalled, and this in turn will reduce the likelihood of recall of each of these words in the chain. The longer the verbal chain, the greater will be the effects of interference on any particular link. Most investigators of verbal sequence learning believe, therefore, that interference is the major influence causing the differences in rate of learning shown in Figure 7. Fifteen items in a chain take longer to learn than 5, and 50 take longer than 15, because of the increased amount of interference in each case. In a 15-item chain, each link becomes *harder to remember* because of both proactive and retroactive interference from 14 other links.

If a suitable experimental procedure is used, interference among verbal links can be demonstrated even with chains as short as 3 verbal items. A small amount of interference may be shown under conditions in which a single word is presented for learning, and the learner is instructed to begin immediately counting backward by threes from some given number. This counting activity interferes with retention of the single word to the extent that recall is only 90 percent probable after an interval of 9 seconds. But when a chain of three words is presented, recall following the same interval of counting is only about 30 percent (Murdock, 1961). The difference in retention is apparently due to the increased interference occurring in the 3-word sequence. In other words, even in a short verbal sequence, a large amount of interference occurs among the units of that sequence.

It is evident, then, that there is still another condition of importance to the establishment of verbal sequences. This is a condition designed to *prevent forgetting*, by overcoming interference from the items in a sequence. How can this be done? One general method is to make the positions of the links highly distinctive. For example, it is known that a highly unusual word occurring, say, in the fourth position of a 10-item sequence will be recalled in this position better than most other items in the sequence. An example of an unusual unit in a 5-unit sequence is as follows: PAL BOY CAT 8 SIR. This factor of distinctiveness may also partially account for the better retention of items at the beginning and at the end of a sequence. Rhythm and meter in a verbal sequence may also have the effect of increasing distinctiveness, making poetry generally easier to remember than the same amount of prose.

But by all odds the most important condition for the prevention of forgetting of verbal sequences is *repetition*. Its effects are seen in Figure 7. The longer the sequence is, the greater the interference, and the more repetition is needed for adequate recall. How does repetition operate in bringing about improved recall of an entire sequence? One good possibility is that repetition is needed to overcome the effects of errors and error tendencies (the latter evidenced by hesitations rather than as overt incorrect responses). As will be mentioned later on, the occurrence of errors implies that *extinction* of a correct link has taken place. If this happens the link may have to be relearned, necessitating an additional repetition. In any case, there can be little doubt that repetition is a most important condition to ensure the retention of verbal chains.

EXTINCTION IN VERBAL CHAINS

The importance of interference in the learning of verbal sequences has by now been quite sufficiently emphasized. The nature of the internal events underlying interference is not as yet well understood. However, a most revealing light has been shed on them by an experiment that deliberately arranged for interference to take place in the response links of verbal paired associates (Barnes and Underwood, 1959) and then examined what happened to these links.

First, the learners acquired a set of eight verbal associates of the form GUZ-*level*. Once these were fully learned, they were set the task of learning a new set of associates with the same initial member and a different final member, as GUZ-*handsome*. After 1, 5, 10, or 20 repetitions of the second list, different groups of learners were asked to write down *all* the adjectives they could remember as associates for the nonsense syllables. Of course, the learners remembered increasing numbers of the adjectives from the second list, the more repetitions they had. But what happened to the adjectives from the *first* set of chains? The finding was that as the second set became more completely learned, increasing numbers of the first set *could not be recalled*. They suffered what may be called (by analogy with types 1 and 2 learning) *extinction*.

The relationship between interference and extinction found in this study is probably a very important one. It clearly suggests that the important event underlying interference is extinction of previously learned connections. In other words, forgetting, as it occurs in verbal chains, is a matter of interference, and this in turn is more usefully conceived as extinction. When a learner makes an error in attempting to reinstate a link in a verbal chain, by so doing he has to some degree brought about extinction of the correct response. The same process may apply to those occasions when the error is not an overt one, but only an omission or a hesitation. When a correct link suffers extinction new learning must occur all over again if the chain is to be reestablished. Hence arises need for repetition to fill in the gaps in a chain that have been occasioned by errors. If it were somehow possible to prevent errors from occurring entirely, perhaps repetition would not be necessary! Unfortunately, the typical verbal chain is so constituted as to make error tendencies highly likely, so that no practical method for eliminating them is apparent.

GENERALIZATION AND DISCRIMINATION IN VERBAL CHAINS

GENERALIZATION • Stimulus generalization of the sort described for type 2 learning can occur within any of the links in a verbal chain. If one first learns a nonsense sequence composed of such units as GEJ, KIV, and HAX, for example, there will be generalizing tendencies to a second list with such units as GEX, KAJ, and HIV. The two sets of units are physically similar both in their appearance and in their sounds, and the response appropriate to a unit in one chain will tend to be connected by generalization to the stimulus of a unit in the other chain. As a consequence, the requirements for discrimination of each link will be severe. The second chain, accordingly, is harder to learn than the first because it tends to give rise to "generalization errors." These in turn have the typical consequences for interference that have already been described, and so make both such chains less likely to be recalled correctly, even when both have been learned fully in the first place. Generalization is shown in such instances to have the effect of making the learning of verbal sequences more difficult by increasing the difficulty of discrimination of the individual links. The same kind of generalization event can also occur among the links of a single chain, with predictable results.

Sometimes, however, generalization seems to work to make a second learning task easier rather than more difficult. The clearest example, perhaps, lies in the generalizing tendencies of *mediating* links. If the learner has initially acquired verbal associates such as BOY-HAPPY, LION-ANGRY, TEACHER-SEVERE, experimental findings show that it is then considerably easier for him to learn the associates BOY-JOYFUL, LION-MAD, TEACHER-HARD. Presumably, the reason is that the coding links for HAPPY and for JOYFUL have considerable similarity, if not identity; and this may likewise be true of a coding link for ANGRY and for MAD, or for SEVERE and for HARD. Although the result is clear, it should perhaps be emphasized here that this reasoning about why it happens involves an extension of meaning of the word "generalization." The original meaning, it will be recalled, pertains to similarity of the physical characteristics of stimuli, and it is a jump from this to speculations about similarities in implicit mediating links. Another possible way of accounting for this latter kind of generalizing will be evident from the discussion of concepts in the next chapter.

SOME EDUCATIONAL IMPLICATIONS

It is apparent from our discussion of verbal chaining that representative human performances can easily be found in everyday life, both in and out of school. Children *do* sometimes learn the sequence of letters in the alphabet, whether or not this is considered good pedagogical practice. Students memorize formulas, or key numbers like the square roots of 2 and 3, and occasionally much longer numbers. Children are often expected to learn the Lord's Prayer, the first verse of "The Star Spangled Banner," the Pledge of Allegiance, and a number of other verses, sayings, or quotations. Students often have to memorize the school cheer, and may, of course, learn many lines as amateur actors. But all these seem to lack an essentiality, an urgency, when considered in terms of the larger goals of education. The sequence of the alphabet, after all, is not involved in learning to read. Formulas can easily be looked up. And although "The Star Spangled Banner" may be of some use in social gatherings, it can gradually "sink in" by being heard many times through mechanical amplifiers. Although few educational scholars would be inclined to say memorization is "bad," it is pretty generally thought to be unimportant. Perhaps it is a matter of priority: students must acquire knowledge and the ability to think, and these goals are heavily emphasized in today's curricula.

It was not always thus in American schools. Half a century ago there was much verbal memorization—the alphabet, the multiplication table, numerical quantities and formulas, poetry, prose writings like the Gettysburg Address, the preamble to the Constitution, and so on. Students practiced reciting the verbal passages they had learned, and declamation contests rewarded oratorical skill in the expression of verbal materials. Verbal memorization is still emphasized today, we are told, in schools in many parts of the world, particularly in Asian countries, and to some extent in Europe.

Is there an educational value to the memorization of verbal sequences? What are the considerations that should enter into a determination of priority for instruction of this sort? The answer to these questions lies in a recognition of the most important usage for recalled verbal phrases, sentences, or passages. This is not to be found in the saving of time realized by recalling a formula rather than looking it up. The major usage of recalled verbal sequences is rather in the area of language itself—specifically, in the construction of verbal utterances that communicate ideas. The question is, What degree of skill is it important for students to have in expressing their ideas in oral form, whether in simple conversation, in informal conference, or in lectures and speeches? To what extent are we interested in providing students with skills of communication and persuasion?

It is no accident that some of the most renowned American orators of previous generations have been men who knew such literature as the Bible and the writings of Shakespeare to the extent that they could repeat whole passages verbatim. These and other literary sources are fundamental to our language. People who are skilled in oral communication are able to recall words, phrases, or entire passages of flowing English, and to weave them into their own vocal utterances in highly effective ways. They are able to do this, not simply because they have *read* these classics of English literature, but because they have *memorized* them. In the terms used in the present chapter, they have learned many varieties of verbal sequences, and can recall them readily. They are able to utilize at will such phrases as "dedicated to the proposition that all men are created equal," or "a tide in the affairs of men," or "seeking the bubble reputation," or "the slings and arrows of outrageous fortune," or "in the course of human events," or "I shall not want," or "with what measure ye mete, it shall be measured unto you," and many, many others.

Naturally, such memorized verbal sequences may also become a source of clichés in both writing and speaking. Phrases such as "stark naked," "utterly exhausted," "starry-eyed wonder," "justifiable wrath," "global diplomacy," and many others, since they have been encountered so frequently in reading material and in everyday speech, become memorized portions of the individual's language repertoire. An orator may sometimes deliberately use such clichés to exploit the appeal they have for his audience. But a skillful speaker is one who has also learned to "play the changes" on such familiar material, so that the completely familiar is avoided. And it is even more important for the writer to seek to avoid excessive use of such phrases, even though they form an important part of his background.

In sum, then, the most direct and obvious employment for memorized verbal sequences is in the construction of created language, particularly in oral speech. The construction of effective original speech does not depend simply on an understanding of rules for grammatical expression. It requires the ready recall of a large fund of verbal sequences that can be woven into novel passages of spoken English in a countless variety of patterns.

GENERAL REFERENCES

Chaining Motor Responses

    Gilbert, T. F. Mathetics: the technology of education. *J. Mathetics,* 1962, *1,* 7–74.

    Keller, F. S., and Schoenfeld, W. N. *Principles of psychology.* New York: Appleton-Century-Crofts, 1950. Chap. 7.

Chaining Verbal Associates

    Cofer, C. N. (Ed.) *Verbal learning and verbal behavior.* New York: McGraw-Hill, 1961.

    Deese, J. *The psychology of learning.* New York: McGraw-Hill, 1958. Chap. 7.

    McGeoch, J. A., and Irion, A. L. *The psychology of human learning* (2nd ed.) New York: McKay, 1952.

    Skinner, B. F. *Verbal behavior.* New York: Appleton-Century-Crofts, 1957.

    Underwood, B. J., and Shulz, R. W. *Meaningfulness and verbal learning.* Philadelphia: Lippincott, 1960.

MULTIPLE DISCRIMINATION; CONCEPT LEARNING

5

Once basic stimulus-response connections have been learned, they may be put together in a sequential fashion to generate capabilities of greatly increased complexity. They may also be put together in other ways, and two of the major ones are to be described in the present chapter. Specifically, the connections may be arranged, not in chains of one after another, but in a fashion that requires responding to stimuli all at one time, either by selecting any single one, or by reacting to them as a group.

Suppose an individual has learned a simple $Ss \rightarrow R$ to the stimulus provided by a door key. We have already seen that this connection may be combined with others to form a chain that results in the performance of opening a door. But there are other ways of responding to a key, and particularly to collections of keys. To be considered here are the learning of capabilities that may be briefly described as follows:

1. The individual chooses one key to open his front door, another for his back door, another for his car, another for his desk, and a fifth for his file cabinet.

2. The individual responds to a specific assortment of keys as "lock openers," and is also able to identify this function for an entirely unfamiliar object that he is told is a "key."

Both these occurrences begin with stimulation provided by collections of stimulus objects or events. However, these are two rather different kinds of capabilities, and it will be seen that the conditions for their establishment also differ. In the kind of learning first mentioned, the individual becomes capable of making different responses to the different members of a particular collection. This is called *multiple discrimination*. In the second type, the learner becomes able to respond in a single way to the collection as a class, which then extends beyond the particular members that were originally present. This second kind of learning is called *concept learning*. Both these forms of learning are of considerable importance in a practical sense. As will be seen, there is a marked contrast in the versatility of behavior produced by learning of the second kind as opposed to the first.

This chapter, then, deals with two different kinds of learning that may be accomplished when an individual is confronted with a set of stimulus objects. In such circumstances, it may be necessary for the learner to learn to respond to each member of the set of stimuli in a different manner, distinguishing them from each other by name or otherwise, in multiple discrimination. Alternatively, what may be required is for the learner to acquire the capability of responding to this set of stimuli as a class, which is what is meant by "learning a concept." Of course, the learner may be required to respond to the stimulus set in *both* these ways on different occasions, and this is perfectly possible for him to do.

MULTIPLE-DISCRIMINATION LEARNING (TYPE 5)

Acquiring multiple discriminations is obviously an undertaking of great importance in everyday life and in school learning. The young child must learn at a very early age to distinguish among people, toys, articles of clothing, eating implements, objects within the household, pets, and many other aspects of his environment. Adults, too, are constantly being called upon to acquire new discriminations of stimulus objects, such as the locations of doors or streets, the titles of books, the names that go with new faces. As for learning in the school, the student is confronted from his earliest days with the necessity for multiple discriminations in shapes, sizes, colors, lengths, volumes, and printed characters. He goes on to learn distinctions among solids, liquids, gases, parts of the earth and the universe, and a tremendous variety of living things; he learns symbols of mathematics and the sciences; he acquires differentiations of events and people of historical note, the offices and functions of government, and varieties of social and economic institutions.

Multiple-discrimination learning is essentially a matter of establishing numbers of different chains. Perhaps the easiest kind to illustrate are differential verbal chains, in view of the consideration of these as individual learning events in the previous chapter. As was there pointed out, a student of a foreign language may be required to learn "translation connections," the foreign equivalents of English words, and the English equivalents of foreign words. Furthermore, the student may be required to learn a *set* of such equivalents at one time, in order to perform some subsequent exercise. Many language teachers now believe this is not the best way to learn to read or speak a foreign language, but this problem may be disregarded for purposes of the example. A typical lesson in beginning French, for instance, might include the following list of equivalents:

cheese — le fromage
buy   — acheter
give   — donner
face   — le visage
wood   — le bois
store — le magasin
taste — le goût

The student is asked to learn these French words so that he can supply each one to the stimulus of the relevant English word. By so doing, the student is later expected to be able to construct a phrase or sentence indicating, for example, that he wants to buy (acheter) cheese (fromage) in a French store (magasin).

As noted in the previous chapter, each single one of these equivalents may be learned as a verbal associate, a chain containing at least three links. For example, it is likely that the word "give" can readily be associated with its French equivalent by means of a mediating link providing an auditory coding, as follows:

$$Ss \xrightarrow[\text{give}]{} r \underset{\text{donate}}{\sim} s \xrightarrow[\text{donate}]{} r \underset{\text{donner}}{\sim} s \xrightarrow[\text{donner}]{} R \text{ "donner"}$$

Thus an entire set of multiple discriminations would be represented as follows:

$$Ss \xrightarrow[\text{give}]{} r \sim s \xrightarrow{\hspace{1cm}} r \sim s \xrightarrow{\hspace{1cm}} R \text{ "donner"}$$

$$Ss \xrightarrow[\text{wood}]{} r \sim s \xrightarrow{\hspace{1cm}} r \sim s \xrightarrow{\hspace{1cm}} R \text{ "le bois"}$$

$$Ss \xrightarrow[\text{taste}]{} r \sim s \xrightarrow{\hspace{1cm}} r \sim s \xrightarrow{\hspace{1cm}} R \text{ "le goût"}$$

and so on.

The middle $s \rightarrow r$ in each chain represents the coding link, whereas the others may be thought of as stimulus link and response link, respectively.

But what happens to the situation, so far as learning is concerned, when the learner must acquire all the chains at once, rather than only one? First, it is apparent that the task of discriminating the stimuli one from the other increases the difficulty of learning. When *give* is presented alone, the discrimination task is not very demanding, but when *give* is presented along with *buy*, the chances of confusion owing to lack of discrimination is increased. This point can be illustrated more vividly by the presentation of a somewhat different list of French equivalents, such as the following:

arm	— le bras
leg	— la jambe
elbow	— le coude
shoulder	— l'épaule
wrist	— le poignet
knee	— le genou
hand	— la main
foot	— le pied
finger	— le doigt

Even the English words providing the stimuli are subject to some confusion, although they are pretty well learned in the adult. But as a set of stimulus associates for multiple discrimination, they need to be well discriminated one from the other, preferably so that they can generate very different mediating responses. It would not be undesirable, therefore, to be sure that the learner, before proceeding with the learning of chains, possessed well-learned discriminations of these parts of the body.

Another site of discrimination difficulty is in the final link in the verbal associate chain—the response link, as it is sometimes called. It may be noted that this is still a matter of stimulus discrimination, this time of the stimuli generated by responses—the small "s's" of the $Ss \rightarrow R$. If they are not to cause confusion difficulties, French words like *fin, faim,* and *femme* must be well discriminated as stimulus-response connections. This is so despite the fact of their marked differences in meaning; they need to be discriminated as learner-generated sounds.

The second major change in the multiple-discrimination, as opposed to the single-discrimination situation, is that a great potential for *interference* exists, which tends to favor forgetting. No sooner has the learner acquired French associates for *arm* and *leg,* than he must further learn the equivalents for *knee* and *foot.* When he attempts to recall any of these, interference occurs, and reduces the probability of recall.

Bearing in mind these two sources of difficulty for multiple discrimination learning, let us return to our first example of an English-French word list, beginning with *cheese–le fromage.* Each of these associates will be most readily learned, by itself, if the optimal conditions for verbal chaining are in effect. First, the word "cheese" must be well learned. One can assume this, perhaps, in an adult, but not necessarily in a child. If one wants third-graders to learn from printed word lists, it is essential that they can read the English words! For another thing, the word "fromage" must also have been previously acquired, so that the learner really knows how to say what he is expected to say as a response. And third, a coding response must be available. Of course, this will vary among individuals. *Cheese-foaming-fromage* would probably serve the purpose. Obviously some associates are going to suggest more readily available codes than will others; *face-visage* seems to be a particularly easy one. Easiest of all, of course, are the near cognates and cognates of the two languages, like *reality-réalité*, and *latitude-latitude*.

Having ensured that all these prerequisite learnings have occurred, the learner faces a task that is not a particularly difficult one. Initially, each chain is produced by "prompting"; that is, the instructor may say "cheese" and then "fromage," or perhaps expose both words together in printed form. For each single associate, the learner is then able to reinstate the entire chain by himself, when the stimulus (the English word) is presented.

But the task of *retaining* what he has learned is considerably more difficult when a multiple set of associates is being learned. The solution (the best available, and perhaps the only one) is to proceed to learn the associates one by one, and then to return and give them more repetitions one by one, in a somewhat different order. (This last condition is used for the purpose of avoiding the use of cues for sequence, which tend to establish chains that have to be unlearned later.) The question of how many to learn before undertaking recall and repetition is one that has not received a clear answer from laboratory experimentation. It is likely that a kind of "progressive part" learning works as well for this purpose as it does for chain learning (cf. McGeoch and Irion, 1952).

Another example of multiple discrimination may be described here in order to illustrate the kind of evidence that has been obtained in systematic experimental studies. Gibson (1942) set two different tasks for her experimental subjects, each requiring the multiple discrimination of thirteen verbal chains. The stimuli for these were nonsense figures, of which six are illustrated for each task in Figure 8. For each of these tasks, the final links were the same monosyllabic words.

Obviously, these two tasks differ considerably in their discrimination requirements, since the stimuli of the first task are much more similar to each other than are the stimuli of the second task. In both cases, the stimuli were first presented together with their associates. On subsequent trials, the stimulus was first presented, and after a brief delay during which the learner attempted to supply the correct associate, the combination stimulus and associate was again exposed. This is a standard experimental method used in studying multiple-discrimination learning, called the *anticipation method*.

The results obtained in this study have been often replicated with different materials. The set of multiple discriminations con-

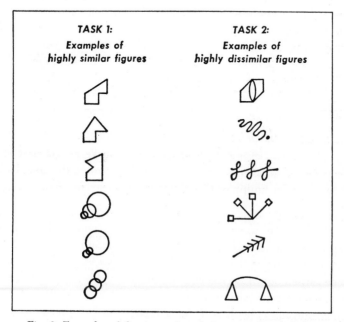

Fig. 8. Examples of figures used to design sets of verbal chains having highly similar stimuli (task 1), and highly dissimilar stimuli (task 2). (E. J. Gibson, Retroactive inhibition as a function of degree of generalization between tasks. *J. exp. Psychol.,* 1941, **28**, 93–115).

taining highly similar stimuli required, on the average, 19.8 repetitions to learn, whereas the set with stimuli of low similarity needed only 8.9 repetitions. Increasing the similarity of the set of stimulus objects involved in multiple-discrimination learning, then, has the quite definite effect of increasing the difficulty of learning. The interference that takes place during the learning session is greater when there is more stimulus generalization. The effect is to increase the need for repetition in overcoming the forgetting that occurs when an entire set of chains must be learned at once.

It is of some interest to note that once the multiple discriminations are learned, whether they have been difficult or easy, they then are subsequently remembered just about equally well. This was Gibson's finding when she measured retention of these two different sets of verbal chains after one day, and it has been confirmed in other studies (Underwood, 1953). In other words, once the multiple discriminations have been fully established, retention is no longer affected by interference *within* the set. It may be, of course, and undoubtedly is, affected by interference from other sources, such as the learning of still other verbal chains.

CONDITIONS OF LEARNING MULTIPLE DISCRIMINATIONS

The various examples described should make possible a fairly complete formulation of some propositions regarding the conditions of learning for multiple discriminations.

Conditions within the Learner

1. One way to specify the conditions for optimal learning is to say that the learner must have previously acquired, *in isolation*, each of the chains that make up the set to be learned. Were this to be carried out, it is clear that learning would be a simple matter of exposing these chains to the learner all at once. But this is rather unrealistic, because if the learner has in fact already learned the individual chains, then getting him to reinstate them merely confirms the fact that they are learned.

2. Usually, the learner has not learned all the chains that make up the multiple discrimination, and he may not have learned any of them. In view of this, it may be said that he needs to have accomplished *for each chain*, the same prerequisites that have been previously described for verbal-associate learning (type 4). This means that the initial stimulus links must have been previously discriminated from each other, and that the response links must also have been previously learned as discriminated $Ss \rightarrow R$ connections.

Referring to our previous example of English-French equivalents, learning these "translation" connections will occur most readily if we know that the learner (1) can identify the English words (this could be assumed in an average adult), (2) is able to "say" the French words when he sees or hears them, and (3) can supply a mediating link. The availability of such links will, of course, vary with the individual, and those people who have a greater supply will presumably acquire the set of chains more rapidly than others (cf. Deese, 1961).

Although experimental studies clearly indicate the importance of these prerequisites for acquiring multiple discriminations, it is equally clear that this type of learning has not often been investigated under conditions in which these learner conditions have been present. (In Gibson's study, for example, the learners did not *prediscriminate* either the stimulus figures or the word responses; many other studies can be similarly characterized.)

CONDITIONS IN THE LEARNING SITUATION

1. The entire set of stimuli that are to be associated in different chains must be presented to the learner one by one, so that he is able to reinstate the chain for each. On this initial presentation, an external stimulus must be used as a "prompt" to ensure the occurrence of the required response in close temporal contiguity with the stimulus. In many cases of verbal-associate learning, the printed word itself is used to prompt the response, as: FACE–LE VISAGE. However, it may not always be necessary, for a prompt like this

FACE–le vis . . .

might well bring forth the correct response in an adult learner who has already learned that there is such a French word as *visage*. It is not apparent that it makes any difference what sort of prompt is used, just so long as it serves to bring forth the required response, and thus to establish the chain.

2. If discrimination learning of the links of the various chains has already been accomplished, as previously described, the interference resulting from generalization among similar stimuli will

be greatly reduced. Nevertheless, some interference will occur, and this generates the need for *repetition*. Under such circumstances, the amount of repetition required will increase with the number of chains to be discriminated.

3. The arrangement of repetition to accomplish learning of the entire set of discriminations best is a question that has not yet received a clear experimental answer. Whether one should learn two chains, or three, or four, or ten, before repeating those previously learned is not known. It may not even make much difference.

As was true in the case of chaining, it needs to be emphasized again that repetition in multiple-discrimination learning does not appear to have the function of strengthening individual connections. It simply does not make logical sense to think that it does, when it is known that any *single* chain whose component $Ss \rightarrow R$'s have been previously well learned can readily be acquired in one trial (for example, a chain like MAN-THREE by an English-speaking adult). Of course, a chain whose components have *not* been previously learned (as HOMME-TROIS, in a person unacquainted with French) may require repetition because its component $Ss \rightarrow R$'s (HOMME $\rightarrow$ "homme" and TROIS $\rightarrow$ "trois") must be learned. But that is quite another story, as we have already seen in Chapter 4, and should not be confused with multiple-discrimination learning.

The function that repetition clearly does have is that of overcoming the effects of forgetting brought about by interference. Presumably, interference occurs because learned chains undergo some degree of *extinction* when other chains are learned within the same situation. In any case, the amount of interference will depend on the number of single chains that constitute the multiple-discrimination task. The more chains there are for the learner to acquire (and differentiate), the greater the amount of repetition needed.

4. Again as in the case of single-chain learning, there must be in multiple-discrimination learning a condition that provides for *confirmation*, the matching of the responses with those that are known to be correct. When the learner reinstates a chain, he

must have a way of knowing that it contains a correct terminal response. In practice, this is often done by exposing to him the word that represents a correct outcome, immediately following his response. For example, if he is learning to respond properly to CHEESE- ———, the French word FROMAGE may be shown to him (or said to him) just after he makes his response. Most learning theorists hold that this operation is one of *reinforcement.*

MULTIPLE-DISCRIMINATION LEARNING AND VERBAL ASSOCIATES

Studies of multiple-discrimination learning in the psychological laboratory have to a large extent included investigations of the learning of sets of *verbal paired associates.* Various verbal materials have been used for this purpose, including "lists" of nonsense associates, GIX-REV, WEP-DAK and so on, and meaningful word associates CAUTIOUS-SICKLY, LIQUID-TROUBLED. The generalizations that appear warranted concerning *single* associates of this sort were summarized in the preceding chapter. Here are others applying to *sets* of associates, which are accordingly relevant to multiple discrimination learning:

1. Learning difficulty increases with similarity of the chains. This conclusion applies when the first members of the chains are similar to each other (as in the set DAF-HUF, DAK-ZEP, DAL-POB, and so on), and also when the final members of the chains are similar (as in DAF-HUF, JAL-HUZ, WEP-HUK). As previously mentioned, either of these arrangements implies the need for more precise discrimination of the $Ss \rightarrow R$ links that make up the list. In the typical paired-associate experiment, such discrimination learning has *not* been carried out as a prerequisite to multiple-discrimination learning. When such discriminations are preestablished, learning of the set of associates becomes a markedly simpler task (Saltz, 1961).

2. Learning difficulty is also affected by the degree of similarity in *meaning* of word members of the chains (as in a list like ANGRY-GIDDY, ENRAGED-ROYAL, WRATHFUL-PERFECT), but in a somewhat complex manner (Underwood, 1953). In all probability, this kind of relationship needs further

investigation if it is to be understood in terms of the mediating links of the words, as suggested in the previous chapter.

3. The most prominent phenomenon in multiple-discrimination learning is *interference*. Whenever recall is attempted, whether during the course of learning the entire set or afterward, evidence is obtained of confusion among the links of the chains that make up the set. A response link that has been initially acquired as a part of one chain turns up in recall as part of a second chain, and vice versa. The chains GEX-JOYFUL, DAX-ANGRY, as members of a larger set, have a tendency to be recalled as GEX-ANGRY, DAX-JOYFUL. Such "intralist intrusions" were included as predictions in the theory of interference originally stated by Gibson (1940) and further studied in her investigation of multiple-discrimination learning. They appear to be primarily, if not solely, responsible for generation of the need for repetition in such learning.

Perhaps it is worthwhile pointing out, too, that although different responses learned in multiple discrimination are commonly *names* for the objects differentiated, they need not be. The sender of Morse code learns a set of key-tapping patterns to differentiate the individual letters of the message he wants to transmit. The student of the clarinet learns to distinguish a set of printed notes by means of a set of fingering responses, each of which bears a specific relationship to a particular note. The operator of a panel controlling industrial or other machinery may have to learn a large number of different key-pressing responses that distinguish the various signals he receives. In all these instances, multiple discrimination is required of a set of chains that may have been (and preferably are) previously learned as individual entities. And in all these instances there are strong tendencies toward interference among the chains, interference that is overcome by the use of repetition.

OTHER PHENOMENA OF MULTIPLE-DISCRIMINATION LEARNING

It has already been necessary to speak of the phenomena of generalization, discrimination, extinction, and forgetting, because these are directly involved in the conditions of learning for multiple discrimination. It will be worthwhile to review these points briefly.

GENERALIZATION • The phenomenon of stimulus generalization occurs among the stimuli being differentiated. It also occurs among the stimuli of the other links in each chain, and this includes the terminal or "response" link. The greater the similarity of the elements of the chains that are to be differentiated, the more difficult is the learning.

DISCRIMINATION • Generalization tendencies among the stimuli of each chain create the necessity for discrimination ($Ss \rightarrow R$) learning of each link of each chain. When such learning is completed as a prerequisite to multiple-discrimination learning, the latter occurs most rapidly.

EXTINCTION • Extinction of any particular chain in the set may be accomplished by omitting reinforcement. Accordingly, extinction is important in bringing about the unlearning of *incorrect* response links. When incorrect responses occur, they may be eliminated by omission of reinforcement, or more specifically, by a failure to be confirmed. However, research findings suggest that the occurrence of such errors fosters the extinction of *correct* responses so that they cannot be recalled, and must therefore be relearned. In other words, it seems likely that extinction is the fundamental cause of the interference that is such a prominent feature of multiple-discrimination learning.

FORGETTING • Forgetting of individual chains is produced by the interference generated by learning other chains that make up the total set. This necessitates frequent review of previously learned chains, by repetition during the learning session. Once the multiple discriminations are all learned, they are still highly subject to forgetting. The curve of forgetting for multiple discriminations is similar to that found by Ebbinghaus for chains: retention falls off rapidly at first, then more and more slowly over a period of days and weeks. Again, properly spaced reviews make it possible to keep retention at a high level.

SOME SALIENT CHARACTERISTICS

This kind of learning is obviously not a simple sort. It requires a good deal of previous learning of chains, verbal or otherwise, to bring it off with greatest effectiveness. Although in its ideal form it occurs quite rapidly, by its very nature it is highly subject to interference and thus to the occurrence of forgetting. The conditions required for its establishment include as points of major emphasis (1) increasing the precision of discrimination of the stimuli to be differentiated, by means of previous learning and otherwise; and (2) using repetition (review) to overcome the effects of interference among the member chains of the set.

Multiple discriminations are frequently required in the learning that takes place in school. The young child must learn distinguishing names for a great variety of classes of things and events in his environment—rocks, birds, stars, flowers, coins, and many, many others. He must learn to make different responses to many kinds of printed symbols—letters, numerals, words, and other signs. The student acquires a multitude of discriminations during his education—of gases, liquids, solids, parts of the earth and universe, animals, plants, musical notes, works of art. People must learn new discriminations all their lives, of common objects, novel symbols, new faces. But besides the widespread occurrence of this type of learning, it also plays an important role, as we shall see, in other still more complex learning activities which are yet to be described.

CONCEPT LEARNING (TYPE 6)

One way the individual can learn to respond to collections of things is by distinguishing among them. Another way, even more important as a human capability, is by putting things into a class and responding to the class as a whole. In a sense this latter kind of learning seems just the opposite of the first kind. But it is more than that because it incorporates the first kind as one of its preconditions. This latter type of learning, which makes it possible for the individual to respond to things or events as a class, is called *concept learning*.

Suppose one were to show a seven-year-old child a set of three hollow blocks on a table top. Two of these blocks are for practical purposes identical, but the other is different. The child is told that a small piece of candy is under one of the blocks, but there is no candy under the others. He is to try to "guess" where the candy is, and lift one or more blocks to get it. (We may call the blocks A, A, and B.) Unknown to the child, the experimenter follows the rule of always placing the candy under the *odd* block, the one that is unlike the other two. Initially, of course, the child really does guess, and the connection $S_{\overrightarrow{B}} R_{lift}$ is reinforced. Now the experimenter places a new set of hollow blocks, of different appearance, C, C, and D, on the table, with the candy under D. (Of course, the spatial placement of the blocks is made unsystematic in all cases.) Now the child, after one or more errors, chooses block D, and the connection is reinforced. Other combinations may be tried, such as BBA, DDC, BBC, FEF, and so on. Eventually, it is found, the child *chooses the odd one*. Once this happens, he is able to perform the task without error for *any* set of blocks, such as XXY, with which he has had no specific previous experience. It may then be said that the child is *using a concept*, or that he is behaving conceptually.

In order for such a statement about the child's behavior to be valid, certain things must be true. First, it must be known that his behavior could not have been learned as a simple $Ss \rightarrow R$ connection, or as a chain of such connections. If one used only a single set of blocks, like AAB, the child could learn to choose the odd one on the basis of its appearance alone (B), as an $Ss \rightarrow R$ connection. Similarly, if one always placed the blocks in the same spatial order, so that the odd one was always on the extreme right, the child could learn a simple stimulus-response connection to a particular location as the stimulus. In order to state that the child is using a concept, one must be able to demonstrate that the performance is impossible on the basis of simpler forms of learning. This can be done, as in the example given, by presenting the child with novel stimulus objects in novel positions. If he responds correctly, it may be justifiably said that he "knows what the *odd one* is," or that he knows the concept *odd*.

The example illustrates a way that individuals have of responding to collections of things, which is different from multiple discrimination. In this case, there are collections of objects that may vary widely among themselves in appearance. The individual naturally must distinguish among them. But the important thing he does is something else: he responds to them in terms of some *common abstract* property. In a real sense, he *classifies* them.

What the child does in this situation with the blocks may be inferred to be something like the following. He may initially say to himself "Oh, it's B." Having found that this doesn't work when CC and D are presented, he may say to himself "It's the one on the right," or "It's the blue one." But none of these verbal chains are successful; they are unreinforced and become extinguished. Eventually, he says to himself, "It's the odd one," and this turns out to work every time. Does he *actually* say these things to himself? It is difficult to obtain evidence that proves this. But so far as the ultimately correct performance is concerned, the child behaves *as if* he could say to himself, "It's the odd one." To be able to state that the child uses a concept, one has only to demonstrate that such an "as if" clause is true.

Returning to our example of concept using in the seven-year-old, it is of considerable interest to ask whether he has to go through this trial-and-error procedure in order to demonstrate his knowledge of the concept *odd*. The answer is, of course, no. It is much easier to bring about the performance required in this situation by saying to the child, "Choose the odd one!" For an average seven-year-old, this instruction should bring about the correct performance immediately. What is shown by the use of this new condition, naturally, is that the 7-year-old hasn't really *learned* the concept in this situation at all. He knew it all the time, and an external verbal cue was sufficient to reinstate the correct behavior.

The trial-and-error exercise is often used by psychologists who study concept using in order to make a detailed analysis of the process. It is not a good example of how concepts are usually learned, but only of how they *may* be learned. But it is nevertheless instructive. Suppose the seven-year-old were a Spanish child who knew no English, and therefore had never learned the word "odd" as an $Ss \rightarrow R$ connection. Naturally, the instruction "choose the odd one" would not enable him to perform the task correctly. In order to find out whether he knew the concept, one would have to put him through such an exercise. Or, the same sort of trial-and-error exercise might be used if one wished to determine whether an animal could use such a concept as *odd*. Harlow (1949) has used similar procedures to demonstrate that monkeys can respond correctly to tasks requiring the concept *odd*.

AN EXAMPLE OF CONCEPT LEARNING

Although the meaning of *concept* may have been illustrated by the previous discussion, the description of the learning of a concept is not yet complete. A concept may be acquired by means of a trial-and-error procedure, but this is not necessarily typical, except perhaps for monkeys. How does a human being learn a concept?

Let it be supposed that a child capable of using language does not know the concept *edge*. Assume it is desired that he exhibit the capability of identifying an edge by name, and more importantly, by identifying any one of a class of things called edges in novel situations. How can such learning come about?

The first step might be for him to acquire the word as a self-generated $Ss \rightarrow R$ connection (type 2 learning), so that when the instructor says "edge" and then asks that the word be repeated, the student says "edge." Next, the student will learn to identify two or three specific edges, by saying "edge" whenever an actual edge is pointed to. By this means he acquires individual verbal associates (type 4 learning). Following this, there need to be several occurrences of multiple-discrimination learning (type 5) in which discriminations are established between each edge and a variety of stimulus situations that are not edges. The *side* of a three-dimensional object, the *top*, the *corner*, the *curved surface*—all need to be distinguished from the *edge*. Requiring the student to make these distinctions by means of words is not essential but might readily be done. The important event is the firm and precise attainment of the *edge* discrimination. A similar multiple discrimination may be learned for a flat-surfaced object such as a piece of paper, involving distinctions between *edge* and *surface* and *corner*; still another for a drawn two-dimensional figure, which may show *shading* as well as clear edges.

How many situations need to be used to establish precise discriminations of edge from other stimuli that are not edge? There appears to be no known answer to this question. But it is important to conduct the discrimination learning within stimulus situations that *represent the actual range of the concept being learned*; otherwise, the concept that emerges will be in some sense incomplete. The examples given here seem reasonably appropriate for this purpose. The student needs to know what an edge is in a three-dimensional object, in a flat thin object like a piece of paper, and in a drawn two-dimensional picture.

At this point, all the prerequisite learning has been accomplished. The student can now say "edge" to three different and specific stimulus situations. He is now ready for that particular event called concept learning. The instructor uses a verbal communication, while presenting all three of these stimuli at once (the three-dimensional object, the paper, the drawing). He says, "Each of these is an edge. What is this? (An edge.) And what is this? (An edge.) And what is this? (An edge.)" Finally he takes one more step, and shows the student a new object or drawing with which he has not previously associated the word "edge." The instructor says, "Where is the edge?" The student points to it. A concept has been acquired!

It is not entirely clear whether the use of the final new example is necessary for the learning itself, or whether it is merely a test of what has already been learned. Quite probably, the former is the case. At any rate, the instructor will probably wish to make a more reliable determination that concept learning has really happened, by asking the student to respond to one or two additional examples, each a novel one.

What is the role of the verbal associate—the word "edge"—in this set of events? Obviously, it provides an important shortcut to the learning of a concept. Without it, one would have to engage in rather elaborate means to ensure that $Ss \rightarrow R$'s to each of the specific stimulus situations were all reinstated close together in time. The instructions "This is an edge, and this is an edge, and this is an edge" make it possible for these three common verbal associates to be recalled by the learner in close contiguity. They can be "cued off" by a word, provided only that the student has already learned the chains in which the word occurs. The function of the word is that of an external stimulus to recall, which makes it relatively easy to structure the situation required for learning. When the student knows the word as a common connection for all three examples, instruction becomes a matter of "telling him" what the concept is.

Thus it may be seen that the learning of a concept is not *necessarily* a verbal matter, since concepts can be learned otherwise by animals as well as by human beings. But using verbal cues makes concept learning a relatively *easy* matter for human beings who have already mastered the prerequisites. The kind of verbalization described here, however, needs to be carefully distinguished from the verbalizing that presents a definition. As an example of the latter, an edge might be defined as "a region of abrupt change in intensity of the pattern of light waves reflected to the eye from a surface." It should not be supposed that this kind of verbalizing would be very effective in bringing about the learning of a concept. (Learning of concepts does sometimes occur this way in highly sophisticated adults, but that is another story.) The learner must instead begin with concrete situations, to which he may bring a common verbal associate. When this condition obtains, using the word as an "instruction" is a convenient way of generating the proper conditions for concept learning.

The kind of capability that is established by concept learning may be depicted as follows, using the *edge* example:

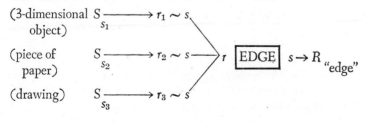

Individual chains to specific edges, established by multiple-discrimination learning, are the first components. These come together in a common event in the nervous system that we infer to underlie the concept EDGE. This makes possible the establishment of a common technical connection, which in this case consists in saying the word "edge."

Adults learn new concepts in much the same way. Suppose, for example, an adult who is studying physiology must learn the concept of *striated muscle*. In such a case one assumes that the basic learning of the words has already been accomplished. But the verbal chains must be established that connect several instances of observed tissue samples (actual or pictured) to the response "striated muscle." Furthermore, a number of multiple discriminations must probably also be acquired; the individual must learn to distinguish muscle tissue from other forms, and of course to distinguish striated from smooth and heart muscle. Once these have been mastered, the basic instructional conditions can be carried out for concept learning. That is, various instances of striated muscle are shown at one time (or in quick succession) and identified by the student, who is then ready to classify a new example of striated muscle as a member of the concept class.

Is this all he must learn about a concept in order to be said to "know" it? The answer is yes, so long as the word "know" means nothing more than to use the new entity as a concept. Of course, an adult will probably go on to learn more about striated muscle in the form of principles (to be discussed in the next chapter). He may learn how striated muscles work, where they occur in the body, their embryological development, and many other things. But these additional learnings will be useless except as sheer verbalizations, unless he first knows the concept by reference to a *class of concrete situations*. It may be noted that this observation about concepts has profound implications for educational practice. It is, for example, the fundamental reason for laboratory work in science instruction. Concepts may be aroused by verbal means, as we have seen. In human beings, their learning is almost always based on verbal chains. But to be accurate tools for thinking about and dealing with the real world, concepts must be referable to actual stimulus situations. These provide them with an "operational" meaning that can come in no other way.

Seven-year-old children show marked differences from four-year-olds in acquiring concepts, presumably because the latter have not yet acquired the verbal chains that make concept learning an easy matter (Kendler and Kendler, 1961). This has been shown by giving children of two age groups a task like that illustrated

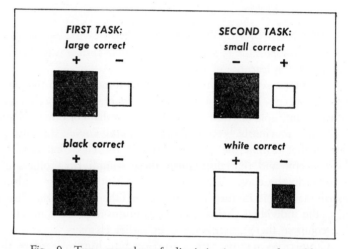

Fig. 9. Two examples of discrimination reversal problems learned by children of two different age groups (four and seven). After learning the first task, the children were shifted to the second (reversed) task. (Kendler, H. H. and Kendler, T. S. Effect of verbalization on reversal shifts in children. *Science*, 1961, **141**, 1619–1620.)

in Figure 9. In the first task, the children were asked to choose between two exposed squares, one large and one small. Although the relative position of the squares was varied, the *large* one was always correct, and the child received a marble for choosing it. Once this task had been learned, each child was given a second task in which the *small* square was now correct. (Another group of children first responded to *black* as correct, and then were shifted to *white*.) The seven-year-olds took an average of eight trials to make this shift, whereas the four-year-olds required twenty-three. It seems probable that the older children in this study were able to use the concept "opposite" quite readily, whereas the younger children had difficulty with it, and tended to continue responding to the situation by means of the simple chain $Ss \xrightarrow[\text{large}]{} R_{\text{choose it}}$. The pre-availability of language (verbal chains) has been shown in still other studies to make considerable difference in the acquiring of concepts by children.

THE CONDITIONS OF CONCEPT LEARNING

It is now possible to summarize in a more formal way the conditions for the learning of concepts.

CONDITIONS WITHIN THE LEARNER • Prerequisites to the learning of concepts are capabilities that have previously been established by multiple discrimination. A set of verbal (or other) chains must have previously been acquired to *representative* stimulus situations that exhibit the characteristics of the class that describes the concept, and that distinguish these stimuli from others not included in the class. Of course, the acquisition of these multiple discriminations is in turn dependent on other prerequisite learnings (the individual chains, and the stimulus-response connections that compose them), as discussed in earlier chapters.

CONDITIONS WITHIN THE SITUATION • In human learners, the situational conditions for learning concepts are largely embodied in a set of *verbal instructions*. To have animals learn concepts often requires a somewhat slow and complex procedure that accomplishes the same things as instructions do with human beings (Gagné, 1964a).

1. The specific stimulus objects, to which chains that include a common final link have been previously learned, are presented simultaneously, or in close time succession. Instructions are used to stimulate the learner to recall and reinstate these chains. In terms of the example used here, the instructor asks, "What is this?" in three different stimulus situations, and expects the answer "edge" in each case.

2. Instructions go on to elicit the same common link to a

stimulus situation belonging to the proper class but to which the learner has not previously responded. Instructions ask, "What is this?" to a new stimulus situation including an edge. Alternatively, the question may be "Where is the edge?"

3. Once these events have occurred, the new capability may be verified by asking for the identification of several additional instances of the class, again using stimuli to which the learner has not acquired specific verbal chains. If these are successfully done, one may conclude that a new concept has been learned.

4. The condition of *reinforcement* is present in the concept-learning situation. The learner's response of "edge" to the new set of stimuli must be confirmed more or less immediately if the concept is to be learned. *Contiguity* is also of importance, as emphasized in condition 1. The specific instances need to be presented contiguously, and their names recalled just prior to the presentation of the "new" instance. The absence of contiguity may well be the factor mainly responsible for the slowness of concept learning when it is done in a trial-and-error fashion, as described earlier in this section. When all the specific instances on which the concept depends are "lively" in memory at the same time, concept acquisition is rapid. As for *repetition*, it does not appear to be necessary when other conditions are optimal. Following the step described as condition 2, the provision of new examples (condition 3) may merely serve the purpose of "testing" the presence of the concept. There is no available evidence regarding the question whether these additional instances aid in concept retention, although this may be true.

GENERALIZING WITH CONCEPTS

The possession of the capability generated in the learner when a concept is acquired is distinguished from all other forms of learning so far described by the characteristic of *generalizability*. Having acquired the concept *edge*, the individual is able to generalize this concept to other different stimulus situations that have not played a part in the learning itself. He can immediately and without hesitation identify an edge to a roof, a cliff, an automobile fender, a lampshade, or any of a great variety of situations. (Of course, this assumes that the initial situations used to exhibit the concept were sufficiently representative of the total class covered by the concept.) If he has learned the concept *raise*, he will be able to recognize this class of event in such diverse circumstances as the raising of an arm, a flag, or a window. *The effect of concept learning is to free the individual from control by specific stimuli.* This kind of learning, then, is obviously of tremendous importance for most kinds of intellectual activity engaged in by the human individual. He reads in terms of concepts, he communicates with concepts, he thinks with concepts.

It is not surprising, then, that the "test" for the presence of concepts is itself a matter of demonstrating that generalizing can occur. Regardless of what stimuli have been used for learning, the acquisition of the concept *odd* is tested by presenting a stimulus situation that has not been involved in the learning. Similarly for *edge*, or *raise*, or any other concept. There must be a demonstration that the learner can generalize the concept to a variety of specific instances of the class that have not been used in learning. Otherwise, it is not a concept, but merely a collection of specific chains.

The generalizing capability provided by concept learning goes far beyond the *stimulus generalization* that is a fundamental property of $Ss \rightarrow R$ learning. Of course, this latter property is still present in the links of the chains used to establish the concept, or to arouse it. But it is limited in extent by the physical resemblances of objects or events. Generalizing by means of concepts, in contrast, is not limited by physical resemblances. When using a concept, the individual experiences no difficulty in identifying an *edge* in a large, round swimming pool or in a tiny letter on a printed page. The property held in common by such widely different stimulus situations as these cannot be described in terms of the resemblances of physical stimulation. An *edge*, in other words, is an abstraction from all the specific situations in which it occurs. This is apparently what some writers mean when they refer to concepts as "relationships of stimuli."

The world experienced by the human individual is largely organized by means of concepts. He thinks of his environment, as well as himself, primarily in terms of concepts of objects, places, and events. He communicates with other people, and they communicate with him, to an overwhelming degree by means of concepts. There are concepts of *things* and *places*, like chairs and tables and trees and lawns and houses and automobiles; up, down, right, left, between, on top of, next to, and so on. The *things* in conceptual form are the nouns of sentences, the *places* are also nouns and sometimes prepositions. Then there are concepts of *events*, which generally are represented by verbs, such as go, stay, take, put, raise, lower, sit, accept, deliver, reject. Children acquire these words as concepts, often in a trial-and-error fashion because of the accidental character of their experiences with them. But a new concept, such as that represented by a technical term, may readily be taught to them in the more systematic manner just described.

SOME EDUCATIONAL IMPLICATIONS

It would be difficult to overemphasize the importance of concept learning for formal education. The acquisition of concepts is what makes instruction possible. One cannot take the time to present to the student even a small fraction of all the specific situations in which he may encounter an edge, or an "odd one," or a cell, or a striated muscle. But if with the use of a few examples he can acquire these as concepts, one may expect that generalizing will occur to the whole of his experience. He is freed from the control of specific stimuli in his environment, and can thereafter learn by means of *verbal instruction*, presented orally or in printed form. He can also communicate his intentions, his actions, and his thoughts to other people, again because the specific words he employs arouse concepts in his hearers that function just as his do.

The young child arrives in kindergarten with many concepts learned, and many not yet learned. He probably has already acquired concepts for a number of common objects in his environment, such as chairs and floors and ceilings and streets and flowers and animals and trees. Most probably he knows such place concepts as *above and below, on top of, underneath, next to, the middle one.* Similarly, he will doubtless respond conceptually to words like "start" and "stop," "go" and "come," "sit" and "stand," and a number of others. But there are many other concepts he still needs to learn that will form the basis of much of his later learning. He may not yet know what "the one before" means, or "the next one," or "double," or "like" and "unlike." As a basis for his reading and writing, he probably has not yet learned to conceptualize word sounds as printed letter combinations. He may not be able to use number names for quantities (whether or not he can recite a verbal chain like "one, two, three," and so on), but he will need to learn these as the foundation of arithmetic. In fact, it is not entirely evident that anyone knows with a high degree of confidence what concepts the typical kindergarten child does not yet have, or what concepts he needs to learn first. The problem is clearly an important one.

As the student progresses in school, he continues to acquire concepts all the time. Once the fundamental skill of reading has been acquired, concepts can often be introduced by means of instructions with accompanying pictures or diagrams. In mathematics this is fairly easy because the stimulus situations that must be responded to with concepts are usually marks on a printed page; adding can be represented by + and subtracting by —. Languages can also be represented in this way, so that the concepts pertaining to language structure (subject, verb, and so on) are learned in response to printed sentences like "John's hat is on the table." But with other subjects, there may be greater difficulty in presenting the fundamental situations to be conceptualized, and pictures and diagrams are often employed. Thus, at some stage of science learning, the concept *fulcrum* may be introduced with the presentation of several diagrams depicting levers, or the concept *cell* may be presented by means of an idealized diagram. Most difficult of all are likely to be abstract concepts like *family* and *legislature*, of the type that make up the disciplines of the social sciences.

The great value of concepts as means for thinking and communicating is the fact that they have *concrete references*. The importance of this characteristic cannot be overemphasized. But since concepts are learned by the human being via language, there is often a danger of losing sight of this concreteness. Learning can become oververbalized, which means that the concepts learned are highly inadequate in their references to actual situations. The learner, one may note, "doesn't really know the meaning of the word," even though he can use it correctly in a sentence. Suppose, for example, a student has merely *read* that striated muscles are made up of bundles of long narrow cells. This verbal information is unlikely to provide him with the kind of concept of striated muscles he needs if he is a student of physiology or anatomy. The danger of verbal superficiality, and the necessity for avoiding it, is recognized in a number of educational doctrines. "Learning by doing" is one of these. Another is the recognition of the importance of the laboratory and the demonstration in science teaching. The concepts of science deal with the real world and therefore must be based on "operations" that are equally concrete.

Besides having concrete references, concepts possess the additional property of freeing thought and expression from the domination of the physical environment. As will be seen in the next chapter, concepts in their generalized form may be linked together in various ways to form principles. "Water boils" is a simple sentence recalling two different concepts to the individual who has already acquired them. But the linking of these concepts results in the conveying of information, of *knowledge*. The tremendous variety of such knowledge that is imparted by means of verbal communication is, of course, a fundamental fact of education. Once concepts have been mastered, the individual is ready to learn an amount of knowledge that is virtually without limit.

GENERAL REFERENCES

Multiple Discrimination

Gilbert, T. F. Mathetics: the technology of education. *J. Mathetics*, 1962, *1*, 7–73.

Postman, L. The present status of interference theory. In C. N. Cofer (Ed.), *Verbal learning and verbal behavior*. New York: McGraw-Hill, 1961.

Underwood, B. J. An evaluation of the Gibson theory of verbal learning. In C. N. Cofer (Ed.), *Verbal learning and verbal behavior*. New York: McGraw-Hill, 1961.

Concept Learning

Harlow, H. F., and Harlow, M. K. Learning to think. *Scient. Amer.*, 1949, *181*, 36–39.

Woodworth R., S. *Dynamics of behavior*. New York: Holt, Rinehart and Winston, 1958. Chap. 12.

Children's Concepts

Flavell, J. H. *The developmental psychology of Jean Piaget*. Princeton, N. J.: Van Nostrand, 1963.

Lovell, K. *The growth of basic mathematical and scientific concepts in children*. New York: Philosophical Library, 1961.

Piaget, J. *Construction of reality in the child*. New York: Basic Books, 1954. (For other works of Piaget, see references in Flavell, J. H.)

Russell, D. H. *Children's thinking*. Boston: Ginn, 1956.

THE LEARNING OF PRINCIPLES; PROBLEM SOLVING

6

THIS CHAPTER deals with some kinds of learning that are truly representative of human intellectual capacities. To some readers, it may seem that the types of behavior being described are, "at last," the kind with which formal instruction most typically concerns itself, and this is probably the case. Moreover, the two types of learning to be discussed here extend to the uppermost limits of human capabilities in the acquiring of knowledge and the solving of novel problems. However, it should be emphasized that these forms of learning do not occur within the medium of a *tabula rasa*. On the contrary, each of them builds on learnings that have preceded them. Although the learning of principles and the solving of problems may well represent some ultimate goals of a formal schooling process, it would be mistaken to believe that these goals can be reached by simply ignoring all other forms of learning, or by pushing the latter into a kind of trash can of unimportant events. The varieties of learning described here are possible only because they have been preceded by the acquisition of a set of prerequisite capabilities that extend down to the simplest stimulus-response connection.

Principles are chains of concepts that make up what is generally called *knowledge*. They represent the relationships among concepts, in all the variety these relationships may take. They range from the simplest kind of "empirical" principle like "The sun sets in the west" to the statement of theoretical relationships such as $F = ma$ or $E = mc^2$. Additionally, when one uses his knowledge of principles to solve a problem, practical or theoretical,

141

he may have an "insight" into the solution that is accompanied by the generation of a "new" principle (new to the individual, that is). This sort of "higher-order" principle is usually the result of successful *problem solving*, and it becomes in turn a part of the individual's repertoire of capabilities. Such principles seem to be retained very well; it is as though the individual's intellectual effort in arriving at them makes them highly resistant to forgetting. These varieties of learning will be described in the order named.

PRINCIPLE LEARNING (TYPE 7)

The simplest kinds of principles are naturally those that the young child learns. He is not able to learn the complex principles of which adults are capable, first, because he may not have acquired all the prerequisite concepts, and, second, because he has perhaps not yet acquired the subtle discriminations that underlie certain complex principles. It will be most useful, therefore, to begin our description with very simple principles and later to show how they can grow in complexity.

SOME EXAMPLES OF PRINCIPLE LEARNING

A young child may be told, "Round things roll." Such a statement obviously represents two different concepts: (1) *round things* and (2) *roll*. Under what circumstances might it be expected that learning has occurred from the making of such a statement? What are the conditions under which one can be pretty certain that the child has learned the *principle* that round things roll?

It seems fairly evident that if learning of the principle is to be expected, the child must already know the concepts *round things* and *roll*. If he has not already acquired the concept *round*, he may end up learning a more restricted principle, such as *balls roll*, and therefore be unable to show that a half-dollar will roll, or a saucer. Accordingly, if he is to acquire this principle in its fullest sense, he must know the concept *round* in its full sense, as it applies to a variety of objects including round discs and cylinders as well as spherical objects like balls.

Similarly, he should have previously acquired the concept of the event *roll*. Naturally, this must be distinguished (by multiple-discrimination learning) from such events as *sliding* and *tumbling*. Such a concept as this may be considerably more difficult to learn than *round*, in fact, since the stimulus events of rotating about an axis may not be easy to discriminate from other events involving the motion of bodies. But again, if the child is to be set the task of learning the principle, and not just a partial principle, he must have acquired the concept *roll*.

Having these prerequisites accomplished, the remainder of the situation for learning is contributed by a representative set of stimulus objects and by a set of verbal instructions to which the learner responds. The stimulus objects might include a set of unfamiliar blocks, some of which are round, some not, and an inclined plane. The instructions might go like this: "I want you to answer the question, what kinds of things roll? . . . You remember what *roll* means (demonstrate with one round object). . . . Some of these objects are *round*. Can you point them out? . . . (Student responds). . . . Do all *round* things roll? (Student answers 'Yes'). . . . Show me. . . . (Student responds by rolling two or three round objects). . . . Good! . . . What kind of things roll? (Student responds 'Round things roll'). . . . Right!" With the completion of this exercise, it is reasonable to conclude that the principle has been learned. However, to test this, a new and different set of blocks may be presented to the student, and he is asked to answer the question, Which of these will roll?

To an adult, this instruction may seem elaborate and detailed, but it surely will not have this appearance to a kindergarten teacher. Why does one not simply say to the child, "Round things roll; remember that"? There are two major reasons. The first is that the child may not recall the concepts *round* and *roll* at the time they are presented to him in the sentence. Special pains are taken to be sure that these concepts are highly recallable at the moment the principle is stated. The second reason is to ensure that the child does not simply learn as a verbal chain the words "round things roll." This, of course, is very easy for him to do, since the statement is a short chain and he already knows the links. But the purpose of the instruction in this case is not to have him learn a verbal sequence; rather, it is to have him learn a *principle*. Consequently, he must be asked to exhibit terminal responses that are possible only if he can in fact put together the concepts *round* and *roll*. Knowing the principle means being able to demonstrate that round things roll, not simply to say the words.

Adults often have to learn principles that are structurally no more complex than this. A student of biology, for example, may encounter the principle *insects metamorphose*. It seems quite evident that in this case, too, if he is to learn this principle, the adult must have the concept *insect* that is well discriminated from other categories of animals, and he must have learned the event concept *metamorphose* so that it is distinguished from other kinds of developmental changes. One may suppose that the adult who has the intention to do so can learn the new principle entirely from the verbal statement itself. To do this properly, he might think of an actual example or two of insects and the changes they exhibit when exhibiting metamorphosis. It may be noted, though, that he is more likely to be able to do this if he has seen metamorphosis in the laboratory or museum, on a field trip, or in a picture. For one cannot be sure that when an adult is confronted with a verbal instruction such as "insects metamorphose," he will in fact learn it as a principle, although this may well be what he is expected to do. Just as the child can learn this statement as a verbal chain, so, too, can the adult.

For adults, then, the external conditions of learning principles are often reduced to verbal statements in textbooks or lectures. Provided the component concepts have been previously learned, verbal instruction *can* be sufficient, although it may not be. The way to tell whether it has been, of course, is to give a test. But the test must probe for the principle, not simply for the verbal sequence. A test that says "Insects _____" (or something equivalent to that) will not do. In contrast, a test that presents a picture of a mosquito undergoing metamorphosis, requiring the student to respond by saying "an insect metamorphosing" (or something equivalent) will be able to determine whether the required principle has been learned.

As these examples show, the principles having the simplest formal structure are composed of two concepts. One can think of these as being arranged in a chain, since one usually has precedence over the other, in the sense that it occurs first in time. "If A, then B," where A and B are concepts, is the typical structure of the simplest form of principle (Gagné, 1964a). The concept A describes the class that must be included in the stimulus situation for this chain, whereas B refers to the class of objects or events that stimulate the terminal link in the chain. To what extent these conceptual chains resemble the more directly observable $Ss \rightarrow R$ chains is not known, although some learning theorists postulate that their properties are the same (Kendler, 1964). The need for contiguity, however, in the members of a conceptual chain that is a principle seems to be just as important for learning as is true with other chains (see Chapter 4).

Since principles are chains of concepts, they naturally can vary in length. A simple principle like *birds fly* can be expanded to *birds fly south in the winter*, containing four concepts rather than two. Definitions, which are one variety of principle, can sometimes become pretty lengthy, as in the following examples: (1) forgetting is a decrease in performance from the level exhibited immediately following the learning which has produced that performance, occurring after a time interval during which no practice has occurred; (2) mass is that property of an object which determines how much acceleration will be imparted to the object by the action of a given force. Usually, such principles as these are stated at the end of a sequence of instruction, rather than at the beginning. To learn them typically requires breaking them up into simpler parts, which are then finally put together as a total principle. Of course, the learner may know them as principles without necessarily being able to state them in an exact verbal form. Knowing them, as has been said, means being able to demonstrate their use in specific situations, whether or not they can be repeated as verbal sequences.

CONDITIONS OF PRINCIPLE LEARNING

It is time now to make the attempt to draw together in a

somewhat formal fashion the conditions of principle learning that derive from these examples.

CONDITIONS WITHIN THE LEARNER • The prerequisite for acquiring the chains of concepts that constitute principles is knowing the concepts. *Birds fly south in the winter* is easily learned as a principle when the learner has already learned *all* four concepts involved in it. There is, of course, a kind of "partial" learning of a principle that may result when the individual knows only some of the component concepts. Should a learner know all the concepts except *south*, it is apparent that some kind of principle could still be learned, but it would be an inadequate one.

As previously emphasized, knowing the concepts means being able to identify any members of the class they name. It is only when such prerequisite concepts have been mastered that a principle can be learned with full adequacy. Otherwise, there is the danger that the conceptual chain, or some parts of it, will become merely a verbal chain, without the full meaning that inheres in a well-established principle. It is unfortunately true that inadequate principles *can* be learned. It is a challenge for instruction to avoid these, and it is a challenge for measurement techniques to distinguish them from adequate ones.

CONDITIONS IN THE LEARNING SITUATION • The major external conditions of principle learning are embodied in *verbal instructions*. The example of instructions used with *round things roll* will be useful to recall here.

1. The conditions of principle learning often begin with a statement of the general nature of the *performance to be expected when learning is complete*. In the previous example, the instructor says, "I want you to answer the question, What kinds of things roll?" Why does he say this? Isn't he simply stating the principle, giving it away, so to speak? The main reason for making such a statement, which the learner "holds in mind" during learning, appears to be this: It provides the learner with a means for obtaining immediate reinforcement when he has reached the terminal act. Having this statement for a model, he will be able to know when he has *finished learning*, and in many cases, when he has ac-

quired the correct principle. Since principles may be long chains, the learner may need to have a conveniently retained reference to tell him when the end is reached. The instructor, though, cannot be said to be "telling the principle." He doesn't state the principle itself, but only the kind of performance that will demonstrate the attainment of the principle.

ala Mager

2. Verbal instructions continue by *invoking recall of the component concepts*. The instructor says, "You remember what *roll* means. . . . You remember what *round* means." In many cases, the recall of these concepts is stimulated entirely by verbal means. In others (as in the example previously given) the class of stimuli that represent the concept may also be shown; the student may be asked to recall the *roll* event by identifying one, and a *round* thing by picking one out. Pictures, of course, may be used for this purpose as well.

3. Verbal cues are next given for the principle as a whole. In our simple example, the verbal statement "Round things roll" accomplishes this purpose. However, it should be noted that these verbal cues to the principle need not be an exact verbalization of the entire principle; they are in this case only because the principle is such a short one. If the principle were one from elementary geometry like "An angle is formed by the intersection of two rays," the verbal cues may be contained in such statements as "Here are two rays. They intersect. We have an angle." Such statements do not correspond exactly to an acceptable verbal definition. Yet they function as well or better in providing verbal cues to stimulate the learning of the principle.

4. Finally, a verbal question asks the student to demonstrate the principle. The instructor says, "Show me." The exact form is not of great importance so long as it truly requires the student to demonstrate the principle in its full sense. Added to this may be the requirement of asking the student to state the principle verbally, as when the instructor asks, "What kinds of things roll?" But note particularly that such verbal statement is not essential to the learning of the principle, nor does it prove the student has learned the principle. Then why is it done? Probably for a very practical reason: the instructor wants the student to be able to

talk about the principle later on, and so he teaches him the right words to say. This is undoubtedly useful, but it is important to note that this kind of verbal chaining ("learning the definition") is an unessential part of principle learning itself.

5. The presence of some familiar learning conditions may be recognized in principle learning. *Contiguity* appears to be an important condition applicable to the time interval between the recall of component concepts (step 2) and the verbal cuing of the principle with these parts properly sequenced (step 3). *Reinforcement* is provided when the principle is exhibited in its complete form. The instructor may say, "Right!" Even prior to this, the student may receive reinforcement by matching his terminal act with a form remembered from the initial instruction (step 1). *Repetition* has not been shown to be an important condition for this kind of learning, nor for its retention (Gagné and Bassler, 1963). However, the particular finding cited was obtained when the principles learned occupied an isolated position within other varieties of principles. The possible need for repetition in the form of review exercises to overcome the effects of interference should not be discounted. Forgetting, after all, is a highly likely occurrence with any kind of learned capability.

The capability acquired when a principle is learned must be somewhat abstractly represented, since by its very nature it cannot be related to *specific* stimuli, but only to the classes of stimuli that arouse its component concepts. As previously stated, a simple principle like "birds fly" may be considered a chain of two concepts, and diagramed as follows:

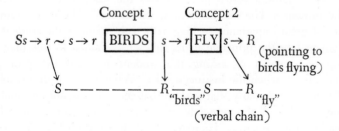

The terminal response, here designated as "pointing to birds flying," may take many forms, so long as it constitutes a demonstration of the principle. Also indicated is the possibility of formation of the verbal chain "birds fly," which is the verbal statement of the principle, not an integral part of the principle itself.

THE INSTRUCTIONAL SEQUENCE · The conditions for learning principles that are in the situation, then, are largely incorporated in an *instructional sequence*. Perhaps it will be worthwhile here to recapitulate that sequence (cf. Gagné, 1963a), since it may be considered to represent the requirements for instruction of principles whether practiced by a teacher, a film, or a textbook:

Step 1: Inform the learner about the form of the performance to be expected when learning is completed.

Step 2: Question the learner in a way that requires the reinstatement (recall) of the previously learned concepts that make up the principle. *(invoke recall)*

Step 3: Use verbal statements (cues) that will lead the learner to put the principle together, as a chain of concepts, in the proper order.

Step 4: By means of a question, ask the learner to "demonstrate" one or more concrete instances of the principle.

Step 5 (Optional, but useful for later instruction): By a suitable question, require the learner to make a verbal statement of the principle.

HIERARCHIES OF PRINCIPLES

Although it is useful to discuss the learning of a single principle, most principles are not learned in isolation, except perhaps by the young child. Instead, the school student or the adult typically learns related sets of principles pertaining to a larger topic. What he learns is *organized knowledge*. The individual principles of such knowledge may have demonstrable relationships to each other in a logical sense. They are also related to each other in the *psychological* sense that the learning of some are prerequisite to the learning of others, just as concepts are prerequisite to the learning of principles. Here the interest centers on the psychological organization of knowledge, and not on the logical organization. The distinction should be kept clear, although it is possible

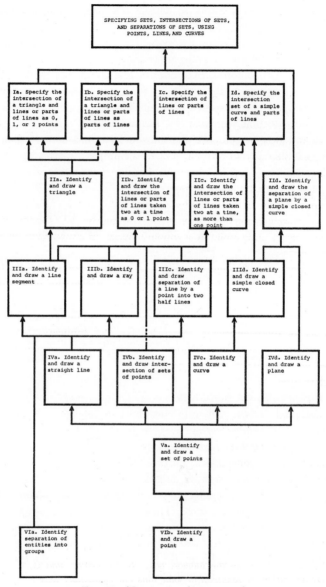

Fig. 10. (*Caption on facing page.*)

that there is some rather fundamental relationship between these two forms of organization.

The psychological organization of knowledge may be represented as a *hierarchy of principles*. As previously shown, two or more concepts may be prerequisite to (and in this sense subordinate to) the learning of a single principle. Similarly, two or more principles may be prerequisite to the learning of a superordinate principle. Once the latter is learned, it may combine with another principle to support the learning of still another higher-level principle, and so on. The entire set of principles, organized in this way, forms a hierarchy that may be called the *structure of organized knowledge* about a topic.

An example of a hierarchy of principles for a topic in elementary nonmetric geometry is shown in Figure 10 (Gagné and Bassler, 1963). The topic as a whole consists of knowledge about points, lines, and curves, their intersections and separations. In other words, what is being taught is a hierarchy of principles by means of which the individual student can specify the properties of these well-known geometrical entities. He must learn not simply to recognize points, lines, and planes, but to demonstrate the existence of these entities as dependent on the application of certain principles. (It will be evident that the kind of principle involved here is usually called a *definition*.)

Although it is not possible to describe the entire topic in detail, it will be worthwhile to comment on some of the contents of this hierarchy, to see how it represents the knowledge that is learned. At the lowest level, the boxes numbered VI and V represent *concepts* that must be known at the start. VIa is the concept *separation (of entities into groups)*. VIb is *point*. Va is *set of points*, a new name for what most uninstructed students would simply call a "line." Beginning with these fairly simple concepts, which must be acquired in the manner described for type 6 learn-

---

Fig. 10. A hierarchy of principles (definitions) to be acquired in a topic of elementary nonmetric geometry. The topic to be learned is shown in the topmost box. (R. M. Gagné, and O. C. Bassler, Study of retention of some topics of elementary nonmetric geometry. *J. educ. Psychol.*, 1963, **54**, 123–131.)

ing, the learner is ready to attain a new set of interrelated *principles*.

First he learns to identify and draw a straight *line* (IVa), which is a set of points extending indefinitely in both directions. Later, he learns the principle which defines a *line segment*, namely, that part of a line which consists of two points and the set of points between (IIIa). Then, he learns to identify and draw a *ray*, the set of points formed by a point on a line and one of the half-lines made by this point (IIIb). Later still, he learns to define and make a *triangle*; this is made up of three points not on the same straight line and the line segments that join these points (IIa). Picking up another thread of principles that build on each other, the student has also learned about *intersections* of lines and parts of lines (IVb, IIb, IIc). Finally, putting together these ideas of a *triangle* and of *intersections*, he comes to learn principle Ia, which enables him to state that the intersection of a triangle and lines or parts of lines as 0, 1, or 2 points. If he has indeed mastered these principles, one building on the other, he is able at this stage to provide examples of intersections of lines with triangles that form sets of 0, 1, or 2 points, and to justify the drawing he makes. Such a drawing must not only "look" right; the learner will be able at this stage to say why it is right.

EVIDENCE OF THE HIERARCHICAL NATURE OF KNOWLEDGE · What happens when learners actually undertake to acquire a set of principles that appear to have this hierarchical structure? Does the mastery of one set actually affect the learning of the next "higher" set, as would be expected? This expectation was tested in a study with sixth-graders, who were asked to learn these definitions of nonmetric geometry from booklets prepared as a self-instructional program (Gagné and others, 1965). These materials had a carefully organized sequence in which the concepts shown at the bottom of the hierarchy (Figure 10) were presented first, then the principles at Levels IV, III, II, and I in that order, until the final task was given as a terminal exercise. Following the completion of this program, a test was given that measured achievement of the principles at Levels III, II, I, and on the final task. The results of this test were analyzed to answer the following kinds of questions concerning the dependence of learning of each principle on the attainment of prerequisite principles: If a student could demonstrate his knowledge of Principle Ia, did this mean he also knew IIa, IIb, and IIc; if he could *not* show knowledge of Ia, did this mean he did *not* know one or more of the prerequisites IIa, IIb, or IIc?

The results showed that the learning of "higher-level" principles was dependent on the mastery of prerequisite "lower-level" principles in a highly predictable fashion. For example, of the 72 students who performed correctly on Principle IIa, only one did not perform Principle IIIa correctly on the test. Of the 18 students who did Principle IIa incorrectly, all 18 did Principle IIIa incorrectly. The prediction that learning IIa depends on knowing IIIa was borne out, therefore, with a frequency of 99 percent. For all the other possible comparisons, as shown in Figure 10, the frequency of correspondence between predictions and findings ranged from 95 to 100 percent. The learning of organized knowledge, according to these results, appears to be predictable from the *pattern of prerequisite principles* that make up the hierarchy of knowledge to be acquired. This conclusion has been verified in a number of studies of the learning of topics in mathematics (Gagné and Paradise, 1961; Gagné, 1962; Gagné, Mayor, Garstens, and Paradise, 1962; Gagné and Staff, Univ. of Md. Math. Project, 1965). There is every reason to suppose that topics with other kinds of content would yield similar results.

Determining the prerequisites for any given principle may be accomplished by asking the question, What would the student have to know how to do in order to be instructed in this principle? For example, if he is to learn the principle IIc, "Identify and draw the intersection of lines or parts of lines taken two at a time, as more than one point," he must know the principles that govern the construction of lines (IVa) and intersections of sets of points (IVb); and also, the principles pertaining to various parts of lines, including the line segment (IIIa), the ray (IIIb), and the half line (IIIc). The reason is that the higher-order principle IIc *incorporates* these other principles as a part of it, in the sense that the behavior it may demand may involve any or all of these subordinate principles on any given occasion. Knowing Principle IIc means being able to deal with intersections of sets of points whether these are line segments, rays, half lines, or indefinitely extended lines. Principle IIc is truly a higher-order generalization, made up of a class of human performances that are themselves made possible by the acquisition of lower-order principles.

If all the prerequisite principles are known, does this mean that the higher-order principle is immediately known also? No, this is not enough. It has to be learned. If the lower-order principles are known, the conditions within the learner are satisfied, but not the conditions of the learning situation. There must be some *instruction*, which includes the steps of informing the learner about the expected form of the performance expected, encouraging recall, and cuing the proper sequence of acts, as described in a previous section entitled "The Instructional Sequence."

ANOTHER EXAMPLE OF A PRINCIPLE HIERARCHY • Many subjects taught in schools, perhaps most, have an organization that can readily be expressed as a hierarchy of principles. Another example of such a knowledge hierarchy, applicable to a topic of restricted scope in physics, is shown in Figure 11, "Vector Resolution of Forces." The principle of identifying horizontal and vertical components of forces as vectors is seen to depend on several subordinate principles. In order to perform correctly in accordance with this principle, the student has to be able to (1) identify the forces acting on the body in opposition to each other (keeping it in equilibrium); (2) represent the forces and their directions as parts of triangles; and (3) identify the trigonometric relationships in a triangle (sine, cosine, tangent, and so on). Each of these principles in turn is based on one or more subordinate principles that must also be learned as prerequisites. Still other "lower-order" principles (such as the definition of a triangle) are not shown in the figure, but could surely be identified as underlying those that are illustrated.

Many other topics learned in school have the character of organized knowledge and may be represented as hierarchies of principles. The principles of syntax and punctuation in English obviously display these characteristics. All sciences, as well as mathematics, are composed of sets of principles that build on each other. In the social sciences, the total structure is often a looser one, but individual topics—the institutions of government; the relation of production, labor, and prices; the structure of kinships; and many others—can obviously be viewed as knowledge having a hierarchical character. A variety of kinds of principle

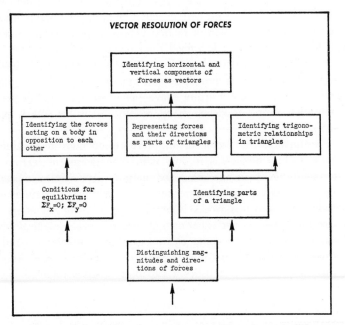

Fig. 11. A hierarchy of principles comprising the topic "Vector Resolution of Forces."

hierarchies can be used to represent the topics of history: the subject can be viewed as being organized by periods of time (the colonial period, the civil war period, and so on), by kinds of events (political, economic, military), and in many other ways.

RETENTION OF PRINCIPLES

As a general rule, the contrast is striking between forgetting the simpler forms of learned capabilities (such as chains and multiple discriminations) and forgetting the more complex forms (concepts, principles). The latter kinds of learning show marked resistance to forgetting, and are frequently remembered with little loss over periods of months and years. In a typical study, it was shown that learners who learned simply the verbal statements of principles forgot most of them within a month, whereas those who learned the principles themselves (so that they could demonstrate them) showed almost perfect retention after the same interval (Katona, 1940). Retention of factual details in prose passages has been found to be much less good than retention of ideas, that is, of the principles contained in these passages (Briggs and Reed, 1943). Many studies of principles and organized sets of principles encountered in school learning have demonstrated high degrees of retention over periods of many months (Ausubel, 1963, pp. 44–45).

Presumably, the factor of interference operates to produce forgetting of principles as it does with other forms of learning. But something about the organized nature of principles appears to resist the effects of interference and to maintain retention at high levels. How this works is not known, although it offers a challenging problem for experimental research. The practical implications, however, are quite clear. Learning principles not only produces a capability commonly referred to as "understanding"; at the same time it establishes a capability that is retained well for relatively long periods of time.

PROBLEM SOLVING (TYPE 8)

The kinds of events called problem solving are of infinite variety; yet they appear to have several formal characteristics in common. An individual may have the problem of parking his car in a spot that is closest to his work but at the same time free of parking restrictions. A student may have the problem of figuring out why the moon has phases. A scientist may have a problem of accounting for a discrepancy in the predicted and measured velocity of a type of nuclear particle. A fiction writer may have a problem of conveying a representation of slothfulness by describing only the actions of one of his characters. All these situations imply the existence of problems that are to be brought to some successful termination by thinking. All these problems are solved by the use of *principles*, simple or complex. Principles are the stuff of thinking.

One might be tempted to conclude, therefore, that problem solving is a set of events in which human beings *use principles to achieve some goal*. This is quite true; yet it is not the whole story. The results of using principles in problem solving are not confined to achieving a goal, satisfying as that may be to the thinker. When problem solution is achieved, something is also *learned*, in the sense that the individual's capability is more or less permanently changed. What emerges from problem solving is a *higher-order principle*, which thereupon becomes a part of the individual's repertory. The same class of situation, when encountered again, may be responded to with great facility by means of recall, and is no longer looked on as a "problem." Problem solving, then, must definitely be considered a form of learning.

SOME EXAMPLES OF PROBLEM SOLVING

At some point in the study of modern algebra, the student may be asked to demonstrate that the following statement, in which a and b are rational numbers, is true:

$$(a + b)21 = a \cdot 21 + b \cdot 21$$

If the student has acquired certain principles previously, he is able to do this in the following steps:

(1) $(a + b)21 = 21(a+b)$; by the commutative property of multiplication
(2) $(a + b)21 = 21 \cdot a + 21 \cdot b$; by the distributive property
(3) $(a + b)21 = a \cdot 21 + b \cdot 21$; by the commutative property

Of course, it is possible for the student to be instructed to take these specific steps, thus acquiring a rather lengthy verbal chain. But the intention here is to illustrate the instance in which he is not instructed by display of the steps themselves (either in a text or on a blackboard). Rather, he is simply given *the problem*:

"Show that this statement is true: $(a + b)21 = a \cdot 21 + b \cdot 21$."
To him, the problem is one of selecting and using certain number principles, which he has previously learned, in an order that will make it possible for him to arrive at a logically correct solution. In considering this example of a set of events as problem solving, it should be borne in mind that it is the *first encounter* of the student with this problem that is being discussed here. Once these operations have been performed, of course, they may be repeated many times with any numbers belonging to the class concerned. Most adults naturally carry out these operations very rapidly, and in fact would be inclined to accept the given statement as true by inspection. But a young student who meets this problem for the first time has no such recalled experience to fall back upon. All he knows is that numbers can be manipulated in accordance with certain principles. To him the situation is a brand new one, and he must *supply* the steps in thinking that will achieve a solution. The most notable things about the problem situation, from the standpoint of such a child, are two. First, instructions inform him of what he wants to achieve, namely, a form of statement in which the product of two numbers is equal to the sum of two products. Second, he obviously has to be able to recall from previous learning some particular principles.

As a second example, let us turn to a problem of a fairly simple and concrete sort, used for the experimental study of problem solving. Here the student is presented with a set of square figures made from arrangements of wooden matches, examples of which are shown in Figure 12. In each case, he is given the problem of transforming one pattern of matches into another in a stated number of moves. The object is for him to be able to make such transformations for a variety of match patterns he has never seen before, not simply to remember the particular patterns on which he practices. In the studies performed with such problems (Katona, 1940), the following results were obtained:

1. The least effective method of establishing the desired capability was showing the learner how to solve several problems by actually moving the matches until the learner could recall the correct moves.

2. Of considerably greater effectiveness was a method in which the learner was instructed in a *verbal principle*. (Two different principles were used, one called "arithmetic," which stated that the matches with double functions should be changed to have single functions; the other called "structural," which instructed the learner to proceed by creating holes and loosening the figures. These were about equally effective.)

3. Best of all for solving new problems was a method that

Fig. 12. Two matchstick problems, with their solutions. (G. Katona, *Organizing and memorizing*. New York: Columbia University Press, 1940.)

proceeded a step at a time to illustrate the changes that would be brought about by using a principle but without stating the principle verbally. Several examples were used to demonstrate the operation of the principle by shading drawings of the squares so as to create "holes" in the original figure. This was called "learning by help," and could equally well be termed "guided discovery." In other words, the performance of the learners subsequent to the presentation of these examples led to the inference that they had *discovered* the principle required for problem solving.

These conclusions throw considerable light on the events of problem solving. As in the previous example, the learners were instructed about the terminal achievement to be expected, the goal of their activity. Again, these results make clear that a higher-order principle is acquired when problem solution is achieved, which principle may be immediately generalized to other new situations presenting problems of the same class. Presenting the *solutions* of problems to the learner was markedly ineffective for learning. Undoubtedly the reason is that such presentations did not require the acquisition of the higher-order principle; the solutions could be learned as simple chains. Using verbal cues to stimulate learn-

Fig. 13. The solution to Maier's pendulum problem. (N. R. F. Maier, Reasoning in humans: I. On direction. *J. comp. Psychol.,* 1930, **10,** 115–143.)

ing, by stating the higher-order principle verbally, brought about problem solving in some learners but not in others. The most dependable method of instruction used illustrations to stimulate the learner to discover the principle for himself.

A third example of problem solving is taken from a famous study by Maier (1930). The learner was first brought into a room about 18 by 20 feet in size, containing only a worktable. He was provided with a set of materials, including some poles, lengths of wire, pieces of chalk, and several clamps. The problem, as told to the learner, was to construct two pendulums so designed that each would make a chalk mark at a designated point on the floor when swung over it. As shown in Figure 13, the correct solution to the pendulum construction problem was achieved by clamping two poles together, wedging them vertically against another pole that they pressed horizontally against the ceiling. From the latter were suspended two wires weighted at their lower ends by clamps that held the pieces of chalk at the proper height so that they marked the floor when the pendulum was swung.

With some of the subjects in this experiment, Maier used an additional set of instructions that seem to have had the function of recalling certain previously learned principles (cf. Gagné, 1964a). These included instructions on (a) how to make a plumb line by using a clamp, a pencil, and string; (b) how to make a long pole out of two short ones, using a clamp; and (c) how to hold up an object against a wall with two poles, by wedging them tightly. With still another group of subjects, an additional instruction was added to the effect that the problem would be simple if he "could just hang the pendulums from a nail in the ceiling." (Nails were not among the materials provided.)

The results of this study showed that the added instructions which fostered recall brought about solution in a greater proportion of learners than did the simpler instructions stating the problem. The final additional set, which Maier called *direction*, improved the probabilities of solution still more. The proportions of college students solving the pendulum problem under each of these three conditions were 0 out of 15, 1 out of 18 (with added instructions), and 4 out of 10 (with instructions plus direction).

It is evident that the verbal instructions used in this experimental situation were fulfilling a number of different functions. Briefly stated, these were as follows:

1. They informed the learner about the nature of the performance expected of him. In other words, they defined his goal—two pendulums that could make chalk marks on the floor.

2. They were deliberately used to bring about the recall of certain subordinate principles.

3. They were employed to "channel" or "guide" the learner's thinking. They did this by emphasizing what was *not* a good

direction for thought (for example, the table was not to be used in the construction, and no nails were available) as well as what *was* a good direction (hanging pendulums from the ceiling).

Although the pendulum problem seems simple when one knows the solution, this appearance is deceptive, since none of the college students was able to solve this problem when only the "problem-stating" instructions were given. To increase the probability of solution, additional resources were needed. These came from within the learner in the form of recalled principles applicable to the problem. They also came from the external situation in the form of verbal cues employed to guide thinking in the proper "direction."

CONDITIONS FOR PROBLEM SOLVING

On the basis of these and other examples, it is possible now to make a summary of the conditions of problem solving, recapitulating a number of the points already made.

CONDITIONS WITHIN THE LEARNER • In order to solve a problem, the learner must be able to recall the relevant principles that he has previously learned. In the pendulum problem, principles of weighting a length of wire, clamping a marking tool, wedging poles to hold an object up, and clamping two poles to make a longer one must all be recalled if the problem is to be solved. For matchstick problems, some principles governing the construction of multiple patterns of squares need to be recalled, either in "arithmetical" or "structural" terms. For the mathematical problem, the principles of commutativity and distributivity must be known and recalled. Thus, so far as the individual is concerned, a problem is never solved "in a vacuum." Problem solution always depends upon previous experience of the learner, or more specifically on the recall of previously learned principles.

CONDITIONS IN THE LEARNING SITUATION

1. There is *contiguity* of the principles that are to be "put together" to achieve solution, and the stimulus situation that sets the problem. The component principles, in other words, must in some sense be "held in mind" all at once, or be reactivated at will in close time successi⌐

2. The required contiguity may be made more highly probable by recent recall of relevant principles. One function of verbal instructions is to ask the questions that stimulate such recall. Thus, in the pendulum problem, the problem solvers were reminded that they knew the principle of weighting a string to make a plumb line, and the principle of wedging sticks together to hold up an object, among others. For these learners, these particular principles were "vivid" and readily available for recall when they entered the problem situation.

3. Verbal instructions that are externally provided may "guide" or "channel" thinking in certain directions. (Such guidance may, of course, be provided by the learner himself in self-instructions.) Guidance may vary in amount or completeness, always short of describing the solution itself. At a minimum, guidance of thinking takes the form of informing the learner of the goal of his activity, the general form of the solution; this amount appears to be required if learning is to occur at all. Greater amounts of guidance function to limit the range of hypotheses to be entertained by the learner in achieving solution. For example, the emphasis given in Maier's "direction" instructions limits consideration to the ceiling as a locus for the hanging of a pendulum, while at the same time excluding hypotheses concerning the use of a nail as a device from which to suspend it.

When these conditions are present, the learner is able to solve the problem, although the time required for this solution is likely to vary with the amount of guidance provided, as well as with certain innate capacities of the learner. It is possible that there are still other conditions, internal or external, that may affect the time for solution, but these are not known at present. The factor of repetition appears to have no part to play in the process of solving problems, except insofar as it may be involved in the recall of subordinate principles. Once problem solution is achieved, learning appears to be unaffected by repetition, and what is learned is highly resistant to forgetting.

It will also be evident that the capability established by problem solving is one which generalizes immediately and without repetition to an entire class of problems. The learner is able to demonstrate the truth of a class of mathematical sentences, or to solve a class of match problems, or to construct pendulums in a class of problem situations. He has acquired a *higher-order principle* that is capable of being generalized in a wide variety of stimulus situations belonging to a given class.

PROBLEM SOLVING AND DISCOVERY

In a fundamental sense, the capability learned by problem solving (type 8) is no different from that which may be learned by combining subordinate principles in the manner described as type 7 learning. Both kinds of learning result in the establishment of higher-order principles. The two kinds of learning appear to differ only in the *nature and amount of guidance* provided by verbal instructions. In the former case, the instructions include a sentence or question that verbally cues the solution, but in the latter case they do not. For example, one group of learners of matchstick problems was told to "remove those matches which serve a double function," while another group was not given this instruction. The first group may be said to have engaged in principle learning, the second in problem solving. A higher percentage of the second group was successful in achieving the higher-order principle (Katona, 1940, pp. 88, 95), and retention of it was also superior in this group.

Problem solving as a method of learning requires the learner to *discover* the higher-order principle without specific verbal help. Presumably, he thus constructs the new principle in his own idiosyncratic manner, and may or may not be able to verbalize it once he has done this. The evidence of experimental studies (cf. Ausubel, 1963) certainly does not demonstrate that higher-order principles *must* be learned by discovery. The guidance provided by verbal instructions may be so complete that the principle to be learned is stated verbally during the course of learning. The key to achievement of a higher-order principle does not lie solely in the discovery method. Nevertheless, the evidence strongly suggests that achieving a higher-order principle by means of problem solving produces a highly effective capability which is well retained over considerable periods of time. For example, the hierarchy of principles of nonmetric geometry described in the early part of this chapter was learned by sixth-graders using a method of instruction that encouraged discovery; that is, the verbal instructions did not state the "solution" until the learners had had a chance to construct it for themselves. Retention of the final task was found to be very high when measured after nine weeks (Gagné and Bassler, 1963).

"The discovery method" is liable to gross misinterpretation in practical learning situations. Some writers and practitioners have treated problem solving as though it could be achieved with a *minimum* of instructions and prerequisite knowledge of principles. This is obviously an incorrect point of view, as the evidence shows. College students who tried to solve matchstick problems *without* prerequisite knowledge of principles and *without* guidance were markedly unsuccessful. Similarly, students who were told only the goal of problem solving for the pendulum problem, without being reminded of subordinate principles and without "direction" were unable to solve the problem. Problem solving, or discovery, is only the final step in a sequence of learning that extends back through the many prerequisite learnings that must have preceded it in time. To be successful, problem solving must be based on the knowledge and recall of the principles that are combined in the achievement of the solution, the higher-order principle. Of course, the individual learner may be set a problem which is "beyond him" in the sense that he must acquire all the subordinate principles himself before he achieves a solution. Solving a problem under such circumstances may happen on certain occasions and in particular individuals, but to advocate such an approach as a practical learning method makes no sense.

To summarize, discovery or problem solving involves the combining of previously learned principles into a new higher-order principle that "solves" the problem and generalizes to an entire class of stimulus situations embodying other problems of the same type. Problem solving occurs when the instructions provided the learner do not include a verbally stated "solution," but require him to construct such a solution "on his own." When this happens, the individually constructed higher-order principle is effective in generalizing to many situations and is at the same time highly resistant to forgetting. But the capability acquired by this means does not appear to differ in a fundamental sense from that which may be acquired when instructions include the statement of a "solution" (unless, of course, the latter is learned simply as a verbal chain). What is learned in either case is a higher-order principle, which is based upon some previously learned simpler principles.

PROBLEM SOLVING AND CREATIVITY

No one can fail to stand in awed admiration of the great intellectual discoveries of history—Newton's laws of motion, Kepler's principles of planetary movement, Einstein's general theory of relativity. Equally awe-inspiring are artistic creations in painting, sculpture, music, and literature, which have also been generated by individual discovery. What do these remarkable achievements of genius have to do with problem solving as described here?

A great scientific discovery or a great work of art is surely the result of problem-solving activity. The solution to a problem, we are told, often comes to the thinker in a "flash of insight," although he may have been turning the problem over in his mind for some time. As problem-solving behavior, these creative acts are based on a tremendous amount of previously acquired knowledge, whether this be of the "public" sort known to science, or of the "private" sort known to the artist. Many creative thinkers testify that they have previously immersed themselves deeply in the subject matter of the problem, often over considerable periods of time. Indeed, it would be strange if they had not done this. Nothing in such testimony supports the idea that there is anything very different about the problem solving that leads to discoveries of great social import. The act of discovery, even in the relatively predictable sense that it occurs in everyday learning, involves a "sudden insight" which transforms the problem situation into a solution situation. As we have seen, it, too, requires that the learner have previous knowledge of the principles involved in the solution.

But the major discovery, in contrast to the common garden

variety, involves a feat of generalizing that goes far beyond what may be expected in the usual learning situation. There is an "inductive leap," a combining of ideas that come from widely separated knowledge systems, a bold use of analogy that transcends what is usually meant by generalizing within a class of problem situations. An excellent example of such inventiveness is provided by the kinetic theory of gases. What was known, on the one hand, was a set of principles concerning the behavior of gases, the relations among the variables of temperature, pressure, and volume. On the other hand, there were the laws of motion, the effects of force in imparting acceleration to objects of specified mass. The stroke of genius in this case was one of hypothesizing that the gas was composed of particles (molecules) that had mass and whose reactions to force could therefore be considered to obey the laws of motion. From this single new synthesizing idea, this remarkable higher-order principle, the consequences follow that permit the confirmation of the theory. But the central idea itself was arrived at by putting together subordinate principles from two widely disparate systems of organized knowledge. A problem of this magnitude had to be solved by combining two sets of principles that originally seemed to have only the remotest connection with each other.

What has learning to do with the great creative discovery? The most obvious and dependable answer is that discoveries of great social importance have been made by men with a great deal of knowledge. They are men who have acquired many kinds of hierarchies of principles. They have been deeply immersed in the principles of the discipline within which they work, and, often, in the principles of other disciplines also. How did they learn these principles? Just as everyone else does—by combining sets of subordinate principles; partly perhaps with the aid of verbal instruction, and partly by making the "small" discoveries that may be involved in the acquiring of the higher-order principles of any particular topic or knowledge system.

Some scholars are highly dissatisfied with this kind of answer concerning the relation between learning and Discovery with a capital "D." Surely, they say, it is reasonable to suppose that if discovery is used constantly as a method of learning, this will predispose the individual to make the great Discovery? So far as any present evidence is concerned, such a proposition is wishful thinking at best; at worst, it is mere verbal sophistry. The use of discovery as a method of learning principles, as we have seen, may lead to individual capabilities that are highly effective from the standpoint of generalizability, applicability, and retention. In other words, this method of learning may generate a solid basis of *knowledge* in the individual. Furthermore, because it is a method rich in reinforcement value, the solving of problems within structures of knowledge to be learned may create a love of learning, a "thirst for knowledge" in the individual learner. But it is a vastly different thing to suppose that this kind of learning will necessarily predispose the individual to become a "creative" thinker, capable of making a great contribution to science or art. To be sure, the variables that produce genius are surely not entirely innate, and must prominently include factors in the individual's experience, arising from his environment. But except as a method for acquiring prerequisite knowledge, "practicing discovery" seems an unlikely choice of antecedent variable to be involved in the production of genius.

THE LEARNING OF STRATEGIES IN PROBLEM SOLVING

Turning back again to the conditions governing the type of learning called problem solving, the present description has emphasized the importance of verbal instructions in providing guidance to the thinking process. It is clear also that these instructions may be furnished by the individual himself when he is engaged in solving a problem without the aid of tutor or textbook. The formulation and use of such *self-instructions* is naturally an event that is itself dependent on a learning process. Among the other things learned by a person who engages in problem solving is "how to instruct oneself in solving problems." Such a capability is basically composed of higher-order principles, which are usually called *strategies*. The manner of learning this particular variety of higher-order principle is not different in any important respect from the learning of other principles. But whereas the higher-order principles previously discussed deal with the content knowledge of the topic being learned, strategies do not. The first type may therefore be called content principles, whereas strategies are heuristic principles. Strategies do not appear as a part of the goals of learning, but they are nevertheless learned.

Strategies have not been studied in connection with the learning of school subjects, but only in abstract laboratory situations. One example is a task in which the individual is asked to predict which of two lights, one on the left and one on the right, will come on in a series of trials. Unknown to the experimental subject is the fact that the lights have been arranged to come on in completely random patterns, but with predetermined frequencies (such as 6 right to 4 left). It has been shown that what the individual tends to do in this situation is to try out, one after the other, a great variety of *strategies*. For example, he may begin by instructing himself, "Alternate right and left," and progress to "Two right then one left," and to considerably more elaborate self-instructions, such as "Single alternate, then double alternate, then one right, then three left, and repeat" (Goodnow, 1955). It seems quite apparent that the strategies used in such a situation are based on simpler principles and concepts.

The use of strategies in forming complex concepts has also been studied in the laboratory (Bruner, Goodnow, and Austin, 1956). In this group of studies, learners were asked to identify a concept of classification in sets of cards, each containing two figures that could be categorized in various ways—on the basis of shape of figure, color of figure, number of figures, and number of borders. The concept sought might be the class of cards containing *two yellow rectangles*. It was found that learners adopted several different kinds of strategies, which might be said to characterize their "style" of solving this kind of problem. Some of these strategies were relatively "conservative," in the sense that a wrong choice did not require starting all over again with a new hypothesis, whereas others were relatively "risky" in the sense that they jumped to a hypothesis before the evidence was complete. The study confirms the idea that a variety of strategies is used in solving problems, and that particular kinds of strategies tend to be favored by particular people. It also makes clear that a given problem of this type may be equally well solved with one strategy as with another.

The implication of these studies is that, when they are engaged in solving problems, individuals may learn to instruct themselves, to adopt strategies which guide their thinking. Presumably, these "self-instruction principles" are learned much as other principles are. But they do not appear as a part of the problem solution itself; they simply aid the process of problem solving. In a similar manner, it is reasonable to suppose that strategies are learned and used by individuals in solving any kind of problem. If it is a mathematical problem that the individual is engaged in solving, he may have learned a strategy of applying the relevant subordinate principles in a certain order. If it is a problem in genetic inheritance, he may have learned to test out recessive characteristics before dominant ones, or vice versa.

Obviously, strategies are important for problem solving, regardless of the content of the problem. The suggestion from some writings is that they are of overriding importance as a goal of education. After all, should not formal instruction in the school have the aim of teaching the student "how to think"? If strategies were deliberately taught, would not this produce people who could then bring to bear superior problem-solving capabilities to any new situation? Although no one would disagree with the aims expressed, it is exceedingly doubtful that they can be brought about by teaching students "strategies" or "styles" of thinking. Even if these could be taught (and it is possible that they could), they would not provide the individual with the basic firmament of thought, which is subject-matter knowledge. Knowing a set of strategies is not all that is required for thinking; it is not even a substantial part of what is needed. To be an effective problem solver, the individual must somehow have acquired masses of structurally organized knowledge. Such knowledge is made up of content principles, not heuristic ones.

GENERAL REFERENCES

Principle Learning

Ausubel, D. P. *The psychology of meaningful verbal learning.* New York: Grune & Stratton, 1963.

Miller, G. A. *Language and communication.* New York: McGraw-Hill, 1951.

Mowrer, O. H. *Learning theory and the symbolic processes.* New York: Wiley, 1960, Chaps. 4, 5, 6, 7.

Problem Solving

Bruner, J. S., Goodnow, J. J., and Austin, G. A. *A study of thinking.* New York: Wiley, 1956.

Gagné, R. M. Problem solving. In A. W. Melton (Ed.), *Categories of human learning.* New York: Academic Press, 1964.

Johnson, D. M. *The psychology of thought and judgment.* New York: Harper & Row, 1955.

Katona, G. *Organizing and memorizing.* New York: Columbia University Press, 1940.

Patrick, C. *What is creative thinking?* New York: Philosophical Library, 1955.

Wertheimer, M. *Productive thinking.* New York: Harper & Row, 1945.

Woodworth, R. S. *Dynamics of behavior.* New York: Holt, Rinehart and Winston, 1958. Chap. 12.

LEARNING AND THE CONTENT OF INSTRUCTION

7

Each of the eight varieties of learning conditions, whether it occurs more or less accidentally or is deliberately employed in formal instruction, establishes a different kind of capability in the learner. This capability may be narrowly specific, as in responding to a signal, or it may range in generalizability to the kind of competence attained in principle learning and problem solving. But in all cases, the capability itself embodies some identifiable *content*. People do not learn in a general sense, but always in the sense of a change in behavior that can be described in terms of an observable type of human performance. As previously pointed out, a successful act of learning is inferred from the fact that the individual can now do something he could not do before. The content of the capability with which the learner begins, as well as the content with which he ends up, are both essential for this inference.

PLANNING SEQUENCES OF INSTRUCTION

The existence of capabilities within the learner that build on each other in the manner described in previous chapters provides the possibility of the *planning of sequences of instruction* within content areas. If problem solving is to be done with physical science, then the scientific principles to be applied to the problem must be previously learned; if these principles in turn are to be learned, one must be sure there has been previous acquisition of relevant concepts; and so on. Thus it becomes possible to "work backward" from any given objective of learning to determine what

172

the prerequisite learnings must be; if necessary, all the way back to simple verbal associations and chains. When such an analysis is made, the result is a kind of map of what must be learned. Within this map, many alternate routes are available, some of which are quite as good as others in achieving the desired objective. But what is *not* possible in such a plan is to "skip over" some essential intervening capabilities.

The importance of mapping the sequence of learnings is mainly just this: that it enables one to avoid the mistakes that arise from "skipping" essential steps in the acquisition of knowledge of a content area. Without such a plan, mistakes of this sort are unfortunately easy to make. It would be pleasing to everyone, for example, if a learner could progress to the capability of extemporaneously composing sentences in a foreign language without previously learning to use individual words. But in fact such "skipping" cannot be done and, if it is tried, may result in serious "blocking" on the part of the student that may persist for a long time. Attempts to skip essential capabilities in mathematics can lead to similar consequences. The same is true of almost any content subject. Following a preplanned sequence, then, and thus avoiding the omission of prerequisite capabilities along any route of learning, appears to be a highly important procedure to adopt in achieving effectiveness for instruction. One of the most readily apparent implications of the descriptions of learning conditions contained in previous chapters pertains to the planning of the sequence of instruction. If one is to take into account the differences in conditions applicable to each type of learning, the feature of *differential starting points* is crucial. Before any act of learning is undertaken there needs to be a plan for learning any given content.

DESCRIPTION OF LEARNING CONTENT

In educational circles, the contents of learning are often referred to as large categories of subject matter—"English," "mathematics," and so on. Although these categories may have a certain usefulness as entities for planning and managing schools and school systems, they nevertheless have some rather unfortunate characteristics as content terms. Chief among these is that the categories are so large that each includes a considerable variety of different kinds of human performances. The existence of such general "subject" categories makes it difficult to determine what human capabilities they do or should include. As a single example out of many possible ones, it is reasonable to think that one kind of capability a child ought to acquire in the primary grades is making an *accurate description of an unfamiliar object*. But is this "English," or "language," or "science"? An even more subtle and at the same time seriously unfortunate consequence of "subject-matter categories" is that they tend to engender a belief in their reality apart from their component human competencies. Thus there may be a tendency toward the false belief that "English" as a content for learning is something more than being able to read, write, and speak English competently; or that learning "mathematics" is something more than learning to solve problems logically and quantitatively.

These difficulties in identifying the content of learning would be avoided if care were taken to put the emphasis where it belongs, which is on the attainments of learners. When an act of learning occurs, the individual is enabled to accomplish something he could not accomplish previously—whether this be spelling a word, or constructing a German sentence, or writing a sonnet, or performing an experiment. Such newly acquired accomplishments need to be identified in terms that are much more circumscribed than the "subjects" of the current-day curriculum.

In the remainder of this chapter, the attempt will be made to examine the *learning structure* of some of the more important curricular "subjects." To do this, it will be necessary to break them down into smaller units of student competencies. Since these do not necessarily correspond to the "topics" into which a subject is customarily divided, a certain degree of novelty can be expected. In addition, it may be noted that these structures represent hypotheses about the content and sequence of each subject that have not been verified, although they obviously are capable of verification. Accordingly, they do not represent anything like a final answer to the problem of subject-matter content, but only an initial suggestion of such an answer. However, they do make it possible to state the relationships between the content of instruction and the requirements of learning conditions as these latter have been described in previous chapters.

The following sections describe, for mathematics, science, foreign languages, and English, what may be called a *learning sequence* for each of these subjects. It is of importance to note that there is no intention of describing a "development sequence," relating the learning of an individual to his stage of growth or chronological age. Simple kinds of learning (types 2, 3, and 4, for example) occur throughout the learning history of the individual, no matter how old he may be. For example, a student of calculus must learn to identify the printed symbol for integration under essentially the same learning conditions that obtain when a student of arithmetic learns the printed symbol for division. In both cases, a sequence of learning can be identified in which increasingly complex forms of learning build on these simpler forms. It is this kind of sequence, independent of the stage of growth of the individual, that is the focus of interest. At the same time, it is inevitable that some correlation between the sequence of simple-complex learning and the sequence of earlier-later events will be present. The individual learns simpler things first, then more and more complex things; while all this is happening, he is also growing older.

SOME LEARNING STRUCTURES

LEARNING STRUCTURE IN MATHEMATICS

Mathematics has a learning structure that has been considerably illuminated, particularly in its early phases, by developments in the teaching of the "new mathematics." Some issues of proper sequencing of this subject have not yet been settled by mathematics scholars interested in pedagogy. Others, though, have been clarified tremendously, and there is reason to hope that many of the inconsistencies that may have tended to make students "block" on the subject have now been removed.

Before proceeding to consider a possible learning structure for a particular mathematical topic, it will be worthwhile to attempt a general view of the kinds of learning as they relate to the activities involved in mathematics performances.

PHASE 1: STIMULUS-RESPONSE LEARNING · At the earliest stage, children often learn to say the names of common numbers from one to ten, and perhaps beyond that, before they go to school. Later on, they may learn to say many other new technical words, such as "multiply" and "cube root" and "secant" and "hyperbola" and "rhomboid" and a host of others. Acquiring these as self-generated responses is the major portion of what is acquired in mathematics under conditions of simple stimulus-response learning. One other simple connection of some importance is learning to hold and make marks with a pencil.

PHASE 2: CHAINING · The nonverbal chains that are basic to mathematics learning include primarily the printing of letters and symbols, and the drawing of larger figures, such as geometrical forms. Some of these may be learned in preschool years, whereas others are learned in the early grades.

PHASE 3: VERBAL SEQUENCES · Many kinds of verbal sequences are important and fundamental to mathematics learning. Before he goes to school, the child may have learned to name a sequence of numerals in their proper order, from one to ten, or from one to twenty. Such a child may be said to "know how to count," although the learning of a verbal sequence of this sort is not what is meant by "counting" in mathematics education. More useful sequences are of the verbal associate variety, in which the child learns to name printed numerals, to say "seven" when he sees 7. Later on, and throughout many years of studying mathematics, he will learn to associate names with new printed characters; he will learn the names of an exponent, a radical, an origin, a parabola, a parallelogram, and many, many others.

PHASE 4: MULTIPLE DISCRIMINATIONS · Some of the fundamental discriminations the child learns permit him to differentiate one specific object (a marble, say) from two, two from three, three from four, and so on up to six or seven. For more objects than this, he must learn to count, as will be seen later. Actually, the only multiple discriminations that are assumed as being essential in formal instruction on numbers are those between nothing and one, and between one and two. But more than these are usually informally learned, nevertheless; primitive and uninstructed human beings can readily discriminate four fingers from five without recourse to counting. Another basic set of multiple discriminations that must be acquired early are the distinctions between printed numerals and other symbols. The printed 9 must be distinguished from the printed 6, $+$ from $\times$, and so on. Later on, there are other discriminations to be learned that will be a source of difficulty if they are not mastered: the positions of the coefficient, the exponent, and the subscript; parentheses and brackets; separations and intersections; the extents of angles; the directions of lines; adjacent and opposite angles and sides of triangles and other geometrical figures; and a variety of symbols, such as Greek letters and the operation signs of logic. Whenever potentially confusable symbols or figures are newly introduced in mathematics, multiple-discrimination learning must occur. To assume that it has already happened, or to deliberately skip over it, is to invite later difficulties with more complex forms of learning.

PHASE 5: CONCEPT LEARNING · *Alike* and *different* are two concepts that are essential to later learning in mathematics, as they are for most other subjects of the curriculum. Sometimes these concepts are learned by children in preschool years. Attaining them as concepts means being able to say about *any* objects, pictures, or symbols that they are alike or unlike. As indicated in Chapter 5, the conditions for such learning require the use of a variety of concrete examples of representative kinds of objects and pictures. It is worth emphasizing, too, that, if he is to be successful, the child who sets out to learn these concepts must have previously acquired multiple discriminations of the specific objects introduced as examples.

A fundamental concept of early instruction in numbers is the *set.* A set is the concept of quantity abstracted from a variety of groupings of specific objects—marbles, balls, beans, pieces of chalk, boys and girls, or whatever. One of the earliest tasks of mathematics instruction, many scholars believe, should be the acquiring of the concept of set by the student. At the same time, or perhaps even earlier, the concept of the *member*, the single unit, of a set needs to be acquired. The point of such instruction, of course, is to free the notion of quantity from control by specific stimuli. When the child has learned *set* and *member of set* as concepts, he is able to generalize them to any and all objects, whether or not he has seen the objects previously. By combination with previous learning of verbal associates, he is then able to name such sets as one, two, and three, and to assign these names to quantities of objects independently of their other stimulus characteristics.

There are other simple concepts involved in early mathematics instruction, which can often (although not always) be assumed to have been previously learned. Some examples are the event concepts of *adding to* and *taking away*. These are important for later learning, when instruction will be concerned with adding something to a set, or taking something away from a set. The concepts of *separation* and *combining* are similarly important. A set of objects may be made into two sets of objects by separating some of its members from others, that is, by actually introducing a physical distance between them. Also, two physically disparate sets may be combined into one by eliminating a boundary or spatial separation between them.

Many other concepts are learned as the student proceeds with the study of mathematics, including add, subtract, multiply, divide, fraction, proportion, base, decimal, and so on to quite a lengthy list. Included, of course, are geometrical concepts like point, line, plane, triangle, rectangle, parallel, and countless others. As mentioned in Chapter 6, it is usually desired at some stage to have the student learn the *definition* of, for example, a triangle. The definition, however, is a principle, and requires that the student has previously learned triangle as a concept; knowing the concept *triangle* means only that the student can *identify* triangle as a class, not that he can define it. The concept stage of learning is an essential one, and should not be skipped over in instruction in the desire to have the student formulate "exact" definitions.

PHASE 6: PRINCIPLE LEARNING • Returning to the earliest content of mathematics instruction, it is evident that it is the intention of modern mathematics to teach the child to count and to add by acquiring *principles.* Having the concepts *set, member of set,*

adding to, and *taking away* makes it possible for the child to acquire principles that, if stated verbally, would run somewhat as
follows: "The set called '2' is formed by adding a member to the
set '1'; the set called '3' is formed by adding a member to '2'; the
set called '4' is formed by adding a member to set '3'; and so on."
Once acquired, these principles make it possible for the child to
order numbers, in other words, to count. Another principle he is
able to acquire is how to form zero (not to be confused with the
simple discrimination "not any"). Zero is that set which may be
formed by taking one member away from the set 1. Progressing
from this point, the child learns how to add by applying certain
principles of combining (joining) sets. By combining the sets 3
and 2, or the sets 4 and 1, the set 5 is obtained, and the child learns
that the statements $3 + 2$, $4 + 1$, and 5, all name the same numbers.

To trace the sequence of learning through even a small number of topics of mathematics is obviously impossible in this space.
Needless to say, mathematics is filled with principles, and they
build on each other in cumulative fashion. An example of a
hierarchy of principles that may be acquired in early geometry instruction has been given in Figure 10 (page 150).

PHASE 7: PROBLEM SOLVING · Principles can also be learned
in mathematics by a judicious use of the discovery method of instruction; in other words, by problem solving. For example, having
learned the counting principles, children can be led to discover
the principles governing the placement of numerals as a means of
naming sets 10 through 20, and thus begin to learn to use the
decimal system. Again, building further on this principle and
those previously learned, they can discover how to add two-digit
numbers; and so on until an ever-growing structure of interconnected principles has been mastered.

THE ORDER OF LEARNING TYPES · These examples from
mathematics provide an answer to this kind of question: Is there a
sequence of forms of learning, from simple to complex, that should
be followed in instruction? The answer is yes, but such a sequence
cannot be applied to whole "subjects" like mathematics; it can
be made to apply only to individual "topics" of mathematics. It

would be incorrect to suppose that the learning of all of mathematics begins with stimulus-response learning and progresses through various other types of learning to problem solving. As we have seen, there is some stimulus-response learning as well as some multiple-discrimination learning even in an advanced topic like integration, whereas some problem solving can occur even in the elementary topics of counting and adding.

Within a "topic," however, it is clear that there *is* a progression of learning types from the simple to the complex. One such progression is illustrated in Figure 14, which summarizes the kinds of capabilities contributing to one of the most elementary topics in mathematics, which may be called "ordering numbers." Not all mathematics educators will necessarily agree that the progression of required learnings must be exactly as shown. This is not a matter of extreme importance, however. What is important is that there must be *a progression something like this*, in which the principles to be learned are put together from prerequisite concepts, while these in turn depend on previously learned multiple discriminations, chains, and $Ss \rightarrow R$ connections. The essentiality of any one of these prerequisites can readily be determined by empirical studies, or by experience in teaching the topic. The most serious errors in instruction occur when the existence of the hierarchy, whatever its detailed structure, remains unrecognized.

LEARNING STRUCTURE IN SCIENCE INSTRUCTION

The hierarchy of capabilities that is learned when an individual studies science has several features in common with that of mathematics. There appear to be two primary reasons for this. First is the fact that both subjects must start with a consideration of concrete objects in order that the earliest forms of learning will be made possible. And second, the student of science very early begins to use the concepts and principles of mathematics, as, for example, in counting and measuring natural phenomena, or in dealing with proportions and directions and sizes.

The typical student who begins the study of a particular topic in science, say in the seventh grade, has already learned many of the basic prerequisites that he needs in order to acquire the new

NUMBER OPERATIONS

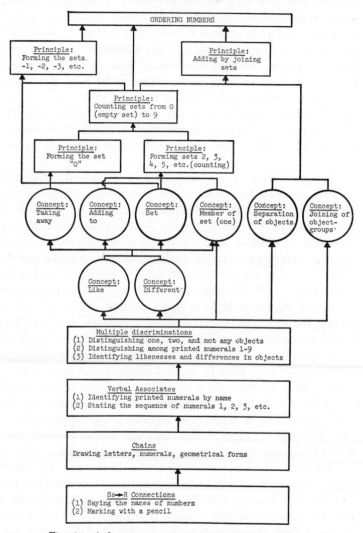

Fig. 14. A learning structure for number operations.

concepts and principles he will encounter. There remains some question, however, whether all the previously acquired capabilities he needs are actually present, because there is room for doubt that present-day curricula in science in the elementary grades are designed to provide all these capabilities. Some of them may have been acquired in studying mathematics, to be sure. But others may not be present; and if this is true the student may be expected to have difficulty with the principles of science. At any rate, for present purposes it is necessary to reflect what seems to be required for early science instruction, rather than what actually exists.

PHASE 1: BASIC TYPES OF LEARNING • It would not be particularly profitable here to try to spell out in detail all the relevant instances of basic learning that are prerequisite to the study of science. Suffice it to say that many $Ss \rightarrow R$ connections, such as the names of common objects and events, are needed, as well as others pertaining to the use of the hands in using a pencil and the eyes in scanning the environment. Chains related to hand movements must also be learned, and others involved in moving the limbs and the entire body in going forward, backward, and in moving the eyes and head in looking up, down, right, and left. Verbal associates are also of fundamental importance to later learning in science. The names of all sorts of common objects and events in the environment must be learned—chairs, tables, houses, floors, ceilings, trees, flowers, cats, dogs, and many, many others, as well as specific events like going, coming, standing, sitting, running, and so on. Most of these basic capabilities are acquired before the child goes to school. When they are not so acquired, early instruction needs to make provision for their learning.

PHASE 2: MULTIPLE-DISCRIMINATION LEARNING • The fundamental content of science is natural objects and events. The very early kind of learning that the child can and must undertake is the *discrimination* of the sensible characteristics of objects and events. Yellow objects need to be distinguished from blue ones and green ones; bright objects from dull ones; rounded objects from angular ones. Loud sounds are to be distinguished from soft ones; high sounds from low ones; brief sounds from extended ones. Heavy objects must be distinguished from light ones; smooth objects from rough ones; sharp objects from dull ones. The taste of sugar is differentiated from the taste of lemon juice; and the smells of various objects become recognizable. The numerousness of sets of objects is distinguished (see Figure 14). The events of body movements are also to be distinguished: near and far, up and down, right and left, large and small.

It is probably a mistake to suppose that all these discriminations will have been mastered before kindergarten attendance is begun. To an adult they appear painfully elementary. Yet a certain proportion of adults are unable to identify yellow as distinct from orange, or to know whether an object has a rounded edge. It seems probable that such deficiencies can in many instances be traced back to some learning deprivation in their initial school years. Early school instruction therefore needs to take pains to avoid gaps in the multiple-discrimination capabilities of the child. The physical characteristics of objects need to be observed and discriminated with systematic thoroughness, using all the externally oriented senses.

PHASE 3: CONCEPTS · The concepts useful for learning mathematics are needed also in learning science, and some other intriguing ones in addition. All the differential *attributes of objects* previously learned as multiple discriminations need to be used for establishing concepts. *Yellow* becomes not just the color of an object, but the name of a class of (yellow) objects. *Round* becomes not just a characteristic of a ball, but the name of a class of objects that may include coins, cans, drawn circles, and many sizes of spheres. *Smooth* becomes not simply the feel of a water-washed rock, but a class of characteristics applicable to silk, cream, polished wood, a baby's skin, and many other things. Similarly, *near* is not just a position of the hand, but a class of distinctions along a gradient of distances from the individual observer that may be occupied by any sorts of objects (as distinguished, of course, from another set of distinctions called *far*).

Still other concepts must likewise be established on the basis of previously learned discriminations. These include such "positional" concepts as *before* and *following*, *next to* and *separated from*, *above* and *below, in front of, behind,* among others. There are "directional" concepts like *parallel to, at right angles to, diagonal to,* as well as *vertical* and *horizontal,* which are common to the beginning study of geometry. Also in this category are concepts of common shapes, such as *circle, square, rectangle, triangle, cube, sphere,* and *pyramid.* Finally, there are the fundamental categories of science, which in this phase probably consist of several concepts of *size* (*length, area, volume*), *time* (*minute, hour, day, week*), *force* (as a push or pull), *weight* (as heaviness), and possibly also *mass* (as related to the phenomenon of inertia).

It should be apparent, as indicated in Chapter 5, that these basic concepts of science do not attain a high degree of abstraction in this early phase of instruction. On the contrary, they are relatable to quite concrete stimulus situations. And it is just this concreteness that is essential if adequate principles are to be learned later. For example, a later principle will be the relationship between length and area of a rectangular figure. To learn such a principle, however, the child must already be able to use the concepts *length* and *area* and *rectangular.* (Using them as concepts means simply that he be able to *identify them,* not describe or define them.) For members of an entire class of closed figures, he should be able to choose the ones that are rectangular, identify the sides that have differing lengths, and the region that has the property of area.

The priority in learning for meanings that are concrete (sometimes called "intuitive," although that is not a clear word) is a matter of great importance to instruction in all subjects. It may be, though, that its importance can be illustrated most clearly within the framework of science. College texts in physics, for example, are concerned about teaching the highly abstract principle contained in the statement $F = ma$. Yet it is common to find that the *force* in such a statement must be related for the student to the basic concept *push* or *pull.* There is nothing shameful in this, or even inaccurate. Before he can master a principle, the student must be able to identify the *concept force,* to point to situations in which a force can in fact be observed. Acceleration and mass are other variables in this equation that must be related to concretely referenced concepts before the principle can be learned. The student must master concepts, imprecise and qualitative as they seem to be, before he can be expected to learn principles.

PHASE 4: PRINCIPLE LEARNING · To return now to early instruction in science, the preceding phase has seen the establishment of a variety of fundamental concepts. Is the student now ready to tackle the learning of principles like $F = ma$, or inheritance through dominant and recessive genes? Probably not, unless one is willing to take the dangerous risk of having him learn to parrot verbal sequences. There are some fundamental *principles* he must learn first which relate to the fact that any science is a highly organized discipline. Some kinds of principles are much more basic than others, and at the same time much more generalizable than others, in the sense that they cut across all the specific scientific disciplines. They are used again and again throughout the study of scientific subjects. In the treatments of introductory science commonly seen in high school and junior high school textbooks they are usually *assumed* to have been learned previously. What kinds of principles are these?

A rather large number of principles could be named that are common to all sciences, and no attempt will be made here to exhaust the list. These principles, however, seem to fall into certain logical categories, and these might well be considered as proper *topics of elementary science* (Commission on Science Education, 1963) in contradistinction to the disciplines of chemistry, biology, physics, and the like, which will later be studied as specific subjects. These categories are as follows:

1. *Classifying.* These are principles that apply to the subdividing of sets of originally unfamiliar objects into several categories of increasing inclusiveness, forming classes and subclasses. Classifying means forming categories based on the appearance of objects, and also on "derived" or "inferred" characteristics. For example, animals may be classified not only on the basis of their appearance (fur-bearing, non-fur-bearing), but also in accordance with their functions (herbivorous, carnivorous, and so on). Besides objects, events also need to be classified; for example, there are

slow and fast chemical reactions, and different rates of transmission of light and sound.

2. *Measuring.* Principles of measurement pertain to the assigning of numbers to objects ordered along certain physical dimensions. Certain measurement principles are common to both science and mathematics. The student learns to specify units of measurement, and to apply these units to lengths, areas, and volumes. In addition, he learns to use principles of time measurement, and to relate different units of duration to one another. Other important principles relate to the measurement of inferred variables, as in using the time taken to change the color of a chemical indicator to measure the "strength" of a solution.

3. *Space-Time Relationships.* A number of science principles pertain to space, movements in space, and the rates of object displacements in space. For example, some important principles relate the appearance of three-dimensional objects to their representations in two dimensions. Other principles, initially nonquantitative, relate amounts of displacement, amounts of force, and rates of movement in simple machines. As an example, the movement of the shorter arm of a Class I lever imparts motion to an object at the end of the longer lever arm that is greater in amount, smaller in force, and opposite in direction. Such qualitative principles as these underlie later learning of quantitative "higher-level" principles.

4. *Communicating.* There are some principles of communicating the observations of science, the need for which derives from the publicly observable character of scientific knowledge. These are principles of systematic description of objects, of events, and of the relationships between events, such as that between temperature and the vaporization of water. Other principles of communication relate to the describing of inferences, and to the distinctions made in the description of systems when the point of view of the observer changes (Karplus, 1962). In a genuine sense, these principles of communication are relevant to the proper scientific usage of the English language.

5. *Inferring.* The basic principle of importance in this category is the distinction between observations and inferences. Many in-

ferred variables of science are defined by means of inferred principles; potential energy, valences, and genes are all examples. One form of inference is *predicting*, in which the observations made in one situation are generalized to a different situation on the basis of an inference that the same mechanisms are at work. The principles to be learned pertain to the deliberate and systematic use of inferences founded on observations.

PHASE 5: PROBLEM SOLVING · As is the case with other subjects, problem solving can profitably be employed in instruction to establish both basic and higher-order principles of science. Novel principles of classification can be discovered by students having suitably designed instructions that guide thinking but do not "give the answer." New units of measurement can be originated for objects or events that have not been previously experienced. In fact, virtually all the principles listed above can be taught by means of instruction using discovery methods. It may be that there is a particular value to instruction which emphasizes problem solving for science subjects, in view of the fact that problem-solving strategies play such a prominent role in science activities themselves.

It is apparent that the principles described here have not frequently been considered suitable topics for introductory science in the elementary grades (see, however, Commission on Science Education, 1963). What relation do they have, for example, to observations of the growth of a bean plant in a window box, a typical subject for the kind of elementary science instruction currently in vogue? The growth of plants can readily be employed in the acquisition of the kinds of principles just described. For example, *classification* principles may be exhibited by means of a demonstration containing several kinds of plants, growing at different rates. *Measuring* principles have an obvious applicability to the growth of plants. *Space-time* principles may be exhibited by the changes in size of plants in several dimensions, as well as by the differential rates of growth of the components of the plants. Observations on plant growth can readily be turned into an exercise having a *communication* objective, for example, by inquiring whether other students are able to recognize the change in a plant described by a particular student. Finally, there is plenty of opportunity for the acquisition of *inference* principles, distinguishing between the observed events of changes in size and the inference of "growth" or other "changes of state."

If one has the purpose of having young children learn these

HYDROLYSIS OF SALTS

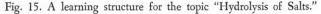

```
                    ┌─────────────────┐
                    │  PRINCIPLES OF  │
                    │   HYDROLYSIS    │
                    └─────────────────┘
                            ▲
            ┌───────────────────────────────┐
            │  Principles of degree of      │
            │  dissociation in salt solutions│
            └───────────────────────────────┘
```

Fig. 15. A learning structure for the topic "Hydrolysis of Salts."

principles, it can be done with magnets, with small animals, with simple machines, with growing plants, and with many other phenomena of the natural world. Alternatively, one can begin with the same observations and end up with not-very-useful verbal sequences. For example, first-graders can easily be taught to answer such questions as "What do plants need in order to grow?" (Sun, earth, and water.) The instructional question becomes, Which kind of capability is a prerequisite for the rigorous study of any science—general principles of the processes of science, or general information (chiefly verbal) about the natural world? On reflection, the second of these alternatives seems trivial in importance as compared with the first.

AN EXAMPLE OF A LEARNING SEQUENCE IN SCIENCE · The dependence of learning of "higher-level" principles of a specific science topic on the previous mastery of "lower-level" principles that are general to science may be illustrated by an analysis of the topic "Hydrolysis of Salts" in solution. To be learned are the principles that permit the prediction of degree of dissociation of the ions of a salt in water, and the consequent production of a solution that yields a basic reaction, an acid reaction, or a neutral reaction. The principles relate the nature of the salt solution to the degree of dissociation of the hydrogen and hydroxyl ions in the acids and bases that have reacted to form the salt. An outline of the principles and concepts that appear to be involved is shown in Figure 15.

As the figure shows, the principles of hydrolysis that constitute the objective of instruction in this example are in a learning sense based on a number of subordinate principles that have specific "chemical" content. These include such principles as "ion composition of acids and bases," "measuring the strength of acids and bases," and others. But if one asks the question of prerequisite knowledge for these content principles, he is bound to arrive at principles that are more general in their applicability. The principles of *inferred measurement*, for example, are involved in the measurement of the strength of acids and bases. Inferred measurement, in turn, depends on some even more general principles concerning *units of measurement,* and the *use of indicators* in measurement.

At a still lower level of prerequisite knowledge, there are concepts. The concepts of the chemical elements are content-specific. But there are others that are general to all of science and that must be acquired as prerequisites to the principles to be learned. Measurement principles depend on previously acquired *number* concepts. Using indicators requires the previous learning of *object attributes*—color, opacity, amount of precipitation, and so on. Principles of chemical combination are similarly based on concepts of *separation* and *joining.* The classifying of ions depends on some principles of classification that derive from concepts of *electrical events* (electromotive force).

Thus it can be seen that knowledge of the principles of a specific science topic requires the previous learning of subordinate principles that are *general* to science, in the sense that they deal with the *processes* of obtaining scientific information, regardless of whether this is biological, physical, chemical, or whatever. Moreover, these fundamental principles in turn necessitate the learning of prerequisite concepts. It would be possible to show that these latter concepts also depend on simpler forms of learning of the varieties described in previous chapters. Science learning, like mathematics learning, has a hierarchical structure that is crucially supported by a number of concepts and principles that are not content-specific; rather, they are general to the study of any and all sciences.

SEQUENCE IN THE LEARNING OF FOREIGN LANGUAGES

The nature of instruction for the learning of a foreign language is of particular interest to the present discussion because such instruction encompasses almost the entire range of learning types. In the design of instruction, there has come to be an increasing awareness during recent times of the necessity for devoting considerable attention to the early parts of language learning, to those capabilities that are generally called "skills." Only when such early skills are mastered, it is now generally conceded, is the student ready to progress to later stages of language learning.

In the description which follows, it is assumed that the objective of "language learning" includes the capabilities of understanding the speech of native (foreign) speakers, of constructing utterances which are required in conversation with foreign speakers, and of reading printed media in the foreign language.

PHASE 1: STIMULUS-RESPONSE LEARNING · One of the interesting features of foreign language learning is that it must begin with the simplest type of learning, stimulus-response learning. In other words, the student needs first to acquire $Ss \rightarrow R$ connections that copy the *sounds* of the language. The more different are the foreign language sounds from those already learned (in English), the more essential this phase is. Spanish, for example, is often considered "easy" because its sounds are relatively similar to those of English; by the same token, Chinese is "difficult." The sounds of the syllables of a word like *gemütlich* are quite different from those in English words; at least, the *ü* and the *ch* are encountered very infrequently as sounds in English. If the learner is expected later to acquire the capability of recognizing these sounds either in speech or in printing, he must first acquire them as simple $Ss \rightarrow R$ connections, so that he can generate them himself as voluntary acts.

The precision with which such sounds must be learned in the earliest phase of language instruction has been the subject of some discussion among language educators. It will be clear from the present and following discussion that a "good accent" is *not* the purpose of this phase of language learning. Discrimination learning needs to occur only with the precision that will result in the differentiation of such sound as *ü* from other confusable sounds, particularly English ones, like *oo* and *uh* and *ee*. To insist on finer differentiations than this (such as "sounding like a native speaker") at this stage of language instruction, although perhaps doing no permanent harm, can certainly delay the progress of acquiring facility in a new language. The degree of precision of discrimination needed in these basic stimulus-response connections is simply that which will enable the *student* to differentiate the sounds in his own utterances.

PHASE 2: CHAINS AND VERBAL SEQUENCES · A certain number

of common expressions may well be learned as simple chains in order to increase the student's initial confidence in the language. Expressions of courtesy and convenience—like *wollen Sie bitte* or *pardonnez-moi* or *wieviel Uhr ist es?*—fall into this category.

But the most important chains to be learned are the verbal associations between objects and actions on the one hand and foreign words on the other; in other words, in the development of a noun and verb *vocabulary*. As stimuli for these verbal chains, pictures can probably be used to good advantage. It is, after all, the chain (money as physical object) → "Geld" that one wants to establish, and not the "translation" chain (English word *money*) → "Geld." However, the importance of the mediating link in such chains is considerable, and should not be overlooked. Thus it seems entirely likely that a picture of coins *plus* the English word "gold" as stimuli would be, on the whole, more effective in establishing a verbal chain ending with "Geld" than would the picture alone. There is no reason at all to think that adding the English word to the stimulus complex in this case produces interference, or somehow increases the difficulty of the task. Quite the contrary would seem to be the case—the English word should have a facilitating effect on learning, because it can provide a highly useful mediating link in the chain to be learned.

Longer verbal chains may also have considerable importance to later learning of self-generated conversational utterances. To acquire a store of such poetical sequences as "Wer recht in Freuden wandern will, Der geh' der Sonn' entgegen . . ." is to have available for ready recall a certain reservoir of expressions and sentence structures that can serve as excellent models from which spontaneous speech can be derived and on which it can be patterned. Prose sequences, of course, can serve the same function equally well.

A second variety of verbal chains that must be learned is the printed vocabulary used in reading. Since learning to *say* the words to be recognized is a prerequisite, the oral production of speech sounds needs to be undertaken first (phase 1). If the objective of language learning were confined to reading, it would probably be more efficient to proceed directly to the learning of printed symbol → word recognition chains. But since this is usually not the sole objective, it may be preferable to provide instruction in the picture → word recognition first. Obviously, these two kinds of verbal chains are both necessary—one beginning with the stimulus of a printed word, the other with the stimulus of an object or its picture, and both ending with the response of the foreign word. There is no reason to suppose that the learning of one kind of chain will interfere with the learning of the other; converging chains of this sort are commonly learned without undue difficulty. If there is a best order of introduction, including the possibility of simultaneous learning of the two kinds of chains, this has not been determined.

PHASE 3: MULTIPLE DISCRIMINATIONS · Potential confusions of foreign words need to be removed by learning exercises designed to overcome the effects of interference, as described in Chapter 5. Every foreign language contains words that sound very much alike, and other words that look very much alike in printed form. As previously pointed out, both the stimulus-connection part of the chain (as in the printed words *regen* and *regnen*) and the response-connection part (as in the utterance of *faim* and *femme*) need to be well differentiated from words of similar appearance and sound.

PHASE 4: CONCEPT LEARNING · The learning of concepts in a foreign language follows much the same course as it does in the native language. Initially, the concept intended by a new foreign word may be most readily conveyed by an English "equivalent." For many nouns and verbs, particularly, this use of an external verbal prompt (the English word) may bring about a very high proportion of the concept learning required. *Fromage* may readily be prompted by the English word *cheese*, *écriver* by the English word *write*. But, as language scholars are fond of pointing out, such external prompts may be insufficient to convey the "true" conceptual meaning of a foreign word. *Cherie*, for example, may be initially prompted by the English word *dear*, but this would be quite insufficient to identify the class of situations in which *cherie* may properly be used. Does one use *cherie* in saying (in

French) "dear mother," "dear sister," "dear friend," or is it confined to "dear sweetheart"?

There is no mystery here. Adequate learning of a concept, as mentioned in Chapter 5, requires the learning of chains in response to a *representative variety* of stimulus situations. Accordingly, in order to learn the concept reflected in a new foreign word, one must encounter it and use it in some representative contexts. To the extent that these contexts have been unrepresentative, the concept learned will be an inadequate one. To the extent that a suitable range of stimulus situations is encountered by the learner, the concept learned will be a satisfactory one.

The necessity for an adequate number of contextual examples is particularly apparent for the learning of such words as prepositions and conjunctions. As every beginning student of French knows, *de* does not always mean the same as *of*, and *a* means many things besides *to*. Again the obvious implication for instruction in these concepts, and many others like them, is to provide a sufficient variety of stimulus contexts in which these small words occur. For such words, although prompting with English probably does no harm when the foreign word is initially encountered, any such procedure is grossly insufficient for the learning of the concept in its full meaning. In order to achieve the latter, the range of situations in which the word occurs must be presented to the learner and responded to by him.

PHASE 5: PRINCIPLE LEARNING · Putting concepts together as connected discourse, whether in understanding spoken speech, in responding to other speakers, or in reading, is a task that obviously requires the use of principles. In traditional language instruction, these are the "rules of grammar and syntax." To learn these rules in verbal form seems a perfectly reasonable thing for a student to do, just so long as the danger of learning "mere verbal sequences" is avoided. If he learns a verbal rule for German such as "*in* in the sense of 'moving into' is followed by an accusative form of the noun," this is a highly useful principle so long as he can identify concretely the concepts that compose it (such as "moving into," "accusative," and "noun"), and has not merely memorized it as a verbal sequence.

Some language teachers state a preference for the inductive formulation of rules by students; in other words, for the use of a discovery method of instruction. As pointed out previously, such a method may actually take longer, but seems to have advantages. In practice, the student would be made to encounter a number of contrasting expressions like *in der Welt* and *in die Welt*, and would discover from the context the rule about dative and accusative forms (without necessarily using these technical terms) following the preposition *in*.

In the learning of language principles, a point deserving great emphasis is the importance of prerequisites. And the necessary prerequisites, as has previously been pointed out, are concepts. The contents of the principles that are exhibited in the form of phrases, sentences, and conversations are, of course, the concepts of the foreign language, that is, its *words* in their conceptual form. It should be almost self-evident that ideas cannot be expressed unless one has previously learned their unitary parts. Thus the learning of vocabulary is of considerable importance in facilitating the learning of the principles of grammar and syntax. The greater the number of verbal concepts one knows, the easier it should be to learn the required principles of language structure.

In traditional language instruction, the learning of principles is usually interspersed with the learning of vocabulary. The student learns a little vocabulary, and then practices using a few principles of grammar. It is at least a likely hypothesis, however, that if a student had acquired a sizable vocabulary, the learning of "structure" would proceed quite rapidly. On the other hand, there would seem to be little merit whatsoever, from the standpoint of learning efficiency, in the attempt to teach structure *before* vocabulary. Whatever is learned in this manner cannot be learned efficiently, because the learner is so frequently "at loss for words."

PHASE 6: PROBLEM SOLVING · As has already been pointed out, discovery of principles of grammar and syntax is a possible method of learning. At somewhat more advanced stages of foreign language facility, the use of problem-solving situations may also be the best kind of learning condition to employ. A native speaker sets the problem situation by inquiring, "What would you like for dinner?" The student must generate a reply that makes sense not only in being understandable, but also in representing the contents of an actual dinner. The setting of many kinds of problem situations of this sort is of great value for acquiring facility in understanding and speaking the foreign language. It need hardly be emphasized again that a reasonably adequate vocabulary is a prerequisite to successful learning by means of such exercises.

A LEARNING STRUCTURE IN ENGLISH

Instruction in one's native language has many points in common with the conditions of learning a foreign language. This is particularly true in the early stages of education, in which the youngster learns to use the language in communicating and in reading. For the sake of brevity, the following discussion of English language learning will be primarily confined to these early stages. Later study of English concerns itself increasingly, as would be expected, with higher-order principles of writing and appreciation of literature. These can be undertaken successfully only after the individual has thoroughly mastered the more fundamental capabilities of English expression and comprehension.

PHASE 1: STIMULUS-RESPONSE LEARNING • First of all, oral units of the sounds of English must be acquired. These consist of the sounding of commonly encountered letter combinations like *bat, rat, mat, sat,* as well as *-ly, -tion,* and the like. Presumably, what are being acquired are the pronunciations of English phonemes (Fries, 1963). It is of some importance to note, too, that these are *discriminated* connections in which the precision of sounds has a certain importance. Shortly following this, however, or even at the same time, the child learns to respond to orally produced *words,* and to use them in oral speech of his own. The more words he learns, the fewer he will need to learn later. Actually, for oral speech, the child may be expected to acquire a vocabulary of reasonable size and to progress to some rather complex and lengthy chains of words before he goes to school. But his degree of progress, of course, depends on the demands made on him by his social environment, including his parents. If parents are not highly communicative and "verbal," the child is unlikely to acquire many words or verbal chains.

PHASE 2: CHAINING · As one progresses to the fundamental skills for reading, it is necessary to recognize that symbolic (printed) representations of English sounds are quite arbitrary, illogical, and essentially meaningless. This sets the stage for a conflict in views about reading instruction that has persisted for many years. On the one hand, the child "knows" a fairly large number of words, in the oral sense, because he has already learned them. But he is now faced with the necessity of learning to recognize the sounds of these words, *and other words he does not yet know*, in printed form. To some scholars, it appears that the child is being asked to take a backward step. And this is true in the sense that he must now learn chains which are composed, not of words, but of *letter combinations*. He must do this because printed English is designed to represent sounds, not words, as is Chinese orthography. Consequently, the initial verbal sequences that underlie reading capability are more like motor chains than they are like verbal sequences. They are chains in which stimuli like B and D are linked to responses like "buh" and "duh"; and a stimulus like A is linked to the responses "ā," "ă," and "ah."

At this stage, the child is learning to distinguish letters by saying the *sounds of letters* to printed stimuli. If the letters have different sounds, as do the vowels, he must learn these; if they have single sounds, as do many of the consonants, these may be learned even more readily. However, it needs to be stated clearly that the purpose of this stage of learning is *not* to learn how to pronounce printed words (a later stage), but rather to develop what Fries (1963) calls "rapid recognition responses" to printed letters. Actually, it may be argued that the particular kinds of responses he learns to the letters are unimportant; and many children have been taught to "name" the letters rather than to "sound" them. It seems reasonable, however, that sounding the letters, in recognizing them, represents a use of responses that will interfere least with later learning.

PHASE 3: VERBAL SEQUENCE LEARNING · Whether or not the individual begins by learning chains to identify English letter sounds, he undoubtedly must learn the verbal sequences that identify printed *words* as he begins to read. This is particularly true, of course, of the most frequently occurring words, "the," "an," "but," "boy," "dog," "tree," and so on. If he has learned to respond to letters and to distinguish them correctly, he may be able to put together chains like *m ă n* (in a sense, to "discover") the word "man"; if he has not, someone must first tell him what the printed word "man" sounds like. In either case, what is being learned is a verbal chain that associates the stimulus of the printed word through a typical set of connections with the saying of the word.

The previous learning of whole words in oral form is an important prerequisite for the kind of verbal chains established at this stage. The response member of the chain must be present in order for the chain to be linked together most readily. In other words, the learner who does not already know how to say the words orally is going to have difficulty learning to read, since he has no way of linking the previously learned orally sounded word with what he sees in print.

PHASE 4: MULTIPLE-DISCRIMINATION LEARNING • In this phase of reading instruction, the learner must acquire discriminations of verbal chains whose printed stimuli have similar appearances—*run* and *ran, hat, bat, rat,* and *cat,* and so on. Distinctions between words having different vowel sounds when different combinations of letters are used, as in *rat* and *rate,* are also of considerable importance. Confusable words are sometimes contrasted in reading instruction, but the attempt to establish discriminations of this sort is not always systematically carried out. There are many potential confusions among common English words, and the deliberate arrangement of learning conditions to reduce the interference resulting from such confusions would seem to be a worthwhile aspect of instruction in reading. According to Fries (1963, p. 194), what the child must learn at this stage is to distinguish the *spelling patterns* of English words, beginning with small words that are familiar to him in oral form.

The objective of this stage of learning English is to enable the child to say orally such a word as "concatenation," which he has never seen or heard before. Whether he knows the meaning of

the word is quite irrelevant. The all-important capability he is acquiring at this stage is the ability to say, when he sees it in print,
the word "concatenation" in a way that is discriminably different
to him from the printed word "concentration." The reason for de-
siring this capability is that he will be able to match the *sound* of
"concatenation" (or "concentration") with the sound of the word
he hears or learns from oral communication. For the child, the
normal sequence in understanding printed text is from words that
are already known in oral speech ("concentration" is a possible
example) to the printed representations of these words.

Is it important to the ultimate skill of reading for the child to
acquire these fundamental distinctions among spelling patterns
that enable him to identify unfamiliar words? The evidence on
this point is not entirely clear-cut. Naturally, the adult reader has
arrived at a stage in which the vast majority of printed words he
encounters have previously been identified in their oral form. In
such an adult, however, the difficulties experienced with a novel
word provide a fairly sure clue to the existence of a gap in his
early instruction resulting from the omission of phase 4, in which
emphasis is given to the sounding of spelling patterns. On the first
encounter, he may be unable to read a word like *obsequiousness*,
which, to an individual who has learned to identify sounds, is
ridiculously simple.

PHASE 5: CONCEPT LEARNING • In many respects, the concept
learning necessary for the understanding of printed (as well as
spoken) English is similar to that previously described for learning
a foreign language. Of course, for many words, conceptual meaning is acquired with the oral form and simply transferred via a
verbal sequence to the printed form. Before reading instruction is
begun, a *house*, a *tree*, a *dog*, a *cat*, a *chair* have all acquired conceptual meaning for the average child as connections terminating
in oral responses. By verbal chaining, the printed form of these
same words becomes linked with the responses controlled by the
concepts previously learned. Thus the printed word "house" can
come to serve as a stimulus for the concept *house*, meaning any
member of the class *house*, rather than being the label for a particular house. New words that are first encountered in reading may

be illustrated by a suitable variety of objects, demonstrations, or pictures in order that their conceptual meaning can be correctly acquired.

Concepts that denote relationships, as do prepositions, are typically learned by being encountered in sequences with other words. The phrases "of the man," "of the boy," "of the tree," and many others like them, provide the variety of examples needed to establish the possessive meaning of the concept *of*. Connective concepts like *but, however, moreover,* and so on, are similarly established by being encountered in a suitable variety of reading contexts.

Phase 6: Principles • As is well known, the sequences of English are highly predictable. It is not difficult to supply missing words in such a sentence as The man's hat was blown off — — — — — —. Although a limited number of alternative forms of completion of this sentence is possible, a great many more are not; hence the probability of completing it in the way it was originally written is quite high (Miller, 1951).

It is these principles of ordering English sentences that are learned by practicing reading with a variety of subject-matter content. As greater facility is achieved, it becomes possible for the reader to attain progressively faster speeds at the task, primarily because he is able to make better and better predictions of what a sentence says without actually looking at every printed word. There are also higher-order principles to be learned, pertaining to the organization of paragraphs, sections, and chapters. All such principles are quite complex, and are typically learned not as formally stated rules, but by a process of discovery from the act of reading.

A summary of the hierarchy of capabilities learned during instruction in reading is shown in Figure 16. It may be noted that some of the basic learnings included in this figure are those of producing language sounds and recognizing printed letters by sound. These are typically not included in the "word method" of reading instruction. With such a method, the capability called "recognition

READING

Fig. 16. A learning structure for the basic skills of reading.

of printed words" is limited to words that have specifically been encountered during previous learning.

LEARNING AND INSTRUCTIONAL SEQUENCES

The four different content examples described in this chapter are intended to demonstrate that the subjects of school instruction possess hierarchical organizations with respect to required types of learning. Each can be analyzed to reveal prerequisite learnings that grow progressively simpler as one works downward from principles to $Ss \rightarrow R$ connections. The learning of the principles that are usually the most obvious *objectives* of instruction requires the previous learning of other principles, and these in turn require prerequisite concepts, multiple discriminations, verbal sequences, chains, and $Ss \rightarrow R$ connections.

The implications for the design of instruction are quite clear. If learning at any level is to occur with greatest facility, careful attention must be paid to the prerequisites of such learning. It will be difficult for the child to learn the definitions (principles) of geometry unless he has previously acquired the concepts of line, angle, triangle, intersection, and so on. It will be difficult for a learner to acquire the principles of any specific science unless he already knows some more basic principles of classifying, measuring, and inferring. It is demonstrably difficult for a learner to construct meaningful utterances in a foreign language unless he has learned the concept words that compose such communications; and it is difficult for him to learn these words unless he has previously learned to say the sounds of the language. Learning to read English comes hard to those who have not first learned to speak many English words. It cannot be said that any of these "shortcut" kinds of learning are impossible, because learning is a marvelous capacity of living organisms that will occur whether one wants it to or not. Nevertheless, shortcuts carry their own handicaps, and typically result in deficiencies that show themselves as limitations in generalizability of the capabilities acquired.

The fundamentals of instruction are not clearly conveyed by such expressions as "reading, writing, and arithmetic." The most general capabilities are much more fundamental than these. In subjects like mathematics and science, the most basic capabilities are to be found in the stimulus-response connections, chains, and concepts that make up the activities of observing, discriminating, drawing, and classifying. In languages, native and foreign, they include the basic forms of learning that characterize the acquisition of word sounds, the discrimination of these sounds, and the mastery of verbal concepts. The systematic planning of instruction in the elementary school grades in terms of such capabilities would probably have a marked positive effect on facility of learning the more advanced principles of all school subjects.

8 types

GENERAL REFERENCES

Learning Prerequisites

Ausubel, D. P. *The psychology of meaningful verbal learning.* New York: Grune & Stratton, 1963. Chap. 6.

Gagné, R. M. The implications of instructional objectives for learning. In C. M. Lindvall (Ed.), *Defining educational objectives.* Pittsburgh: University of Pittsburgh Press, 1964. Chap. 4.

Gagné, R. M. Problem solving. In A. W. Melton (Ed.), *Categories of human learning.* New York: Academic Press, 1964.

Knight, F. B. Some considerations of method. In G. M. Whipple (Ed.), *National Society for the Study of Education, Twenty-ninth yearb. Report of the society's committee on arithmetic.* Bloomington, Ill.: Public School, 1930. Chap. **4.**

The Structure of Selected Subjects

Brooks, N. *Language and language learning: theory and practice.* New York: Harcourt, Brace & World, 1959.

Commission on Science Education. *Science: a process approach. Teachers Guide.* Washington, D.C.: American Association for the Advancement of Science, 1963.

Congdon, A. R. *Training in high school mathematics essential for success in certain college subjects.* New York: Teachers College, Columbia University, 1930.

Durrell, D. D. *Improving reading instruction.* New York: Harcourt, Brace & World, 1956.

Fagerstrom, W. H. *Mathematical facts and processes prerequisite to the study of the calculus.* New York: Teachers College, Columbia University, 1933.

Fries, C. C. *Linguistics and reading.* New York: Holt, Rinehart and Winston, 1963.

National Council of Teachers of English, Commission on the English Curriculum. *The English language arts for today's children.* New York: Appleton-Century-Crofts, 1954.

National Council of Teachers of English, Commission on the English Curriculum. *The English language arts in the secondary school.* New York: Appleton-Century-Crofts, 1956.

National Council of Teachers of Mathematics. *The learning of mathematics its theory and practice. Twenty-first yearbook.* Washington, D.C.: The Council, 1953.

UNESCO. *The teaching of modern languages.* New York: Columbia University Press, 1955.

THE MOTIVATION
AND CONTROL
OF LEARNING
AND TRANSFER

8

THE PREVIOUS CHAPTER has described one of the principal ways in which programs of education need to take into account the conditions of various forms of learning. The attainment of new capabilities by human learners requires a systematic plan for the acquiring of subordinate discriminations, concepts, principles. Learned capabilities become most readily generalizable when they are soundly based on previously mastered entities.

As every teacher knows, other kinds of arrangements besides these must be made for effective education. The enterprise of learning must be managed. For one thing, there is the necessity of creating certain additional preconditions of learning (cf. Gagné and Bolles, 1959), the conditions that will ensure student *motivation.* Then as one proceeds into the events of learning themselves, there is the need to institute the conditions that influence learning —in other words, to manage *instruction,* including the assessment of its outcomes. There is still a third major aspect of the total educational process, concerning which little has been said up to now. This is the matter of establishing conditions to ensure the *transferability* of what has been learned.

The importance of motivation to the educational enterprise is widely recognized, and need not here be given detailed justification. The essential questions to be answered may be put as follows: How does one motivate the individual to undertake the enterprise of learning? How does one keep the learner interested in continuing the learning exercise, as well as in seeking further learning after completing it? Obviously, such questions imply that some state internal to the learner, which functions as a precondition of the events of learning themselves, needs to be established and maintained.

Assuming that the two kinds of internal states—previously learned capabilities and motivations—can be suitably established, the remaining components of instructional procedure are *external* to the learner. The main external category comprises the specific conditions of learning, as described in previous chapters, translated into practical procedures for each particular content objective. They are composed of techniques for ensuring the conditions of contiguity, reinforcement, and repetition necessary for the acquisition of particular capabilities by the learner. They include also the requirements of verbal communication, whether in the form of oral or printed language. Accordingly, the management of instruction becomes a matter of suitable arrangements of oral communication (usually by a teacher), printed communication, pictures and other graphic representation, as well as the objects and events that are to be directly observed. The kinds of instructional procedures that are possible in achieving the conditions of learning previously described will be discussed in a later section.

A final category of external events pertains to the arrangement of conditions that will ensure that what has been acquired will be *generalizable*, or *transferable*, to a suitable variety of new situations outside the immediate learning environment. One must seek transferability of acquired knowledge in two senses. First, the capabilities that are acquired need to be generalizable to as wide as possible a variety of *applications* in specific situations of the same class. If the individual has learned how to compute the value of a hypotenuse, it is of importance to know also whether he can do this properly in a variety of newly encountered situations that involve such computation. Second, it is expected, in accordance with the principles described in the preceding chapter, that a capability will be transferable to the *learning of new knowledge*, particularly of the sort specifically related to it in a superordinate sense within a learning structure. Computing the hypotenuse is presumably transferable to a principle such as finding vectors of forces, in the sense that it makes the learning of this higher-order principle readily possible. Perhaps these two meanings of transferability do not exhaust the possibilities for this important concept, but they at least represent the minimal essentials.

Assuming, then, that a suitable learning structure has been planned, the manager of the educational process must turn his attention to the establishment of motivation in the learner, to the execution of specific instructional procedures which will ensure that learning will occur, and to the institution of further procedures to bring about transferability of what has been learned.

MOTIVATION FOR LEARNING

The motivation of human behavior is such a large and complex subject that only a small portion of it can be treated here. Of course it is of great interest to everyone, and not only to the psychologist who studies motivation intensively, to know what varieties of motives exist, how they originate and develop within the individual, and to understand how they determine the "force" and direction of human behavior. Many investigations of motivation have been and are being made, and there are many books on the topic (McClelland *et al.*, 1953; Brown, 1961; Hall, 1961).

It will be apparent to the reader that the present work cannot deal with the topic of motivation in any except a fairly restricted sense. This is not because its importance is unrecognized. In fact, many students of the educational process are convinced that the problem of controlling and developing motivation is quite the most serious issue faced by the schools. This broad conception of the motivational problem includes a consideration of the motives that make the student want to seek knowledge, to utilize his talents, to desire self-fulfillment as a human being, to relate to other people in a satisfying manner, and to become an effective member of society. Such goals as these are of tremendous importance to any system of education. The exploration of the motivational development they require is a subject deserving a separate volume.

In this chapter it will be possible to deal only with those varieties of human motivation that are most highly relevant to the process of learning and the procedures of instruction. Before discussing these specifically, it will be desirable to speak of two specific varieties of motivation that seem to represent two contrasting extremes, and that also seem to be outside the scope of the present treatment.

MOTIVATION TO ATTEND SCHOOL

With respect to the practical problem of providing instruction to students, it is evident that they must want to place themselves in the environment where such instruction occurs in order to be able to be affected by it. Young children sometimes have rather weak motivation to attend school, preferring the familiar environment of home and mother. Such lack of motivation is often a concern of the kindergarten teacher, as it is to parents. Usually, social motives of conformity to group pressures, as well as other motives of curiosity about the new environment and perhaps pleasant rivalries with new children, gather sufficient strength to overcome the negative effects of this motivation to avoid school.

Negative motivation toward a school environment is not entirely lacking in older children, either. For example, studies of lower-class children (Riessman, 1962) have emphasized the fact that these students may consider going to school a kind of "sissy" occupation, dominated by females who extoll the virtues of neatness, cleanliness, orderliness, and so on. In essence, this was Huckleberry Finn's attitude toward school. It is noteworthy, however, that these same children do not have negative motivation regarding learning, or the value of an education (Wilson, 1959), but only toward school attendance.

If learning of traditional subjects is to take place in schools, it is evident that the problem of establishing positive motivation toward school attendance is both real and important. Nevertheless, it is not a kind of motivation that can be directly treated here. Ensuring positive motivation toward school is something that must be dealt with to a large extent in terms of the family and the community. If the student's family accepts and values the school, the chances are that he will also. If there are community pressures for school attendance, these will be reflected in the individual's behavior. For purposes of the present discussion, the desire or willingness to attend school must be assumed.

THE RESOLVE TO LEARN

Far at the other extreme of an ordered set of motives is the kind of motivation that may be called a "resolve to learn." Some discussions of the problems of motivation speak of "motivation to learn" as if this were a specific kind of resolve by means of which the student could say to himself, "I must learn this," and learning would then follow. But if there is this kind of specific motivation, it does not appear to be very effective. A number of studies have shown that under many circumstances learning occurs about as well when such a resolve is absent as when it is present: this has been the general finding in investigations of "incidental learning" (Postman, 1964).

But such a specific resolve needs to be carefully distinguished from motivation to *achieve*, which, as later discussion will show, is of tremendous importance to successful learning. If the student's "motivation to learn" means that he resolves *to be able to do something*, a something that can be achieved as a *result* of learning, then this is positive motivation of a substantial character.

In general, then, subsequent sections will attempt to discuss the kinds of motivation relevant to successful learning; but in doing so, they will avoid the twin extremes of "motivation to attend school," on the one hand, and the specific "resolve to learn" on the other.

MOTIVATION TO ENGAGE IN LEARNING

What makes an individual want to undertake learning? How can one establish the kind of motivation required for the student to be selectively attentive to the stimulus events that will bring about the change in behavior that is the sign of learning?

ALERTNESS • If a student is to respond to stimulation, regardless of how it is presented, he must have a state of *alertness* that corresponds at least in one sense to the commonsense word "attention." It is of considerable importance that recent studies of the nervous system have identified this alertness function and located it in certain centers of the brain. Unless these neural centers are active, the effects of external stimulation do not reach the cerebral cortex, and consequently cannot play their role in bringing about learning. It is not a fiction, therefore, that the student's "brain must be awake" in order for learning to occur. The alerting center must be active.

It is too soon to be able to specify how the alertness function may be controlled. Activity in this center is presumably decreased when the individual is sleepy or fatigued. Perhaps it can be stimulated by certain drugs. In all probability, a state of alertness is subject to signal learning (type 1): this may be one kind of response that can be conditioned to a warning signal or to an alarm clock. For the purposes of conducting instruction, however, little can be added to the prescription that alertness must be present in the student. So far as is known, learning does not occur without it.

Motivation to Achieve · One of the most powerful and effective motives that can be called into play in setting the stage for learning is motivation for *achievement*. The simple acts learned by a young child seem to be very largely dependent on this kind of motivation. Wanting to be able to open a door, a child acquires the chain by which he reaches for and turns the doorknob; wanting to get a parent to give him his ball, he acquires the verbal sequence that "names" the ball. Later on, the individual may want to be able to name the letters of the alphabet, or to identify all the varieties of new automobiles, and this motivation is an essential precondition for the learning of multiple discriminations. Later still, the student may want to be able to identify a chromosome, or a chemical element; or he may be motivated to be able to add fractions, or to demonstrate the truth of logical propositions, or to conduct a scientific experiment.

From the earliest age onward, however, it is important to note that motivation to achieve means *wanting to be able to do something*. The individual conceptualizes his goals in terms of action. The action itself may be more or less socially useful; college teachers sometimes suspect that the kind of achievement students have in mind is being able to hold a "bull session" on a topic, whereas the teachers hope for action of a kind having a greater social importance than this. But even if only "being able to talk about" something is the goal, it is nonetheless a form of action. In contrast, wanting "to comprehend" a subject, or "to really understand" it, or to "appreciate" it are not the kinds of achievements to which students can normally relate their own individual desires. It takes a very sophisticated, mature individual to understand what is meant by a "desire to understand."

Much use is made of specific achievement motivation as a basis for learning in the school. Wise teachers know the power of telling a student what he will be able to do when a particular learning session or topic is completed. The young student of science may be told, for example, that the learning of certain principles will enable him to predict the size of a plant, or to express its rate of growth in graphic form. The student of mathematics may be told that, having learned certain principles, he will be able to construct a novel number system, or to find the lengths of the sides of triangles. The student of English may be told that he will be able to read the "funnies" by himself or, at a later stage, to enjoy the novels of Henry James or to interpret the legal language of an insurance policy.

However, it is relatively easy to overlook this kind of motivation, and this is a common mistake of elementary textbooks. A chapter may begin by saying, "Now we are going to learn about valence," but such a statement is extremely weak, from the standpoint of human motives. How much better if the chapter can initially inform the student that the principles of valence will enable him to predict the molecular composition of compounds resulting from chemical reactions, or some other desirable action he can readily grasp. Again it is apparent that the key to achievement motivation is the *conception of action* on the part of the student. He must want to be able *to do something.*

There is, of course, a broader aspect to achievement motivation. Suppose the student says he does *not* want to be able to predict the rate of growth of a plant. What then? The most straightforward answer is that he must learn to want it. At an earlier age, perhaps he can learn to connect this particular want with a more general one of amazing his friends or parents, thereby receiving social approval. Later on, it should be possible to relate this specific motivation to a variety of more general goals, such as wanting to go to college, wanting to make his own living, wanting to own a farm, wanting to be a scientist. But these relationships (which the reader will recognize as principles, in the terminology used here) of specific to general motives are not innately apparent to the student, obvious as they may be to his parents and teachers. He must learn them, and this means they must be communicated to him.

One of the most important functions of the teacher is to become a source of adult guidance for the student. By assuming such a role, he is able to teach the principles that make it possible for the student to associate the specific achievement goals of a particular topic of instruction with larger, more general goals. At the simplest level, such principles may merely relate a particular entity to be learned, like adding decimal quantities, to a subsequent topic like using decimal equivalents of fractions, or to a concrete action like adding dollars and cents. Beyond this, the achievement of adding decimals may be related to more advanced and spectacular "feats" of mathematics; the student need only grasp what these are, but not necessarily how to do them, in order to be motivated for achievement. At a still more general level, specific achievements can be related to the student's interests, to his desire for skill and competence, and to his own life goals. There is, of course, no simple "key" to the establishment of such motivation. What is suggested here is that the establishment of achievement motivation needs to be pursued vigorously and with great frequency. Naturally, home influences will contribute toward this task. But the school is one of the important places where achievement motivation can be acquired.

MOTIVATION TO CONTINUE LEARNING TASKS

Once the learner is motivated to "put himself into" the learning situation, the first part of the problem is solved. As has been said previously, if the commitment to learning is made, and the proper prerequisites have been met, learning is virtually an inevitable consequence. However, the learning of an entire topic, or subject, requires the learner to continue to maintain the goal he has set for himself during a period of time in which he may be engaging in quite a variety of activities. Accordingly, it is still necessary to devise means of keeping the student interested. A means must be found of keeping up his motivation to continue the learning task until it is finished.

ACHIEVEMENT OF SUBTASKS · It is perhaps not surprising to find additional usefulness for achievement motivation in maintaining interest in a learning task. In this case, though, the learner must undertake to achieve the goals of *subtasks* along the route. For example, the task depicted in Figure 10, which ultimately enables the learner to specify points, lines, and curves, contains sixteen or more subtasks, each of which can be represented as a separate goal. At one point in learning, the student is acquiring the capability of "identifying a ray"; at another point, of "identifying intersections of lines"; and so on. Each separate subtask (or single principle) can become for the student an achievement to be met, and therefore a motivational challenge.

If the individual achievements of subtasks are to become sources of motivation, it is evident that they must be systematically communicated to the student. This means simply that he must be told, "Next you will need to learn how to recognize the part of a line called a ray," or something equivalent to this, *before* he actually undertakes the learning. One cannot expect him somehow to infer the goal of the next subtask before he has even begun it. In order to use this achievement as a source of motivation, it must be communicated to him prior to the occurrence of learning. Obviously, to do this for every subtask to be learned requires very careful planning of the whole instructional sequence for any topic.

ENJOYMENT OF LEARNING · If the learner can regularly seek and find rewards for his achievement motivation, it is not unreasonable to suppose that this entire set of experiences will generalize into a positive enjoyment of learning itself. To develop such a "love of learning," the student must be progressively weaned from dependence on the teacher or other agent external to himself. First of all, this means that he needs to develop his own "standards" against which he can compare his achievements as they develop stage by stage during his learning of a topic or a subject. The new student of a foreign language may need the external reference of a native speaker's utterances in order to make the comparisons that lead to reinforcement of pronunciation skills. But the experienced student will be able to judge his pronunciation against his own set of standards. Similarly, learning to write an essay surely requires much feedback from a teacher in its early stages; but as more experience in writing is gained, the student becomes able to compare his output against his own set of standards.

A second kind of motivational development, extending over a period of years, is an increased dependence on self-generated "instructions" and strategies in the prosecution of a learning assignment. In the early years of school, the child needs frequent verbal guidance in the acquisition of new concepts and principles. But to an increasing degree in the higher grades, it should be possible for him to provide his own guidance, and to acquire a variety of learning strategies that will enable him to take control of the entire learning situation. He can approach each new learning task as something that can be tackled with the aid of his own problem-solving techniques and strategies. If, for example, he must read a technical book in a field new to him, he can supply his own set of "organizers" (Ausubel, 1963, p. 24) to the material. A number of writers have suggested that the practice of a discovery method in learning can generate some strategies which exert a lasting effect on motivation to continue learning tasks and to undertake new ones (Bruner, 1961; Schwab, 1962).

THE EXTERNAL EVENTS OF INSTRUCTION

The important *internal* states of the individual who is participating in the process of learning are his motivation and his store of prerequisite knowledge. To be considered next are the *external* events that influence the process. In terms of managing instruction, it is evident from the previous chapter that certain steps can be taken to arrange for the establishment of suitable internal states of the learner. By suitable planning of a sequence or course of instruction, one can ensure that prerequisite learnings have been accomplished. Somewhat less surely but no less importantly, the attempt can be made to establish the kinds of motivation that need to prevail during learning. In turning attention next to the requisite external events for learning, it may be expected that control over their occurrence is a highly practical undertaking.

Control of the external events in the learning situation is what is typically meant by the word "instruction." These are the events that are manipulated by the teacher, the textbook writer, the designer of films or television lessons, the developer of self-instructional programs. It is possible, of course, to look on instruction as a mysterious art, impossible of being analyzed in these terms. But this point of view is opposed to that taken in this volume, as will already be apparent. Instead, the present approach is one that attempts to classify the parts of the instructional situation and to describe the kinds of control to which they may be subjected in bringing about learning. The description of conditions for various types of learning contained in Chapters 2 through 6 should make possible the derivation of general principles of control over external instructional events that are related to the types of learning being undertaken, but at the same time independent of the specific content to be taught.

COMPONENTS OF INSTRUCTION · There appear to be three major parts of the instructional complex that may be controlled or manipulated. First, it is possible to control the *stimulus situation*, by which is meant the objects or events that are the focus of learning interest. In reading, the stimuli are printed words on a page; in science, the stimuli may be plants or tissues or chemical solutions or balances; in mathematics, they may be symbols or drawings of geometrical figures. The second component of instruction is the *verbal communication* employed to direct the learner's attention, to guide his learning, and to institute the proper sequence of actions, among other things. Strictly speaking, such communication is not a part of the content to be learned, but only that part of the instruction which exerts a control over the learner's behavior during learning. When simple forms of learning are being undertaken, this distinction between *guidance* and *content* is easy to make. When such things as principles are being learned, since these are often stated verbally, the distinction is more difficult to draw. Nevertheless, it would be hard to overestimate the importance of the distinction for an understanding of the instructional process. Third, there is the matter of control over the *feedback* to the student from the events of learning. Consideration must be given to the question of how the learner knows he has achieved the objective of a learning act, and how such information can be manipulated to bring about reinforcement.

CONTROLLING THE STIMULUS SITUATION

The objects and events that make up the stimulus situation for learning, naturally enough, vary according to what is being learned. The desired content of instruction will determine whether the stimulus situation is primarily composed of foreign words, of collections of rocks, or of geometrical shapes. But the general forms taken by stimuli, whether objects, pictures, or printed texts, are importantly determined by the *type of learning* that must be undertaken. To deal with this question adequately, therefore, it is necessary to consider the stimulus situation applicable to the types of learning described in previous chapters. For this purpose it will be possible to begin with stimulus-response learning (type 2); it may be assumed that the requirements of the stimulus situation for signal learning (type 1) may be satisfied by the introduction of a signal (almost any physical stimulus will qualify).

THE STIMULUS SITUATION FOR THE LEARNING OF $Ss \rightarrow R$'s AND CHAINS · In learning a stimulus-response connection, the stimulus with which the response is to be associated must be presented in such a way that it is perceived by the learner. If the individual is to learn to grasp a pencil, one needs simply to be sure that he sees this physical object, and also feels it. A second aspect of stimulation that needs to be present comes from the kinesthetic sense, that is, stimulation generated by muscular action. As indicated in Chapter 3, this latter part of the total stimulation must be present if a voluntary act is being learned. Many studies provide evidence that trying to establish a motor act by having the instructor guide or push the moving member is quite ineffective for learning (Carr, 1930). Learning to print or write script provides an example in the school; the student must practice "doing it himself." Only in this way can the necessary stimulation from his own muscles be made to occur dependably as a part of the total stimulus situation.

As these examples imply, the presence of kinesthetic stimulation is equally necessary when single $Ss \rightarrow R$'s are being linked into chains. In this case, however, the primary purpose is not to establish the individual links, but to connect these links in a proper sequence. The stimulation for each following link needs to include the kinesthetic feedback from the immediately preceding link if the chain is to be learned most effectively. Verbal chains are no exception; the stimulation provided by hearing and feeling oneself say word No. 1 furnishes an important portion of the cue to saying word No. 2, and so on.

THE STIMULUS SITUATION FOR MULTIPLE DISCRIMINATION · The basic requirement for multiple discrimination is that the stimuli be associated with different responses so that they will not be confused with one another. In some instances, all the stimulus objects may be presented at once. For example, if the student is being asked to make differential identifications of leaves of oak, maple, elm, birch, and poplar, samples of each of these leaf types may be shown all at once on a table. Under such circumstances it is possible for the student to learn in a circumscribed time interval that the maple leaf is *maple*, and also that it is *not oak*; that the elm leaf is *elm*, and that it is *not birch*; and so on.

Under other circumstances, particularly when the number of discriminations to be made is large, it may be necessary to present the stimuli in sequence, because they cannot all be looked at effectively together. Identifying twenty children in a schoolroom is an example. The important requirement continues to be one of "contrast practice," in which the learner not only has a chance to learn that one object is an X, and another a Y, but also that the first is *not a Y* and the second is *not an X*. Sometimes, the stimuli are grouped into highly similar subsets in order to make easier this kind of differentiation. In formal terms, as was stated in Chapter 5, the primary purpose of "contrast practice" is to overcome the effects of interference.

THE STIMULUS SITUATION FOR CONCEPT LEARNING · The

stimuli for the learning of concept categories are the objects (or events) selected to *represent* the class being learned. For example, if the concept *triangle* is to be learned, it is necessary to represent a variety of these in order for the child to acquire a concept broad enough to apply to all triangles. Similarly, if the concept *reflex* is being acquired, the variety of such events must not be limited to the knee jerk, but needs to include a reasonable variety of reflexes having different bodily sites.

The stimuli for concept learning *may* be words, although the use of these stimuli presents the risk of "mere verbalizing." Educated adults often acquire concepts whose stimuli have been words; thus, an adult may acquire a fairly adequate concept of *meiosis* by reading about it or by looking it up in a dictionary. It is noteworthy, however, that even with sophisticated learners a few pictures may greatly facilitate the acquisition of such a concept. Youngsters, too, are able to acquire the concept *triangle* verbally, from words such as "three points not in the same straight line, joined by three line segments," and this method can be used provided it is clear that the subordinate concepts *point, line, join,* and *line segment* have previously been learned. As will be apparent, such learning is actually a matter of acquiring a concept by learning a principle, with the added effect that the principle thus learned can also be stated verbally. However, as previously noted, this is not the simplest way to learn a concept, and in many cases it is not the best way. A variety of pictured triangles provides the most direct stimulus approach to the learning of this concept.

THE STIMULUS SITUATION FOR PRINCIPLE LEARNING · The stimuli for learning principles are most often verbal ones. The major part of the "content" that makes up an academic curriculum is thus set apart from most simpler forms of learning by being presented via verbal communication. The early grades of school may be considered as having the primary purpose of furnishing the student with the basic language skills that will make it possible for him to learn principles. "Water boils when the temperature reaches 212 degrees F," and "The colonists resented taxation by the English" are the kinds of relatively simple principles that abound in the curriculum of elementary and secondary education. Verbal statements of this sort may be considered typical stimuli for the learning of principles. Presumably, it is not the fact that such statements are English sentences which is their essential characteristic, but the fact that they contain verbal stimuli arousing concepts in close contiguity with each other. The principle concerning water, for example, is a sequence of the concepts *water, boil, temperature, reach, 212, degrees,* and *F.* As previously emphasized, such a sequence of contiguous concepts is highly effective for learning, provided all the concepts it contains have been previously learned and can be recalled.

There is nothing impossible about learning principles without using verbal stimuli; it is simply a more roundabout process. For example, one can imagine a person learning some principles of checker playing without a word being spoken, over a period of time in which he participates in a number of games. Under such circumstances, the individual may "put together" rules by saying them to himself. But obviously the rules of the game, as well as the strategies of the game, can be learned much more rapidly by using verbal stimuli that present verbal statements of principles pertaining to "moves," "pieces," "jumps," "kings," and so on.

The stimuli for learning, then, are dependent on what kind of learning is going to be required, and not simply on what content is to be taught. For simple forms of learning, stimuli are those features of stimulus objects that are to serve as cues to the responses in $Ss \rightarrow R$ connections. In multiple discrimination, contrasting stimuli presented during "contrast practice" are necessary for the establishment of connections that differentiate among these stimuli. For concepts, a variety of stimulus objects is needed to represent the class being learned. And for principles, verbal stimuli presented in the proper sequence are usually employed to arouse the concepts that are being combined to form the principles.

VERBALLY COMMUNICATED "DIRECTIONS"

Another important reason for verbal communications in instruction is to tell the learner what to do—that is, to guide his behavior. Such communications have the form of *directions* of the sort printed on packages to tell purchasers how to open them. They may say "First, pull the tab, then press with the thumb," or something like that. In a similar way, directions to the learner may tell him, "First do this, then do that," or "First remember the word meaning apple, then the word meaning tree, then write them down as one word." The following sections describe the variety of functions performed in learning by verbally communicated directions.

DIRECTING ATTENTION • Obviously, one function for verbal directions is to direct attention to the object or characteristic that is to become the stimulus in a learned connection. With the simpler forms of learning, it is common for the instructor to say, "Now watch this!" while holding up or pointing to a stimulus object or event. "Look at this," "What do you see here?" "Notice this part," or "Listen carefully" are some of the many examples of verbal communications used by a teacher to direct attention to some specific stimulus. Such directions are particularly common when simple kinds of learning are being undertaken.

Although verbal statements are perhaps the most commonly used means of directing attention, there are, of course, other ways. Gestures made by the teacher can be equally effective. The sudden movement of an object is another kind of event likely to direct attention to it. When illustrations are used as a part of instruction, a variety of means of directing attention are available, including overprinted arrows, circles, or contrasting colors. Animated techniques in motion pictures provide many additional ways of directing the viewer's attention to relevant stimuli.

In the acquisition of concepts and principles, since the content itself is represented verbally, methods must be sought to distinguish this content from the verbal directions that focus attention, as well as from directions performing still other functions. It is common to find the concepts to be learned italicized, underlined, or printed in bold type, for the purpose of focusing attention. Similarly, principles may be set apart from the remainder of a text by being printed in different style or size of type. And a variety of other devices can be used for directing attention toward the content to be learned, including setting the latter apart by means of color, or by use of a surrounding "box," as is done in many modern textbooks.

CONVEYING INFORMATION ABOUT EXPECTED PERFORMANCE • Another function of verbal directions in the learning situation is to give the learner information about the class of responses to be expected when learning is completed. If he is beginning to learn about *reproduction*, for example, some such instructions may be used: "There are several different ways in which living organisms reproduce themselves. What you will be learning is how to describe each of these ways, and to give some actual examples of them." Or, if he is learning to *add decimals*, instructions may say, "What you will learn is how to add the numbers such as 124.27 and 16.743 to obtain the sum 141.013."

Telling the learner what is to be his performance when learning is complete is a function of directions that seems to be of considerable importance to the learning process. It cannot be said with certainty why this is the case. Such instructions may provide continuing "direction" to learning, in the sense suggested by Maier (1930). This may mean that they establish a *set* which is "carried in his head" by the learner throughout the period of learning, and which makes it possible for him to reject extraneous and irrelevant stimuli. The use of "advance organizers" as studied by Ausubel (1960) may also be considered as performing a similar function for the learning of meaningful verbal material. Another possibility is that directions telling the learner about expected performance enable him to match his own responses with a response class he remembers, and thus to "know when he is correct"—a reinforcement function. For example, the performance expected in adding decimals, the learner knows, must be an expression that contains a decimal point, and otherwise has the general form of 141.013. It cannot be of the form 141013, nor 141 1/77.

Under many circumstances, the clearest kind of directions about expected performance following learning may be those that actually show the learner, before learning begins, what such a performance looks like. Is this "telling him the answer"? Obviously, it is not really doing this, because one ordinarily expects him to learn a whole class of performances, not just the single one used to illustrate that class. However, if in fact the learner can acquire all he is supposed to learn by simply being told about this class, surely this is economical learning! Presumably, keeping the learner in the dark serves no useful function in such instances.

INDUCING RECALL OF PREVIOUSLY LEARNED ENTITIES • Verbal directions may tell the learner to recall something he has learned previously. When a chain is being acquired, recall of the links may be stimulated in the proper sequence by verbal means. "Wrap the string around the package," "Twist the ends," "Turn the package over," and similar verbal instructions may be used in establishing the chain involved in tying a package. Recall may also be stimulated in connection with the learning of concepts. The verbal instruction "This is a button" may be used to recall a single verbal association that has previously been learned, before proceeding with instruction that exposes new varieties of buttons along with the verbal response "button." And a most important use of directions to induce recall accompanies the learning of principles of various orders of complexity. Before acquiring the principle "sodium is a metal," it is necessary for the learner to recall what "sodium" is and what a "metal" is, and each of these concepts may be made recallable by suitable verbal directions to "remember."

Two different kinds of directions can be used to induce recall of previously learned entities, and either may be preferable in particular instances. When a relatively simple principle is being learned, it may be sufficient for verbal directions to stimulate *recognition* of what has previously been learned. This would be the case with such instructions as "You remember what sodium is and you remember what a metal is." When more complex principles are being acquired, it may be desirable for the directions to require *reinstatement* of the concepts subordinate to principles, rather than simply recognition of them. Thus in the learning of such a principle as that involved in "identifying and drawing the separation of a plane by a simple closed curve" (see Figure 10), it may be desirable for directions to require the *reinstatement* of subordinate principles, by saying "Draw a simple closed curve," and "Which one of these represents a plane?" The learning of the higher-order principle can then proceed satisfactorily with the assurance that the necessary subordinate principles are available for immediate recall.

The necessity for recall of previously learned entities immediately prior to the new act of learning is probably a reflection of the importance of the factor of *contiguity* in learning. As indicated in previous chapters, the establishment of chains, concepts, and principles is made easy when it is certain that the necessary subordinate capabilities are highly "available" in memory, so that they can be recalled in close temporal contiguity to the new set of connections being acquired. In contrast, the attempt to learn when some "piece of content" cannot be recalled results in lengthy delays and frustration to the learner. The use of verbal instructions in inducing recall is accordingly a highly important feature of the total instructional process.

GUIDANCE IN LEARNING BY DISCOVERY · Still another way in which verbal directions are employed as part of the conditions of learning is to *guide discovery* of principles to be acquired. As previously stated, many principles are learned simply by being stated in verbal form, as in "Current flows in the direction of higher to lower electric potential." Such statements, of course, represent the content to be learned, and are therefore not to be considered "instructions." But when the method of discovery is employed, a sequence like the following might become a part of instruction: "Remember that a given point in a circuit may have a greater potential than another point. In which direction would you expect current to flow?" The first of these statements is designed to stimulate recall. The second is a question asking the student to discover the principle governing the flow of electric current. It is an example, then, of a verbal instruction having the function of *guiding* discovery (or problem solving).

Directions that guide the learner's discovery are very often in the form of questions. Of course, more than one question may be needed, in contrast to the rather simple example just given. In general, questions used for this purpose do not include all the language needed in the "answer," but they may include some of it, and they are certainly designed to suggest the kind of answer required. Guidance provided by this kind of verbal instruction is a method familiar to every teacher. It has been found to be effective in experimental studies of principle learning (Gagné and Brown, 1961; Gagné, Mayor, Garstens, and Paradise, 1962), although the question of how much or how little guidance is most effective has not received a satisfactory answer as yet. Presumably, the effect of such verbal questioning is to channel the thinking of the learner in such a way that the extreme incorrect hypotheses he may try out implicitly are eliminated from consideration. The effect of guidance may therefore be to speed up the learning, since the learner does not waste time on discovered principles that are wildly wrong. At the same time, even though guided, he does actively generate the principles himself, rather than simply responding to them in prestructured verbal form.

In summary, the verbal portions of instruction constitute two major parts: *content principles,* and *verbal directions* that tell the learner what to do. Several different functions can be distinguished for the latter directions:

1. They may direct the learner's attention to stimuli. ("Look here!")
2. They give the learner information about the performance expected following learning. ("Now you are going to learn how to demonstrate that $ab + bc$ is equivalent to $b(a + c)$.")
3. They stimulate recall of previously learned capabilities. ("Remember that the atomic weight of hydrogen is 1.")
4. They are used to guide learning by problem solving (discovery). ("If a molecule of water has the composition H_2O, how would you find the weight of such a molecule?")

FEEDBACK FROM LEARNING

Learning is not something that "just happens" to the individual, at least so far as most of its varieties are concerned. (The exception is signal learning, which appears to represent externally "imposed" learning.) Typically, the learner is attempting to achieve some performance, and his motivation toward this achievement may be of critical importance. Accordingly, some means or other must be provided during instruction for him to perceive the results of his activity, to receive from the learning environment some feedback which enables him to realize that his performance is "correct."

SIMPLE FORMS OF LEARNING · According to a considerable body of evidence (Kimble, 1961, pp. 140–156), feedback from the execution of desired responses in stimulus-response learning needs to occur within a few seconds if learning is to progress rapidly. When an animal is acquiring a simple connection like pressing a lever or running along a pathway, acquisition is fastest when the reinforcement (usually in the form of a food pellet) is given immediately following a successful response. As the delay is lengthened within a range of 30 seconds or so, learning takes place more slowly. However, it is possible for animals to learn simple acts of this sort when the delay in reinforcement is a minute or longer. Observations of learning under such feedback conditions have suggested the strong possibility that the animals are actually learning chains, made up of links that they themselves supply and that fill the gaps between their correct response and the occurrence of reinforcement. In other words, chain learning is a means available to an animal to acquire connections under conditions of delay in reinforcement (Kimble, 1961, pp. 196–198). This kind of event, therefore, may serve to emphasize the importance of immediate feedback, rather than to disaffirm it.

FEEDBACK IN THE LEARNING OF CONCEPTS AND PRINCIPLES It is quite apparent that the learning of concepts and principles takes place in human beings under conditions in which reinforcement, however it may be characterized, bears not the faintest resemblance to a pellet of food. In the most typical instance, the learner makes a response that reflects his newly acquired capability, and then is "told" whether he is right or wrong. However, this does not mean that the words "right," "wrong," "correct," "incorrect" have to be used. In the classroom, supplying the correct response may be followed by the teacher's going on to the next point in the lesson. Many other kinds of subtle cues may be employed—a nod, a smile, a glance; there is no need to specify what all the possibilities are. Presumably, the learner needs to have previously learned that these events signify that his response has been a correct one. This can be assumed under most circumstances, since he probably has learned it quite early in his life.

The usefulness of frequent feedback during the acquisition of principles, or of a set of interrelated principles, should not be overlooked. The designers of programmed instruction frequently point to the importance of confirming responses "each step of the way." Many instructional programs are composed of single sentences containing blanks to be filled by the learner, and a printed "answer" that may then be checked against this response. When entire topics are being learned, feedback for the correct accomplishment of each subtopic can probably be of considerable value for the efficiency of learning.

When principles are being learned, feedback need not always come from the external situation, but may arise from other concepts or principles recalled by the learner himself. In other words, there are many instances in which the learner "knows he is right" because of an internal check that he can apply to the responses he has produced. For example, in completing the chemical equation

$$HCl + NaOH \rightarrow H_2O + NaCl$$

the compounds on the right are (let it be assumed) familiar ones, whose chemical composition has been previously learned. Furthermore, the number of atoms of each element involved in the equation is the same on the right as on the left. Thus a learner who managed to discover how to complete this equation would be pretty confident about its being correct without being told. Of course, he might like to have further verification at a later time. But the point is that he has been able to use recalled principles in supplying his own reinforcement within a short time after the completion of his response.

It may be that the internal checking the learner is able to do in the learning of principles and hierarchies of principles is an important source of reinforcement in learning. If immediacy of feedback is necessary for learning, as suggested by studies of simpler forms, self-checking may be the best way to ensure it. Even though the "knowledge that one is right" may occasionally turn out to be incorrect when further verification against external standards is made, the effect of such self-checking can furnish some immediate satisfaction that may speed learning.

APPRAISAL • Another important technique for feedback is an "appraisal exercise" or "test" given at the end of instruction on a topic. If the learner has been informed of the performance expected at the end of learning, it is desirable that this expectation be fulfilled by permitting him the opportunity of checking his performance against an external standard. If appraisal procedures become customary, it is reasonable to suppose that they will have an important effect on the student's motivation to continue learning. Obviously, a "test" given mainly for motivational purposes should have nothing about it that is obscure to the learner or deliberately hidden from him. If the objective of instruction is to add decimals, the appraisal should be of his capability of adding decimals; if he is learning to balance chemical equations, then the appraisal should concern balancing chemical equations; and so on. There should be no attempt to measure other aspects of his behavior simply because he is "taking a test." Of course, testing sometimes has other purposes than this, but the initial appraisal test needs to be a straightforward attempt to assess exactly what the student has learned in the immediately preceding exercise. As such, it can be a source of feedback of value to retention of what has been learned, and to the continuation of positive motivation for learning.

THE MANAGEMENT OF INSTRUCTION

The instructional process may be thought of as a set of procedures designed to accomplish the various objectives described in the present chapter. Once the structure of learning has been planned in accordance with the principles of Chapter 7, the task of initial instruction becomes one of establishing motivation, of presenting a suitable stimulus situation, of delivering verbal communications, and of providing for learning feedback. Each of these functions is essential; should any one of them be omitted, learning would occur only with difficulty.

How do these procedures fit together in a typical instructional exercise? This can be illustrated by an analysis of an in-

TABLE 1

The Instructional Process for an Exercise on "Inferring the Presence of Water Vapor in Air"

Instructional Event	*Function*
1. Teacher directs attention to clouding of windows on a cold day; the ring of water left by a glass of ice water; the cloud left by breathing on a mirror. Questions students about why these events happen.	1. Establishment of *achievement motivation*, based on curiosity and the desire to display knowledge to other children and to parents.
2. Children are given tin cans and ice cubes.	2. Providing *stimulus objects*.
3. Students are told to put the ice cubes in the cans, and to watch what happens to the outside of the cans.	3. Completion of stimulus situation. *Verbal directions* to focus attention.
4. Students are asked to describe what they see. "Fog"; "drops of water"; "large drops running down"; "ring of water at base of can."	4. *Verbal directions* to stimulate *recall* of previously learned concepts. *Feedback* provided.
5. Students are asked what they can infer from their observations. "Liquid is water from the air."	5. Learning of a principle by discovery; for some students, this may be recall. *Feedback* provided.
6. Other alternatives are pointed out to students. Could it be some other liquid? Could it come from the metal of the can? *How can one test an inference?*	6. *Verbal directions* to inform the learner of the *expected outcome* of instruction (how to test this inference).
7. "How can we tell whether this liquid is water?" ("Taste it.")	7. *Verbal directions* requiring *recall* of previously learned principle.
8. "If the water comes out of the metal, what should happen when it is wiped off?" ("Can should weigh less.")	8. *Verbal directions* requiring *recall* of previously learned principle.
9. Students are asked, if the	9. *Verbal directions* requiring

TABLE 1 (cont.)

Instructional Event	Function
water comes from the air, what should happen to the weight of the can after water collects on it. ("Can should increase in weight.") Direct observation is made of increase in weight of can by ice, by weighing on an equal-arm balance.	*recall* of previously learned principles.
10. Students are asked to recall that steam consists of water droplets and water vapor (an invisible gas). Air can contain water vapor.	10. *Verbal directions* requiring *recall* of previously learned principles.
11. Students are asked to state (a) what they observed; (b) what they inferred; and (c) how they checked their inference.	11. Learning of the principles of distinguishing observation and inference, and of operations required to check inferences. *Feedback* provided.
12. Students are asked to make and test inferences in two or three other new situations, and to describe the operations and reasoning involved. These might be (a) water evaporation; (b) the extinguishing of a candle in a closed cylinder; (c) the displacement of water by gas in an inverted cylinder.	12. Additional *examples* of the principles learned, for the purpose of ensuring their recall and generalization.
13. Another new situation is presented to the students and they are asked to describe it in terms of (a) what they observed; (b) what they inferred; (c) how they checked their inference.	13. *Appraisal* providing feedback.

Based on an exercise of the same name occurring in Commission on Science Education, *Science: A process approach, Part 4.* Washington, D.C.: American Association for the Advancement of Science, 1963.

structural sequence in elementary science, entitled "Inferring the Presence of Water Vapor in Air." This exercise has the objective of having the child learn to identify an inference, namely, that the liquid accumulating on a cold surface exposed to the air comes from the air. From the instruction provided, it is expected that the child will be able not only to state the inferred principle, but will be able to tell the operations and steps in reasoning that make possible the checking of the inference. The analysis of instruction for this exercise is given in Table 1.

This table makes it clear that each step in the instructional process can be accounted for in terms of the principles previously described in this chapter and others. There are several reasons why this analysis should be informative for an understanding of instruction. First, it is made apparent that an exercise of this sort has an *objective* to begin with, and is completed only when that objective is reached, that is, when students are able to display the performances implied by the objective. Second, the analysis helps to pinpoint the exact *stage at which learning occurs*. Some learning may occur at step 5, although recall of a previously learned principle may be more likely for some students. Step 11, however, is clearly the point at which one can expect students to be able to state and carry out the principles of interest they are supposed to be learning. As a third and related matter, the analysis given in the table serves to emphasize that a substantial amount of recall must *precede* the act of learning itself. Verbal directions are used to stimulate recall in steps 4, 6, 7, 8, 9, and 10. And finally, the point is well illustrated that learning is not really complete when the required principles are elicited on the first occasion, as in step 11. This must be followed by some *additional examples* of the principle, as well as by an *appraisal* that informs the learner of his own success in achieving a new capability.

Designing instruction for initial learning is thus seen to be a matter of setting up a total set of circumstances within which learning can be embedded. Many preparations need to be made for the act of learning, and together these constitute what is known as *instruction*. These procedures have the functions of establishing motivation; and in addition, of controlling the external situation in terms of the presentation of the stimulus, the verbal direction of behavior, and the provision of learning feedback.

THE CONDITIONS OF TRANSFER

In general, learning is managed and instituted for broader purposes than simply the modification of particular human performances. It is brought about in order to establish capabilities that will be of lasting usefulness to the individual. As mentioned earlier in this chapter, there are two major ways in which learned capabilities can be of use. One is in making it possible for the individual to execute some performances that are not directly learned but are in some sense similar to those that are learned. For example, the teacher of physics hopes that certain elements of the scientific method learned in connection with that subject will transfer to the solution of a problem in biology, or even in social science. The capabilities specifically learned in school should enable the student to perform some acts of practical value to him, whether in his everyday life or in connection with an occupation. This *transferability* of what has been learned may be called *lateral transfer*, since it refers to a kind of generalizing that spreads over a broad set of situations at roughly the same "level of complexity."

The second kind of use for learned capabilities lies in making it possible for the individual to learn additional, "advanced," or more complex things, in the sense described in Chapter 7. The student who has learned the subordinate principles involved in finding the capacitance of an electrical system finds that the learning of such a higher-order principle is easier than it would otherwise be. The subordinate capabilities transfer to the higher-order learning, and facilitate its occurrence. This may be called *vertical transfer*, since it refers to the effects that learned capabilities at one level have on the learning of additional ones at higher levels. Both kinds of transfer are of importance to education.

CONDITIONS FOR LATERAL TRANSFER

The kind of observation which leads to the inference that lateral transfer has occurred is as follows. An individual has learned that the relationship between two sides of a right triangle may be expressed as $A/B = \cos \phi$. He now encounters, for the first time, a problem in physics relating to the acceleration of a body rolling down an inclined plane, and he sees that the plane may be treated as a side of a right triangle. Without additional instruction, he proceeds to express the relationship he is looking for in terms of the cosine of the angle of inclination of the plane with the horizontal surface on which it rests. This behavior may be contrasted with that of another individual who has *not* learned A/B $= \cos \phi$, and therefore does *not* express the relationship seen in the inclined plane in that manner. The behavior of the first individual is said to show *transfer of learning* to the extent that the performance is done more readily than it would have been had not the originally learned capability been present (that is, more readily than the second individual was able to do the same thing).

In the case of this kind of transfer, the question of *how much* appears to be a matter of *how broadly* the individual can generalize what he has learned to new situations. Presumably, there are limits to this breadth of generalization, which vary with different individuals. One could perhaps think of a whole range of situations of potential applicability of the cosine relationship that displayed decreasing degrees of similarity to the situation in which the principle had originally been learned. At some point along this dimension of breadth of generalizability, a given individual will fail to transfer his previously learned knowledge. Another individual, however, may be able to exhibit transfer more broadly to a wider variety of differing situations.

The most important conditions for lateral transfer appear to be *internal* to the individual. Apparently, some students are able to relate what they have learned to a wider variety of new situations than are others. Is this because they are "built that way," or because they know more? This question is a difficult one, and its answer is not known at present. Presumably, though, both learned and innate factors are at work.

Assuming that nothing can be done in an educational sense to alter innate differences in breadth of transferability, a good deal can be done concerning the learned factors. The more broadly based a learned capability, the better chance it will have to transfer to new and different situations. Accordingly, the usefulness of any learned capability will be increased if it is practiced in as wide a variety of situations as possible. Finding the cosine of an angle, once learned, has a greater probability of being transferable if it is practiced in situations that are widely different from each other. A similar statement can be made about almost any learned capability. The transferability of foreign words and phrases will be increased if they are practiced in a wide variety of contexts. The transferability of the scientific process of "formulating operational definitions" will be increased if it is practiced in connection with a wide variety of natural phenomena. The implication for the management of instruction is therefore quite clear: provision needs to be made for encouraging the learner to apply his knowledge broadly and in as great a variety of new situations as can be devised.

CONDITIONS OF VERTICAL TRANSFER

Vertical transfer is observed when a capability to be learned is *acquired more rapidly* when it has been preceded by previous learning of subordinate capabilities. Many examples of this sort of event have been implied by the learning structures described in the previous chapter. In Figure 15, for example, it is implied that the individual who *has* learned the principles of hydrogen and hydroxyl ions in solution will then be able to learn readily the ion composition of acids and bases; whereas the individual who *has not* learned the first (subordinate) principles will have greater difficulty in learning the second (superordinate) principles. In this case, the question of *how much* transfer is a matter of the time taken to learn the higher-order principle by the first individual as compared with the second. Alternatively, one can contrast the proportion of individuals learning the higher-order principle in groups of students who have, and who have not, learned the subordinate ones. It is possible to observe such vertical transfer throughout an entire learning structure, as has been done for tasks on the addition of integers (Gagné, Mayor, Garstens, and Paradise, 1962).

The primary *internal* condition for vertical transfer is the *mastery of the subordinate capabilities.* This kind of transfer is very improbable unless the relevant lower-order chains, concepts, or principles have been learned. Learning of these subordinate capabilities must *precede* transfer. The *external* conditions are the same as those that govern the learning of higher-order capabilities, and that have been specifically described in the previous section; they include the verbal directions given to guide the learner's behavior and to stimulate recall. The most important prescription for managing the conditions of vertical transfer can be stated as follows: ensure that relevant subordinate capabilities have been thoroughly learned before calling on vertical transfer to aid the learning of "advanced" capabilities.

Another internal condition of vertical transfer should be mentioned. This kind of transfer is presumably enhanced by the *variety of previous knowledge* the individual has acquired. The reason for this is that the learning of any particular advanced principle or topic may be approached in various ways, not just in one way. The definition of a *limit* in mathematics, for example, can be introduced in a manner that is based on a number of different subordinate principles. In physics, *mass* can be defined in several different ways and thus made to depend on the previous mastery of different principles. It is possible that these subordinate knowledges may act to enhance each other's effects when a new capability is being learned. For this reason the latter learning may be faster for an individual who has many subordinate capabilities to draw on than it is for one who has few. Vertical transfer may occur more readily in an individual who knows a lot (of relevant subordinate knowledge) than in an individual who knows a little. At the present time, however, such a statement has a hypothetical character, since it has not been systematically studied.

MANAGING INSTRUCTION FOR TRANSFER

Establishing the conditions for transferability of what is learned can be seen to be an educational function of considerable importance. It involves procedures that will have an effect not only on the acquisition of further knowledge, as in vertical transfer, but also on the broad application of learned capabilities to novel and practical situations, as is the case when transfer is of the lateral type. Both these meanings would appear to be included in a phrase like "teaching for transfer," an objective of instruction that has been emphasized by many educational scholars.

It is of prime importance to note that transfer is a phenomenon which depends on previous learning. Educational writers occasionally wax so enthsuiastic about the importance of transferability that they are prone to forget this fact. Of course it is desirable to set up instructional conditions that will "stretch students' minds," "encourage the generalization of knowledge," "challenge students to solve problems in novel situations." Any or all of these objectives state the aim of transfer of learning. But something must first be learned before it can be transferred. The student who is going to transfer the principles of elastic bodies to the membranes of a living organism must first learn the principles of elastic bodies. One of the major prerequisites for transfer is learning.

The second condition of importance in seeking to assure transfer is the variety of stimulus situations to which the student is encouraged to generalize his knowledge. The more varied these can be made, the more useful will the learned capability become. At lower educational levels, this variety may be achieved by deliberate use of various natural objects and events in the classroom, or on field trips. At higher levels, the function of providing contextual variety can be largely performed by verbal communication, of the sort that may take place in a "discussion group," for example.

GENERAL REFERENCES

Managing Instruction

  Ausubel, D. P. *The psychology of meaningful verbal learning.* New York: Grune & Stratton, 1963.

  Hilgard, E. J. (Ed.) *Theories of learning and instruction, 1964. Sixty-third yearb.* Chicago: National Society for the Study of Education, 1964, Part I.

Motivation

  Bandura, A., and Walters, R. H. *Social learning and personality development.* New York: Holt, Rinehart and Winston, 1963.

  Brown, J. S. *The motivation of behavior.* New York: McGraw-Hill, 1961.

De Cecco, J. P. *Human learning in the school.* New York: Holt, Rinehart and Winston, 1963. Chap. 2.

Hall, J. F. *Psychology of motivation.* Philadelphia: Lippincott, 1961.

Hunt, J. McV. *Intelligence and experience.* New York: Ronald, 1961.

McClelland, D. C., Atkinson, J. W., Clark, R. A., and Lowell, E. L. *The achievement motive.* New York: Appleton-Century-Crofts, 1953.

Transfer of Learning

Grose, R. E., and Birney, R. C. (Eds.) *Transfer of learning.* Princeton, N.J.: Van Nostrand, 1963.

Stephens, J. M. Transfer of learning. In C. W. Harris (Ed.), *Encyclopedia of educational research.* New York: Macmillan, 1960.

Travers, R. M. W. *Essentials of learning.* New York: Macmillan, 1963, Chap. 6.

LEARNING
DECISIONS
IN EDUCATION

9

AN EDUCATIONAL SYSTEM is designed to bring about changes in the capabilities and attitudes of human beings. Not all the expected changes from infancy to usefully functioning adulthood are the responsibility of the school, to be sure. Some of them, like early established modes of relating to other human beings including parents, and persisting character traits like honesty, anxiousness, persistence, are usually thought to be greatly influenced by the environment of the home and the individual's contemporary associates. Still others are undoubtedly determined in part by membership and instruction in religious organizations. But the vast majority of behavioral changes, and particularly those identified as underlying the performance of socially useful work, are generally considered to be the province of the educational system. It is this social organization that must transform the highly dependent young child into the adult who, in his own individual manner, lives a life that is satisfying to himself largely because it contributes to the goals of his society.

The modifications brought about in the human individual by the educational system are the result of the process called learning. To be sure, the individual does grow and mature in a physiological sense during the years from five to twenty. But the changes that make him a productive member of society happen because of a process of learning that interacts with this maturation. The growing itself cannot be affected or altered very much. The learning, in contrast, is easily affected by almost every interaction the individual has with his environment, physical and social. To appreciate how prone to learning the human individual is, it would perhaps be wise to start with the notion that he is learning all the time.

Since learning is such a pervasive and persistent process, it is not entirely unreasonable to ask whether an educational system is necessary at all. Why not let the individual grow up, watch what others do, become curious about the world, discover principles for himself, and thus with a minimum of fuss become a "well-educated" man? This is not a completely ridiculous idea, for it is quite conceivable that a certain number of individuals who are inherently bright enough, and who are simply told where to find things when they are looking for them, can in fact become knowledgeable and capable adults. But it seems quite doubtful that more than a few unusual individuals could actually accomplish this feat. The amount of knowledge modern man must have to be even a moderately successful and satisfied citizen is growing all the time. And for the person who is not an intellectual giant, that is, for 98 percent of the population, the system of "educating oneself" simply will not work. By implication, the fundamental reason for an educational system is to *manage learning* so that it will occur most efficiently.

How well is learning managed by our present educational system? During recent years, there have been many complaints that the management of learning is not very efficiently done. Periodically, a sample is taken of what high school graduates know about history, or about arithmetic, and the amount of knowledge revealed is often astoundingly low. Frequently, college professors testify to the inadequate mastery of language skills among their entering students. During recent years, university scholars have increasingly participated with other educators in projects designed to revise and reform the curricula of the earlier grades of school; not simply to "bring them up to date," but to incorporate in them a range of intellectual content that they have not previously possessed. Frequent suggestions are made to introduce content subjects in the elementary grades that have for years been thought suitable only for the junior and senior high school years.

These and other events raise the question as to just how efficiently learning *can* be managed by an educational system. Judged by the needs for intellectual competence in the modern world, is our system of education doing a fraction of what it might? Have our schools become, relatively speaking, mainly community organizations for the care and socialization of the young, rather than institutions for the imparting of knowledge?

The proper answers to these questions need to be approached with an understanding of what the management of learning means, and this is what the present chapter is about. It will be desirable to look closely at the kinds of decisions made within an educational system that affect learning. There are a fair number of these decisions, and not all of them are made by the teacher in the classroom. Some of them, as might be expected, relate to the content of instruction, others to the method, still others to the situation surrounding the student. They range from the initial planning that goes into the determination of objectives for learning, to the procedures used to measure its outcomes. It is, of course, not suggested that all decisions of an educational system affect learning and its management; quite the contrary is true. (A fire escape affects children's safety, but not their learning.) But many educational decisions do have an effect on this central function of managing learning, and the attempt will be made here to discuss at least the most important of these.

THE EDUCATIONAL SYSTEM

To begin, it is necessary to define what is meant here by an "educational system." A familiar meaning of this phrase puts the primary emphasis on the organization of a geographical district into a system of schools, presided over by a superintendent of schools who is responsible to an elected school board. In this meaning of the term, there may be a Zenith City School System, or an Erie County School System, or a Mountainside District School System. Or again, to the extent that a state is given responsibility for the administration of all the schools within its borders, there are State Educational Systems. In a somewhat different sense, one might speak of a national Educational System. Any or all of these might be referred to as "upper-case" Educational Systems.

The reference in this chapter, however, is to a "lower-case" educational system. By this is meant that arrangement of people and conditions which is needed to bring about the changes in the human individual, attributable to the process of learning, which transform him from a dependent child to a productive adult member of society. In other words, the educational system is that system which has the learning of the individual as its primary mission. The indispensable human component of this system is the student, and another very important component is the teacher. It will be apparent that the "lower-case" educational system is not always in perfect harmony with the "upper case" Educational System; in some instances they may not even have compatible objectives. But these are not questions to be dealt with in this chapter, where the concern is only with the system whose purpose is to bring about learning.

The conception of an educational system consisting of Mark Hopkins on one end of a log and a student at the other is in many ways an admirable one. It is a simple and clear model, except for one thing, which is implied but left unstated. There is no indication in the usual brief description of this system of how it functions, this is, of what its "input" and its "output" are. This difficulty needs to be cleared up so that no misunderstanding can arise. The essential input in this system is *to the student*; likewise, the output is *the student's* changing behavior. As a component of the system, therefore, one cannot substitute anything for the student without having a different system entirely. But this is not true for the log or for the teacher who sits on the end; one can use a board for a log and a book for a teacher while still maintaining the same system with its objective of promoting learning. The student, however, must remain. The student and his behavior constitute the crux of the system.

In this simplest of educational systems, the teacher is the *manager of the conditions of learning*. What he says to the student comprises the verbal directions and also the verbal stimulus content of the learning situation. What he points to or has the student look at in the surrounding environment becomes a part of the stimulus situation for learning. This managing function of the teacher does not change when the system is made more complex by incorporating certain technological improvements. Providing the student with verbal content by means of books speeds up the whole process of learning, once the skill of reading has been acquired. Using pictures, filmstrips, or motion pictures makes possible the representation of a great variety of objects and events that cannot be directly seen from a log in one geographical spot. Records and tape recordings can provide auditory stimulation of languages, music, and other sounds beyond the capabilities of a single teacher, even if he is a Mark Hopkins. In more complex educational systems, then, the teacher may be aided by a number of gadgets, and also by a number of other people. But the essential function remains one of managing the conditions of learning.

DECISIONS THAT AFFECT PLANNING FOR LEARNING

The management of learning is surely not an easy function to perform. It requires many decisions, each of which affects in some way or other the conditions of learning and therefore the "input" to the student. The objective of this management is to ensure that learning will be efficient, that is, that the greatest change in the student's behavior will occur in the shortest period of time. The first kind of decision about learning pertains to the *planning* of suitable conditions for learning.

DEFINING OBJECTIVES FOR LEARNING

It is logical to suppose that the initial step in deciding on the conditions for learning is that of defining objectives. In terms of the system model, this means that for any given occasion on which the system is to perform its mission, there needs to be a decision about the *nature of the change in behavior* sought. Only if this is done will it be possible to infer what kind of input needs to be made to the learner, that is, what kind of learning situation needs to be established to bring about this change.

THE NATURE OF OBJECTIVES · A number of writers have emphasized the importance of defining the objectives of learning in terms of *observable human performances* (Gagné, 1964b; Lindvall, 1964; Tyler, 1949). As Mager's (1962) work shows so effectively, to say that a student at the end of a learning session will be expected to *know* something, or to *understand* something, or to *appreciate* something provides an unsatisfactory basis for the planning of the learning situation. These kinds of verbs, which occur so frequently in works on the "objectives of education" (French, 1957; Kearney, 1953) may, to be sure, furnish an agreeable starting point for thinking about the problem. But they are quite inadequate as concluding statements on the basis of which decisions about learning can be made. The idea that a high school student should "understand probability," for example, is a good general statement with which many educators and parents might agree. But it is only the beginning so far as the formulation of defined objectives is concerned. Does it mean, for example, "stating in numerical terms the probability of choosing a black bean from a set composed of n black beans and m white beans?" Or does it mean "deriving a general expression for the probability of n events taken m at a time"? Or perhaps, "identifying the probability of a hit by a baseball player with a batting average of 220"? Or possibly all these?

It may be noted that each of the latter kinds of statements of objectives carries the air of objectivity with it. One of the evident reasons for this is the use of a certain kind of verb, which describes *overt action*. The verbs are *state* (which means make a verbal statement of), *derive* (which means make a sequence of logically consistent statements beginning with certain assumptions), and *identify* (which means simply point out or choose correctly). One has little difficulty in realizing from these statements what it is that can be observed about the student's performance which would lead to the conclusion that the objective had been attained. Quite in contrast are verbs like *understand* or *know*, which simply set the stage for these "objective" objectives, and cannot themselves be unambiguously observed.

There are, then, obvious differences between statements of objectives that are ambiguous, and true *definitions* of objectives, which are not. What are the characteristics of a definition of an objective? Such a definition is a verbal statement that communicates reliably to any individual (who knows the words of the statement as concepts) *the set of circumstances that identifies a class of human performances.* There is little room for disagreement about such definitions, excluding semantic ones, which can be made rare. By means of this sort of definition one individual should be able to identify the same human performance as some other individual. In other words, these are "operational definitions." The kind of statement required appears to be one having the following components:

1. *A verb* denoting observable action (draw, identify, recognize, compute, and many others qualify; know, grasp, see, and others do not).

2. A description of the *class of stimuli* being responded to [for example, "Given the printed statement $ab + ac = a(b + c)$"].

3. A word or phrase denoting the *object used for action* by the performer, unless this is implied by the verb (for example, if the verb is "draw," this phrase might be "with a ruling pen"; if it is "state," the word might simply be "orally").

4. A description of the *class of correct responses* (for example, "a right triangle," or "the sum," or "the name of the rule."

Using these criteria, it becomes a relatively straightforward task to make adequate definitions of objectives. For example, a mathematical objective might be: "Given a printed statement of the form $ab + ac = a(b + c)$, containing numerals, states the name of the principle exhibited." In the field of English, one could have this objective: "Completes sentences of the form 'The people gave _____,' when given the instruction 'supply a direct object.' " In a foreign language, an example of an objective could be: "Speaks grammatically correct French sentences to questions of the form 'Qu'est-ce que vous avez?' 'Qu'est-ce qu'il a?' and so on, using familiar nouns." Instruction in biology might include as an objective: "Distinguishes, in written description, between *mitosis* and *meiosis*, in terms of the kinds of cells in which they occur."

When instructional objectives are derived and defined in this manner, it becomes readily possible to observe the human performances to which they refer. Moreover, it is possible to assess (or measure) the attainment of these objectives. Thus, as will be seen in a later section, the problem of measuring the outcomes of instruction can be approached in a fairly straightforward manner.

Perhaps the most important implication of this method of defining objectives is that the *type of learning* to be undertaken, and the required *conditions for learning*, are tremendously clarified. For example, if the objective is "distinguishes the atomic structure of the halogens" it is fairly clear that the capability for this performance must be acquired as *multiple discrimination*. If the objective is "identifies similes in passages of English literature," it is apparent that a *concept* must be learned. If the objective is "demonstrates a test of Archimedes' principle (using materials that have not been employed in instruction on this principle)," then of course *principle* learning is called for. "States the scientific problem connecting dew and boiling water" might well call for the learning of a strategy.

The relevant set of decisions for instruction deriving from the definition of objectives are those that determine the type of learning to be employed in attaining these objectives. As described here, such decisions are obviously highly specific. They can usually not be made for an entity of learning as large as a "topic." Instead, they need to be made for each of the individual learning acts that collectively make up a topic, arranged in a hierarchical manner (Chapter 7). The beginning objectives in a topic are likely to imply the learning of *verbal chains, multiple discriminations,* and *concepts.* The later objectives are more likely to be *principles* of considerable complexity. A decision to teach an entire topic under the same kind of learning conditions would evidently be both harmful and inefficient. What is needed is an analysis of the objectives that make up a topic, and a set of decisions about each of them as to the most effective conditions for learning.

DETERMINING THE LEARNING STRUCTURE

If decisions concerning what conditions of learning need to be made for each act of learning within a topic, then obviously the topic must first be analyzed to determine its composition. This is the process of analysis that leads to the specification of knowledge hierarchies such as those described in Chapter 7.

Analysis of a topic begins with the statement of the terminal objective—the performance or performances one expects the student to be able to exhibit after the learning of that topic has been completed. Once this objective has been satisfactorily defined, one can proceed to identify a subordinate set of subtopics, each an individual learning act, that must be considered prerequisites for the learning. Each of these subtopics in turn may be subjected to the same process of analysis, until one has arrived at performances that the students are known to possess, at which point the analysis stops. Each *subordinate* objective, then, is derived by systematically applying to the *next higher objective* the question, "What must the student already know how to do, in order to learn this performance?" [Gagné, 1963a]. The description of what the student must know—in other words, the prerequisite capabilities he must have—identifies the subordinate objectives.

Although a number of examples of the process of analyzing topic objectives have been given in Chapter 7, still another will be used here. Suppose that the topic is, "Using the 'stop' marks in punctuating written prose (comma, period, semicolon, colon, dash, parentheses)." To be somewhat more specific, the objective is "in writing simple prose on an assigned topic, uses the proper 'stop' marks—period, comma, and so on." There would seem to be two lines of prerequisites needed to establish this performance. The first, Line A, is composed of "the concept of the period," "the concept of the comma," "the concept of the semicolon," and so on. The second, Line B, may be called "the 'stop' concepts," which require identification of the places where various "stop marks" are put. The analysis would then proceed in somewhat the following fashion:

> *Topic Objective:* Using proper "stop" marks in writing simple prose
> *Principles:* Given unpunctuated printed prose, inserting proper

punctuation marks to correspond with different varieties of stop

Line A	*Line B*
1. *Concepts:* Identifying by different intonations in oral reading, comma, period, semicolon, etc., occurring in printed prose	1. *Concepts:* Identifying by different intonations in oral reading, different varieties of stop in unpunctuated printed prose
2. *Multiple discrimination:* Distinguishing period as .; comma as ,; dash as —; etc.	2. *Multiple discrimination:* Distinguishing correct and incorrect "stops" in prose that is read aloud

There is much that is instructive in the results of this analysis. For one thing, it is evident that the topic objective cannot be adequately achieved without *both* lines. One may attempt to teach only the concepts of Line A, but the objective will not be reached, because the individual has never learned to identify the varieties of "stop" in prose that is originally unpunctuated. Alternatively, if one were to give instruction only in Line B, the student would "hear" the different stops all right, but would not be able to choose the correct punctuation mark. This is not, then, a matter of choosing between Line A and Line B; both state required prerequisites. Another important point illustrated by the analysis is the progression of increasingly simple forms of learning required to establish each objective as one proceeds downward in the hierarchy: principles, then concepts, then multiple discriminations. The last, of course, require chains or verbal sequences that are assumed to have been previously learned. For Line B, the concept of a "stop" is recognized as the identification of a pause that would be there if the prose were read and thus heard. Accordingly, multiple discriminations of different pauses in "heard" prose must be established as a prerequisite.

Recapitulating the analysis procedure, each objective is subjected to the question, What must the student *already* know in order to learn this performance? Depending on the nature of the objective, what is required to establish it are prerequisite capabilities plus suitable learning conditions. Thus, to achieve the objective that is a

1. *higher-order principle* requires learning conditions for a principle plus prerequisite (subordinate) objectives of principles or concepts;

2. *principle* requires learning conditions for a principle plus prerequisites (subordinate) objectives of concepts;

3. *concept* requires learning conditions for a concept plus prerequisite (subordinate) objectives of multiple discriminations;

4. *multiple discrimination* requires learning conditions for multiple discrimination plus prerequisite (subordinate) objectives of verbal or motor chains; and

5. *chain* requires learning conditions for a chain plus prerequisite (subordinate) objectives of $Ss \rightarrow R$ connections.

DECISIONS ABOUT MOTIVATION

Still another kind of decision precedes the actual events of instruction; this pertains to the motivation of the student. It has frequently been said that motivating the student is one of the most important jobs the teacher can do. The present description of educational decisions leads to the view that motivating should probably be considered the primary task of the teacher. Certainly it is the most important function that the "man on the other end of the log" can undertake. Learning itself takes place within the learner, largely as a result of his activity. But something must drive this activity, and direct it toward the goal of achieving objectives.

First of all, the student must be motivated to enter into the learning situation; he must want to "sit on the end of the log" and to stay there. For the very young child, the motivation may be a desire to please his parents, and the teacher who represents his parents. In addition, one of the strongest sources of motivation undoubtedly is the desire to participate in what other children are doing, to be an acceptable member of a social group. These sources of motivation, however, will not be strong enough to carry him throughout all of his school years. Another kind of motivation needs to be acquired and nourished by the instructional situation itself. *Motivation to achieve* must be established that springs from within the individual.

MOTIVATION AND LIFEWORK • Motivation to achieve derives in some ultimate sense from the individual's aspirations about what kind of person he wants to be, and what lifework he wants to pursue. Most children, if not all, have an intense desire to "grow up," in other words, to become adults and engage in adult pursuits and occupations. Even the somewhat unrealistic aspirations that an eight-year-old boy may have (such as being a fireman, or an airplane pilot) reflect a desire to be able to accomplish things that he cannot now do. But "growing up" is not just a matter of becoming larger and stronger. It is also a matter of learning how to do many things. An airplane pilot, for example, must know how to interpret weather maps, how to compute time of flight, how to interpret instruments and radio signals, and to execute the many other performances that make up his complex job.

One important decision in the area of motivation, then, is to convey to students the general principle that being a useful adult requires the achievement of many kinds of performance capabilities. The teacher, as a representative of the adult world, needs to seize every opportunity to point out the relationships between adult occupations or other activities and the achievements that are a necessary part of them. In this way the child will learn that "being able to do things" as an adult is largely a matter of having learned how.

A related decision has to do with informing students about the entire range of possible adult occupations. This is not the kind of information students come by naturally, and learning it incidentally in the home and community may be quite infeasible. Children of farm families may know of farming as an occupation, but little else; children in industrial communities may know of adult work in particular industrial plants, but little else. One of the most important functions of the school, particularly so far as motivation is concerned, may be to provide information about the range and variety of adult occupations. Children need this information early and frequently if a basis is to be established for achievement motivation. Perhaps the best arrangement would be for teachers to begin imparting such information in the early grades, and never to stop doing so. At best, vocational information would constitute the introduction to every topic being learned.

MAINTAINING ACHIEVEMENT MOTIVATION • To maintain the motivation to achieve during the course of instruction on topics or subjects, a valuable decision will be to keep students informed of the objectives of instruction, and also of their achievement of these objectives. If students are to learn "how to read a weather map," the kinds of performance to be expected when learning has been completed should be made plain from the outset (see Chapter 8). If the topic is punctuation, it should similarly be made clear before learning begins that the objective is "to be able to use correct marks of punctuation in writing prose." It is not suggested, of course, that such an objective can be effectively conveyed simply by repeating it as a verbal statement. Instead, it needs to be illustrated by an example of prose (perhaps one produced by the uninstructed student) that illustrates incorrect and correct punctuation. Achievement motivation cannot be effectively established unless the "mystery" of objectives is completely removed. "Why are we learning this?" is a question that always needs to be answered, as thoroughly and precisely as possible.

Assessment exercises, or "tests," need to be employed at frequent intervals for the purpose of giving the student feedback about his achievement. For many topics the checking of achievement will need to be done on each subobjective, not only on the terminal objective of the topic as a whole. An assessment exercise carried out for this purpose *can* be a fairly simple activity; certainly it does not need to be surrounded with the folderol of "test norms" and "grading." In its simplest form, the situation is like the following: A student has had the objective of "identifying the factors of numbers through 144." When learning is completed, an assessment is carried out in which a selected representative sample of numbers within the stated range is given to the student with the instruction to name the factors of each. If he names them all correctly (allowing for a chance error or omission), then he has achieved the objective. If he does not, then he has not achieved the objective, and needs to engage in further learning. This should be as plain to him as it is to the teacher who administers the "test."

Its most important function, after all, is to provide the kind of feedback that has the effect of maintaining his desire to achieve.

DECISIONS CONCERNING INSTRUCTION

The decisions described in previous sections are clearly matters that affect *planning* for the activity of learning. The objectives of learning are defined, the structure of these objectives within each topic is determined, and the conditions for motivation are decided on. The next step is the design of the instructional situation itself. First, the conditions of learning need to be determined for each capability to be established. In addition, decisions need to be made about the nature and extent of transfer of learning, or the desired "applications" of what is learned. Interacting with both these kinds of decisions are choices governing the assessment of the newly learned competencies. These three kinds of decisions, taken together, are what determine the basic nature of the instructional situation.

CHOOSING THE CONDITIONS FOR LEARNING

The choice of conditions for the learning of each topic and subtopic results in a *design* for learning that determines its effectiveness in a crucial manner. Learning conditions can be predesigned (and thus, in a sense, become a part of planning), or they can be designed on the spot to meet each instructional situation as it arises. These two methods need to be examined somewhat more closely.

Two Methods of Design · The most fundamental question affecting the design of the learning situation is the extent to which it may be predesigned for the individual learner, and the extent to which it must be created while instruction proceeds. The writer of a technical book, for example, usually makes the implicit assumption that he is predesigning the learning situation—that a learner who interacts with the printed matter on the pages of his book will in fact achieve the objectives he has in mind, whether or not they are explicitly stated. In contrast, the writer of a book called something like *Brief French Grammar* is making quite a different assumption. He is, in a sense, stating only the objectives of instruction, and assumes that the design of the conditions of instruction will be made by a teacher during the time the latter is interacting with a student. The first example illustrates intentional *predesign* of the conditions of learning. In the second example, the teacher engages in *extemporaneous design.*

Extemporaneous design of the conditions of learning, during interaction with a student or students, is undoubtedly considered by many teachers one of their most important functions. To be done well, it requires a tremendous amount of knowledge and skill, which may well be possessed by a certain number of members of the teaching profession, but doubtfully by all. There is no evidence at present as to how well this task of extemporaneous design is done. The comparative achievements of students or classes provide no answer to this question, since such achievement is affected by several other factors in the instructional situation, including the student's own self-initiated activities. Everyone remembers one or more "good" teachers, or teachers who have "had an effect" on him, but this appears to be irrelevant evidence. While engaged in the learning process itself, the learner cannot be expected to be able to judge the adequacy of instructional decisions made by a teacher. However, he *is* likely to remember his own motivational changes that resulted from the teacher's efforts, and this is surely a legitimate basis for recalling a teacher favorably.

There is much to be said in favor of *predesign* of the conditions of learning. First of all, it appears to be completely feasible. Once the objectives of instruction have been defined, and the learning structure of any topic has been determined, the only remaining action needed is the establishment of the conditions required for each type of learning described in Chapters 3 through 6, individually for each learning objective. Such a procedure should, if systematically followed, bring about the required learning in the most efficient possible manner. As the description of each type of learning has made evident, there is nothing difficult or obscure about these conditions. Often they consist mainly in communicating to the learner by means of a verbal statement, as is the case when principles are being taught. Often, too, they depend simply on placing two statements in temporal contiguity so that the learner himself can discover the principle to be learned. Probably the most difficult part of the process, though, is *choosing the proper learning conditions.* But the task of doing this is surely made easier if it can be done deliberately by predesign, rather than having to be done extemporaneously.

It may be argued that extemporaneous design can better take into account the individual differences of students. One student, because of previous learning or innate constitution, may be able to discover a new principle with a minimum of learning guidance, whereas another may need a great deal of help. The teacher can detect these differences and react to them, making an extemporaneous design that fits the individual learner. But this is an unconvincing argument. First of all, it may be seriously doubted that the typical classroom is a place where the task of designing learning conditions for each individual student can possibly be done. The teacher is simply unable to deal with each student individually in this manner. More likely, the design that evolves extemporaneously is one that goes too slowly for the well-informed student, moves at about the proper pace for the average, and misses the ill-prepared student entirely. Second, it *is* perfectly possible for predesigned instruction to take individual differences into account. The two most important sources of difference are the degree to which prerequisite capabilities are available; and the degree to which "learning guidance" is needed (as when principles are being learned).

ADVANTAGES OF PREDESIGN OF LEARNING CONDITIONS · The major possibilities of predesigning instructional content to allow for individual differences have been exhibited, not in the classroom or in the textbook, but in *programmed instruction.* It has become increasingly evident to research investigators of this technique that one of its major contributions to instruction is the feature of being adaptable to many varieties of learners (De Cecco, 1964). "Adaptive" instructional programs can be made to select for the student the instructional content he needs in order to have the necessary prerequisites for the learning of each new topic or subtopic. If these prerequisites are present, the student is sent on to the next concept or principle to be learned; if they are not present, then they must be learned first, after which the student is sent on as usual. Amount of learning guidance can similarly be made adaptive to the needs of the individual learner (Gagné, 1963a). There is nothing about predesign as such, therefore, that prohibits the adjustment of the learning situation to the needs of the individual learner. In fact, quite the contrary: adaptive instructional programs take this feature of design as one of the main objectives to be achieved.

The positive advantages of predesign of learning conditions go beyond this particular feature of adaptation to the needs of the individual learner. They include the following:

1. The selection of proper learning conditions may be made as an unhurried choice, rather than in "spur of the moment" decisions.

2. A "quality control" of the choice of learning conditions is ensured and maintained. Quality does not suffer from variations in teachers' skills.

3. Predesign makes possible pretesting. Whether or not a set of learning conditions has been correctly chosen and designed can be determined by trying it out on students, and revising if necessary.

4. Predesign of learning conditions greatly reduces the necessity for the teacher to use valuable time in extemporaneous design, and thus makes it possible for a proper emphasis to be restored to the teacher functions of *managing instruction, motivating, generalizing,* and *assessing.*

The fourth point should not be taken lightly, since these other functions deserve a great deal of emphasis in education, and are likely to suffer neglect by teachers who are overburdened with the very difficult task of extemporaneous design of learning conditions. Managing instruction by advising on the choices of what topics to undertake next, and by suggesting suitable sequences of topics to fit the students' interests and objectives, is surely a most important function for the teacher to perform. Motivating students, insofar as this is not completed by parents, can be most effectively done by a wise and understanding teacher. Generalizing knowledge by the conduct of discussions that stretch imagination and encourage originality is surely an activity the value of which is widely recognized, and for which most teachers would welcome having more time. Finally, the job of assessing the progress and achievements of students is another most essential function that requires the skill and objectivity of the teacher. More time for all these important teacher activities might well be obtained by reducing the time spent in extemporaneous design of learning conditions.

PRINCIPLES OF DESIGN · Whether the conditions of learning are predesigned or extemporaneously designed, they need to be in accord with the principles described in Chapters 3 through 6. Recapitulated in brief form, assuming in each case that prerequisites have been met, they are as follows:

1. *Stimulus-response learning*: Provide repetition of the $Ss \rightarrow R$ connection, applying reinforcement immediately.

2. *Chaining (motor)*: Reinstate $Ss \rightarrow R$ links in the proper order, either by beginning with the terminal link and working backward, or by using prompts. Reinforcement of the terminal link and also a certain amount of repetition are necessary.

3. *Verbal chaining*: Reinstate verbal links in the proper order, including mediating or "coding" links. Confirm correct responses. For longer chains, external "prompts" may be needed to provide sequence cues. Repetition is needed to overcome the effects of interference.

4. *Multiple discrimination*: Present stimuli in a manner that emphasizes distinctiveness. Repetition may be needed to reduce interference among individual connections. Confirm correct responses.

5. *Concept learning*: Present a suitable variety of stimuli to represent the concept class, each stimulus having a connection with a common response. Verify by presenting a novel stimulus that is also a member of the class.

6. *Principle learning*: Inform the learner of the performance to be expected. Invoke recall of component concepts by verbal in-

structions. Make verbal statement of principle. Verify by the direction "Show me."

7. *Problem solving:* Inform the learner of the performance to be expected. Invoke recall of previously learned concepts or principles. Provide verbal guidance that directs thinking, but that does not state the principle being attained. Verify by asking the learner to "demonstrate" a concrete instance.

These conditions are given here with great brevity, and the reader is urged to refer to earlier chapters for a more complete account. At any rate, let it be emphasized again that decisions concerning what learning conditions are appropriate need to be applied to *each learning act* within a topic, and cannot be properly applied to a topic as a whole. Design of conditions for truly efficient learning can only be achieved, therefore, by reference to a learning structure that identifies the individual learning acts of a topic and their relationships to each other.

DECISIONS AFFECTING KNOWLEDGE TRANSFER

Once knowledge has been acquired, it needs to be put to use. Most statements of educational objectives emphasize the broad applicability of learned capabilities, rather than the immediate and specific objectives of the sort referred to in a previous section. Thus, it is generally considered desirable that the student learn not only to recognize structurally correct English sentences, but to apply this knowledge to compositions that he himself generates. Similarly, a goal of science instruction is not simply one of having the student state a concrete example of a scientific principle, but also one of making it possible for him to apply this principle in novel situations, and perhaps even to design an experiment to test a principle of his own devising. Obviously, instruction must include provisions for meeting such goals as these, which demand the transfer of knowledge.

TEACHING FOR TRANSFER · What kind of decisions can be made to support and encourage knowledge transfer? Primarily, the occurrence of transfer seems to be a matter of permitting the student to "think about" and "apply" the knowledge he has acquired. To some extent, this can be done by suitable design of the knowledge structure itself, followed by an appropriate learning situation. For example, a problem that sometimes puzzles mathematics teachers is why students who have apparently mastered the addition and subtraction of integers (signed numbers) then proceed to show that they cannot do "word problems" involving the addition of integers. One important key to this problem lies in the analysis of the learning structure. Suppose students are to respond to questions like "The temperature rose from four degrees below zero to twelve degrees above zero; what has been the total amount of change in degrees of temperature?" The learning structure for such a performance needs to include not only a subordinate objective of "adding negative and positive integers," but also another one that may be phrased as "translating various verbal expressions like 'four degrees below zero' into the form of integers like '−4.'" In other words, one definite method of "teaching for transfer" would require that the learning structure define *all* of the subordinate objectives involved in such a goal, and deliberately set out to include these in instruction.

THE ENCOURAGEMENT OF PROBLEM SOLVING • But there are in addition much broader requirements to the objective of knowledge transfer. The student needs to be encouraged to "think about" the relationships among various categories of knowledge he has acquired and to make his own applications to new situations and problems. Some authors (for example, Bruner, 1961) have suggested that individuals can learn *strategies* of knowledge application and transfer by participating in problem-solving activities designed as a part of instruction. Others (for example, Gagné, 1963b) have emphasized the need for the broadening of knowledge under conditions in which ideas can be made discriminating or "incisive." But there is a good deal of agreement that knowledge should be used for thinking, and that thinking fosters the transfer of knowledge.

One of the instructional techniques that seems to have served the purpose of encouraging students to think is the organized discussion group or discussion class. The inclusion of such a technique in a course of instruction may accordingly be considered a decision in the direction of emphasizing knowledge transfer. When properly conducted, a discussion group can stimulate students to engage in extensive problem solving in the presence of novel situations, verbally presented. Evidence from studies of group problem solving (Taylor, Berry, and Block, 1957) suggests that the individual student may not have the greatest number of ideas in the group situation, nor even the best ones. But the fact that they must be well communicated, and are subject to the "sharpening" of criticism by members of the group, may be a reason why group problem solving is found to be more effective than individual solving of the same problem (Lorge *et al.*, 1955). It seems reasonable to suppose that the group problem solving which can occur in a discussion class provides the same kinds of opportunities and exhibits the same kinds of performance trends as are evident in these controlled studies.

A discussion class, however, can be a failure as an effective technique for knowledge transfer. The most common reason appears to be a condition in which the participants do not have the prerequisite knowledges. Students cannot solve problems concerning the treatment of clowns in Shakespeare's writing if they are not able to conceptualize a "clown," or to describe the behavior various Shakespearian clowns exhibit, or to formulate principles about the clowns' use of language. All these knowledges are *prerequisite* to a discussion class, not a part of it. Similarly, students will not think effectively about the power of the presidency in the government of the United States unless they have already learned the principles of such power as expressed in the Constitution, in laws, and in executive actions. To attempt the initial learning of these prerequisite knowledges in discussion classes is to use a woefully inefficient procedure for learning. But to *follow* such learning by organized discussion is quite another matter. Under the latter conditions, the discussion group can be a powerful instrument leading to the stimulation and refinement of thinking, and therefore to the broad transfer of knowledge.

DECISIONS ABOUT ASSESSMENT

As has previously been pointed out, the management of learning includes provision for assessment of the capabilities that have been learned. For one thing, properly conducted assessment constitutes an important source of feedback to the learner, and thus is intimately bound up with the learning process itself. And for another, the necessity of planning out a systematic course of instruction in which one performance builds on another means that the attainment of each capability needs to be carefully confirmed before the learner proceeds to the next. In order for the next higher principle to be learned effectively, assessment is needed *within* topic learning (Gagné, Mayor, Garstens, and Paradise, 1962); and it is needed *at the end* of topic learning so that the learner can proceed to related or advanced topics.

Despite the existence of a rather elaborate technology, it cannot be said with confidence that the assessment procedures customarily used in developing typical "standardized" tests are entirely adequate to meet current assessment needs. One important problem that does not appear to have been included in current techniques is a method for assessing human performance in terms of the objectives of instruction. Instead, achievement tests often appear to have the goal of demonstrating how disparate human abilities can be, along undefined dimensions. Now, the existence of individual differences is a well-known fact, and it scarcely seems a worthwhile enterprise at this point to continue to refine the techniques of measuring them with increasing degrees of precision and reliability. In fact, it is a legitimate question as to whether such an attempt can ever succeed any more than it has already.

ASSESSING THE IMMEDIATE OUTCOMES OF LEARNING • The aim of tests designed for the assessment of learning outcomes, in contrast, needs to take quite a different tack. In particular, tests should be designed to assess the immediate outcomes of learning, as exhibited by the learner when he has first attained a new discrimination, concept, principle, or an entire topic. The interest in such tests is not on how different one learner is from another, but rather on the extent to which each learner has achieved the defined objective with which instructional planning began. This distinction has been well described by Glaser and Klaus (1962) as between tests that are *norm-referenced* and tests that are *criterion-referenced*.

The former type is a test whose scores are interpretable only by reference to a distribution of scores obtained from an entire tested group; in other words, the scores express the extent of individual differences. Scores of the latter type derive their meaning by reference to an *external standard (criterion)*. Certainly, it is the latter kind of measure that is needed for assessment of a learner's capability in attaining defined instructional objectives.

Tests of immediate learning outcomes cannot be designed merely by changing the purpose of the total test. Attention must also be paid to the form of each item that the test contains. The item must be designed to measure the objective specifically, not in a general sense. For example, there must be an item to measure "spelling verb forms that double their terminal consonants when made into a gerund by the addition of 'ing,' as sum, summing"; not just a collection of items that measure "spelling."

Consider a test item like the following: "Find the thickness of a pipe whose inner circumference is 9π, and whose outer circumference is 21π. (a) 12π; (b) 12; (c) 6π; (d) 6; (e) 3." It is difficult to see how such an item could serve the purpose of assessing *immediate outcomes* of learning a topic in mathematics (although, to be sure, it may be employed for other purposes, as discussed in subsequent paragraphs). The reason is that this item draws on the knowledge of two different higher-order principles, rather than on only one. First, there is the principle relating circumference to diameter. And second, there is the principle, readily exhibited in a drawing, that the outer diameter of a pipe equals the inner diameter plus twice the thickness of the pipe. Should an individual be unable to perform this item correctly, it would not be possible to tell from this failure whether (1) he did not know the first principle; (2) he did not know the second principle; (3) he did not know either principle; or (4) he knew both principles, but because of innate intellectual limitations, was unable to "put them together" in solving a new problem. Thus an item of this sort cannot be used to obtain a direct measure of whether the student has mastered specific objectives. To do this, one needs an item that tests knowledge of the first principle directly and unambiguously, as, "What is the difference in diameter of two pipes, one of which has a circumference of 21π, the other a circumference of 9π?" And in addition, an item is needed to measure the second principle, perhaps one that exhibits a drawing of a pipe in cross section, with values of internal and external diameters shown, asking the question, "What is the thickness of the pipe?"

To assess the immediate outcomes of learning, then, it is necessary to construct a "test" whose items have the following characteristics:

1. pose questions that reflect directly the defined objective of the learning;

2. conform to the class of performances that the learner has been told represent the achievement to be reached at the end of a learning session; and

3. represent this class of performances without being specifically recallable as verbal chains from within the learning session itself (except in those instances in which specific verbal recall is itself the objective).

In other words, measuring specific outcomes of learning cannot be a matter of designing items that are "easy" or "hard," in the sense that they require the use of capabilities other than those which were to have been specifically established by the learning session. It is not the kind of questioning whose general form should be hidden from the student. Such measurement does not have the aim of increasing the contrast among the performances of students. On the contrary, *its purpose is to compare each student's performance with an external standard representing the defined objective.*

It should be clear from this discussion that the primary reason for direct measurement of the outcomes of a learning exercise or session is to ensure that instructional objectives have been met. If a student fails to exhibit the performance required on such a test, he needs to undertake additional learning covering the same ground. It is inefficient, even useless, for him to try to proceed to the learning of advanced topics, in view of the hierarchical nature of knowledge, as described in Chapter 7. Whether by "repeating" the same instruction he has been given, or by using a more elaborately "guided" form of instruction, the defined objective must somehow be achieved if subsequent learning is to be even minimally efficient for this student. This kind of test, then, has the aim of determining whether the learning that was supposed to occur has really happened.

ASSESSING THE GENERALIZABILITY OF KNOWLEDGE · The more general objectives of instruction usually include the aim of knowledge generalization or *knowledge transfer*. The attainment of these objectives also needs to be measured. It will be apparent that such measurement has a different purpose from that designed to assess the attainment of immediate learning objectives. The purpose of this second kind of assessment is to *forecast the direction of future instruction*.

It is to be expected that there will be substantial individual differences among students with respect to the amount of generalization they can accomplish, each having learned a given topic or set of principles. In part, this difference in the capability for knowledge transfer depends on differences in the content of previous knowledge they have acquired. In part also, it may depend on some innate differences in intellectual capacity. These differences, whatever their origin, may be expected to appear prominently in any measure designed to assess the extent of knowledge generalization.

It is difficult to detect in most standard published achievement tests that any consistent objectives have been followed in the design of the items they contain. On the contrary, the impression is gained that many different principles have been used, often in quite inconsistent ways, so long as the tests that result do in fact yield a range of scores. However, if the aim of such measurement is to forecast what should be the future course of instruction for the individual student, it is evident that a more systematic approach to such measurement needs to be employed. One ingenious attempt to devise a systematic method for measuring knowledge transfer has been made by Bloom and his collaborators (1956). These authors describe knowledge transfer objectives under the headings "comprehension," "application," "analysis," "synthesis," and "evaluation." Each of these types of generalization is defined, and each is exemplified by a number of test items in various content fields. At the college level, the use of such categories of objectives has led in many instances to significant improvements in the planning of instruction and the measurement of its outcomes (Dressel, 1954).

The volume by Bloom and his colleagues describes a variety of kinds of measurement that may fairly be said to assess the transfer of knowledge. Two important dimensions of such measurement may be distinguished. The first is illustrated by items that test the *breadth* of generalizability of an acquired principle. This is done by describing a novel, concrete situation, and asking the student to state whether or not it is an example of the principle. For instance, one item that illustrates measurement of such an objective (called "comprehension") is as follows (Bloom *et al.,* 1956, p. 99):

> When a current is induced by the relative motion of a conductor and a magnetic field, the direction of the induced current is such as to establish a magnetic field that opposes the motion. This principle is illustrated by
> A—a magnet attracting a nail.
> B—an electric generator or dynamo.
> C—the motion of a compass needle.
> D—an electric doorbell.

Assuming that the student knows the principle stated as the initial portion of this item, he is first reminded of it. The point of the item, though, is to test whether the principle has been acquired *broadly* enough to make possible the identification required.

A second dimension of knowledge transfer is illustrated by the category the Bloom volume calls "synthesis." Essentially, these test items attempt to determine whether the student can form *new higher-order principles.* This activity, of course, involves problem solving, and may be considered to represent knowledge generalization in the *vertical,* or upward, direction. An example item provides a student with a four-line poem, and asks him to add a second verse of four lines. The student, it is said, must "achieve a novel organization of ideas." In other words, he must put together, without any specific guidance, some principles in the construction of a new principle to be used in solving a particular problem.

Two KINDS OF ASSESSMENT • Decisions about assessment of the outcomes of learning, then, are of considerable importance to the whole instructional enterprise. No better guide can be found to the phrasing of the questions that make up this assessment than the clear and unambiguous statement of learning objectives. Two kinds of objectives need to be distinguished, however, and these lead to the development of two kinds of assessment instruments. First, there is a need to test whether or not each individual student has in fact learned the performances that have been stated as *specific* objectives. And second, the more *general* objectives implied by the transferability of knowledge need also to be represented as assessments of student capabilities. Both types of test are needed, and they should not be confused with each other. The first type is used to identify what the student has or has not learned. The second is most useful in forecasting what future advanced learning he should undertake.

PRIORITY IN EDUCATIONAL DECISIONS

A number of kinds of decisions have been described, all of which affect the primary function of a "lower-case" educational system: to make possible efficient learning in the individual student. In outline form, these decisions are concerned with:

1. learning objectives;
2. the structure of knowledge to be learned;
3. motivation;
4. conditions for learning;
5. the transferability of knowledge; and
6. assessment.

In the simplest form of the educational system—the student and the teacher at opposite ends of a log—it is evident that all these decisions must be made by that tremendously wise person, the teacher. But a modern educational system often assumes a greater degree of specialization than this, particularly since the probability of finding someone wise enough to make all these decisions is continually diminishing. Many people besides the teacher now make decisions about learning objectives—parents' groups, school administrators, university scholars, writers of textbooks, and others. (The objectives they decide on are not always defined, or even made public, but they are chosen, nonetheless.) The structure of knowledge to be imparted is determined by the writer of a textbook or a workbook, or by the designer of a film, as are also many of the conditions for learning. Although they may be influenced by the teacher's decisions, the conditions affecting transfer of knowledge are often constrained by custom, availability of space, and other logistic matters. For many years the designers of "standardized tests" have made important decisions about assessment, a trend which appears to have fostered the notion that only they know how to ask questions of students.

Specialization is doubtless inevitable in the educational system. What is left for the teacher to do? What priority should be given to the following six kinds of decisions, so far as the teacher's job is concerned? To answer this question, one must consider mainly the kinds of teacher functions that are most highly dependent on dynamic interpersonal relationships for their success. At the same time, functions of the teacher should be those that a moderately wise, mature, adult individual can be expected to learn to perform without acquiring an impossibly great amount of specialized professional knowledge. Looked at from this point of view, the decisions for the teacher have something like the following priorities:

1. Motivation • No set of decisions are more clearly dependent on personal interactions with the student than are those concerned with motivation. The establishment and nurturing of personal goals and values, and the relation of these to more specific motives for achievement, can best be done by a person who occupies a position of authority in the everyday life of the developing individual. Specializing this function in the "guidance specialist" does not appear to be a direction of educational change that is likely to succeed in the long run. Every teacher should be a guidance specialist.

2. TRANSFERABILITY OF KNOWLEDGE • To the extent that the teacher on the end of the log is considered to be *discussing* ideas (rather than instilling them), this is a classic teacher function. To some degree, and in suitable circumstances, other students can serve this function too. But whoever the participants may be, the refinement, qualification, and elaboration of acquired knowledge appears to be a process best conducted by interaction between people. The skillful teacher has learned a variety of techniques for conducting discussions that aid the generalizability of knowledge.

3. ASSESSMENT • The teacher should be the best-equipped person to know what questions to ask the student. Teachers need to take a great deal of the responsibility for this function, and need to learn the techniques necessary to perform it well. To some degree, testing is necessarily a specialized function, and methods of testing are much in need of further development by specialists.

4. CONDITIONS FOR LEARNING • Although the teacher should doubtless continue to have some part in determining the conditions of learning, there is a distinct possibility that *predesign* of these conditions will be found to be the more efficient procedure for many kinds of content. As a specialized function, the choice of learning conditions often requires the professional knowledge of the learning psychologist.

5. THE STRUCTURE OF KNOWLEDGE TO BE LEARNED • Determining learning structures has been a specialized function, in which the teacher has played a minor role, for a number of years. (Exceptions occur in some instances of college instruction.) Ideally, it would seem reasonable for the learning structure of knowledge to be determined by people with professional "content" knowledge working together with educational psychologists.

6. LEARNING OBJECTIVES • These decisions are also in a sense "specialized" beyond the realm of teacher responsibility. Parents, scholars, community leaders—all have some part to play in the stating of objectives of instruction. But objectives must also be defined in terms of observable human performances, and this activity requires some specialized psychological knowledge.

GENERAL REFERENCES

Determining Objectives

Bloom, B. S. (Ed.), Engelhart, M. D., Furst, E. J., Hill, W. H., and Krathwohl, D. R. *Taxonomy of educational objectives. Handbook 1: Cognitive domain.* New York: McKay, 1956.

French, W. *Behavioral goals of general education in high school.* New York: Russell Sage, 1957.

Gardner, J. W. *Excellence.* New York: Harper & Row, 1961.

Kearney, N. C. *Elementary school objectives.* New York: Russell Sage, 1953.

Lindvall, C. M. (Ed.) *Defining educational objectives.* Pittsburgh: University of Pittsburgh Press, 1964.

Motivation

See References for Chapter 8.

The Predesign of Learning Conditions

De Cecco, J. P. *Educational technology.* New York: Holt, Rinehart and Winston, 1964.

Galanter, E. H. (Ed.) *Automatic teaching: the state of the art.* New York: Wiley, 1959.

Glaser, R. (Ed.) *Teaching machines and programed learning, II: Data and directions.* Washington, D.C.: National Education Association, 1965.

Lumsdaine, A. A., and Glaser, R. (Eds.) *Teaching machines and programmed learning: a source book.* Washington, D.C.: National Education Association, 1960.

Assessment

Dressel, P. L. (Ed.) *Evaluation in general education.* Dubuque, Iowa: Brown, 1954.

Lindquist, E. F. (Ed.) *Educational measurement.* Washington, D.C.: American Council on Education, 1950.

Tyler, R. W. Achievement testing and curriculum construction. In E. G. Williamson (Ed.), *Trends in student personnel work.* Minneapolis: University of Minnesota Press, 1949. Pp. 391–407.

RESOURCES FOR LEARNING | 10

THE DECISIONS that affect learning have been described in the preceding chapter. When these decisions are wise, they lead to efficient learning; when they are not, learning is inefficient and often ineffective. The educational system also has the function of executing these decisions, and nowadays it has a variety of resources to call on in its operations. There are not only blackboards and textbooks, but also projectors and tape recorders and television circuits and computers. Furthermore, each and all of these may be introduced at many points in the instructional process, and used in a variety of ways. They may become parts of, or even to some extent replacements for, the lecture, the recitation class, the discussion group, the demonstration, the laboratory.

This chapter's purpose is to discuss these resources for learning by describing the functions they can serve in promoting efficient learning. To do this, it will be desirable first to review in a general way the nature of the instructional situation. Following this, it will be possible to consider the purposes that particular "devices" can fulfill in instruction, as well as those they cannot serve. The various kinds of arrangements that the instructional situation can take—the "modes" of instruction—can then be systematically described. The lecture, the class, the tutoring session, the laboratory—each of these modes will be seen to involve different arrangements of instructional media. Finally, the implications of these resources and their modes of usage can be pointed out for the educational system of today and tomorrow.

267

THE INSTRUCTIONAL SITUATION

The focus of the instructional situation is the student, within whom learning actually occurs. Most of the previous chapters have been concerned with describing the nature of these learning changes and how they are brought about. A slightly different viewpoint will be needed in order to delineate the subject of this chapter, namely, a view over the learner's shoulder. The environment of the learner has many components that are important for learning. Taken altogether, these may be considered to constitute the *instructional situation*.

COMPONENT FUNCTIONS OF THE INSTRUCTIONAL SITUATION

Ignoring for the moment the physical appearance of the instructional situation, it is possible to identify several different functions that must be performed by its components. In most cases, they have been mentioned in previous chapters. These are the various ways in which the environment exerts its effects on the learner.

1. *Presenting the stimulus.* Every type of learning requires a stimulus, and usually these stimuli must be located within the learning environment, outside the learner. If a chain is being learned, an external cue must be provided for each link, even though these cues may become unnecessary later. If multiple discrimination is to be accomplished, the stimuli to be discriminated must be displayed so that correct connections can become differentiated from incorrect ones. If concepts are being learned, a suitable variety of objects or events representing a class must be displayed. If principles are being acquired, the stimulus objects to which they are expected to apply must somehow be represented to the student. And if problem solving is undertaken, the "problem situation" must similarly be represented and displayed. Obviously, these various stimuli can be presented in many different ways by objects already in the learner's environment, or by means of pictures, printed books, or oral communication.

2. *Directing attention and other learner activities.* Environmental components also act on the learner by directing his atten-

tion to certain stimuli or aspects of stimulus objects and events. In very young children, vivid or suddenly changing stimulation may be used for this purpose. Very soon these can be supplanted by oral commands, and later still by printed directions such as, "Notice the number of electrons in the outer ring," or "Look at the graph in Figure 23." Activities other than attention may also be directed by such instructions, as implied by the statements, "Remember how a line is defined," or "Complete the following sentence." These activities are not themselves learning; they are simply actions that must be taken by the learner in order to create the proper conditions for learning. Verbal directions that have these purposes can be presented either orally or in printed form.

3. *Providing a model for terminal performance.* The importance of the function of informing the learner about the general nature of the performance to be acquired has been emphasized previously on several occasions. There is no single way of doing this, and many different components of the instructional situation may be employed. Most commonly, the "model" of performance to be expected following learning is conveyed by oral or printed communication.

4. *Furnishing external prompts.* In learning chains as well as multiple discriminations, cues may be provided in the instructional situation to establish a proper sequence of connections or to increase the distinctiveness of stimuli. As learning proceeds, these extra cues may be made to "vanish" when they are no longer needed. Stimuli that function as extra cues may take a variety of forms. For example, they may be pictorial, as when a sequence is depicted in a diagram reading from left to right. Or they may be auditory, as in emphasizing the differences in sound of such French words as *rue* and *rouge*. Verbal stimuli are often employed for both these purposes, as well as for the purpose of furnishing distinctive "coding links" in verbal chains. In Gilbert's (1962) example of learning color coding for resistors, the word "penny" is provided as a link between *brown* and *one*, the word "nothingness" as a link between *black* and *zero*.

5. *Guiding the direction of thinking.* When principles are being learned, and particularly when learning takes the form of

problem solving, the direction of recalled internal connections (thoughts) may be guided by instructions from the learner's environment. As described previously, such guidance is presumed to have the effect of increasing the efficiency of learning by reducing the occurrence of irrelevant "hypotheses." Generally, instructions having this function of "hinting" and "suggesting" take the form of oral or printed prose statements.

6. *Inducing transfer of knowledge.* Providing for the transfer of learned concepts and principles to novel situations may be accomplished in a number of ways. The conduct of discussion is one of the most convenient. Obviously, this is a special kind of interaction between the learner and his environment, and it is not possible to specify exactly what form will be taken at any given moment by stimulation from the environment. The process is usually initiated, however, by verbally stated questions of the "problem-solving" variety. An important alternative method is to place the individual within a problem situation more or less directly, without the use of words to describe it. A science demonstration may be used to serve this function. Also, motion pictures can be used with considerable effectiveness to initiate problem-solving discussion by "getting the students into the situation" in a highly realistic manner.

7. *Assessing learning attainments.* The environment of the learner also acts on him to assess the extent to which he has attained a specific learning objective or subobjective. It does this by deliberately placing him in representative problem situations that concretely reflect the capability he is expected to have learned. Most frequently, this is done by asking him questions. Although it is conceivable for the learner to formulate for himself the questions to be asked, this is difficult to do even for the experienced adult learner. Preferably, the questions must come from an independent source, so that they will be uninfluenced by the learner's wishes, but will accurately represent the objective.

8. *Providing feedback.* Closely related to assessment of learning outcomes is the provision for feedback concerning the correctness of the learner's responses. The questions that are asked the learner, followed by his answers, must in turn be followed by in-

formation that tells him whether he is right or wrong. Sometimes, the provision for this feedback function of the learner's environment is very simple to arrange: a foreign word pronounced by the student may sound like one he hears on a tape; the color of a chemical solution may indicate the presence of an element he is searching for. At other times it may be considerably more complex, as when the adequacy of a constructed prose paragraph describing an observed event is assessed, and the results fed back to the student.

These eight functions, then, represent the ways in which the learner's environment acts on him. These are the external conditions of learning that, when combined with certain prerequisite capabilities within the learner, bring about the desired change in his performance. Obviously, there are many ways to establish these conditions in the learning environment, and many combinations of objects, devices, and verbal communications may be employed in doing so. Probably the most important consideration for the design of the learning environment, however, is not that several alternative ways of accomplishing the same function are usually available. Rather, the important point is that for a given function, certain means of interacting with the learner are quite ineffective. Accordingly, the characteristics of various *media of instruction* in performing these functions need to be considered carefully in making a choice.

MEDIA FOR INSTRUCTION

The phrase *instructional media* is used here to refer to the various kinds of components of the learning environment that generate stimulation to the learner. In this broad sense, the teacher is usually a major source of such stimulation. Besides the teacher, there are various objects and devices, ranging from books to television receivers, that have this general function of providing inputs to the learner. There is no intention here to detract from the teacher's importance by considering his function of stimulus generation along with that of inanimate systems. Naturally, inanimate systems can perform their function effectively only when their stimulus contents are designed by people who also have in mind the purpose of instructing. However, it is illuminating to distinguish all the sources of stimulation for the learner in the situation immediately surrounding him, and thus to include the teacher as one of these.

Some media for instruction have formed a part of the learning environment for many, many years. Besides the teacher, these include printed or written media provided by blackboards and books, natural objects that are directly imported into the instructional situation, and photographs or drawn representations. Newer media for instruction are motion pictures, whether presented by means of a movie projector or a television system, and teaching machines, which may be considered a means of combining the characteristics of books and pictures with certain other instructional functions. For what purposes are these various media appropriate, and for what purposes are they inappropriate, or at least relatively ineffective?

OBJECTS FOR INSTRUCTION

The stimuli for the instruction of the child in his preschool years are primarily the objects in his restricted world: his toys, the furniture in his house, the simple tools he uses, the ground and trees and telephone poles and streets, and, of course, the other human beings with whom he interacts. When he goes to school, the variety of these objects changes somewhat. Now there are special collections of leaves, or shells, or rocks that display all in one place the individual things he has encountered before. In addition, there are other objects that he has not yet seen before, perhaps new kinds of animals and plants, or specially constructed blocks. The use of objects to present stimuli continues throughout his school years, with the objects themselves growing more refined and complex. Particularly is this true in the science laboratory, where the new objects may be chemicals and solutions, new varieties of animals and plants, and instruments such as balances, microscopes, ammeters, and chronometers.

Instruction needs to be fundamentally based on the stimulation provided by objects and events (that is, changes in objects), assuming, of course, that these objects may be people. As emphasized in Chapter 5, objects and events are the stimuli from which concepts are derived. Although instruction comes to depend heavily on verbal communication, the words merely "stand for" things that may be directly observed. This is the fundamental reason why scientists place such a high value on the laboratory and the field exercise. Scientific knowledge depends ultimately on the direct observation of things and events.

Naturally, the objects used for instruction must be carefully chosen. If multiple discriminations are being established among varieties of rocks, care must be taken to select the samples so that the differential features will be emphasized. If the addition of unit quantities is to be learned, a set of objects (blocks) of sizes graded in these units must be provided. If the concept of magnetic attraction is to be learned, a suitable variety of magnets and pole orientations must be employed. The kind of learning that is contemplated therefore has considerable significance for the choice of objects selected as media for instruction.

DEMONSTRATION

Demonstrations consist of actual objects that are typically made to interact with each other so as to display an event or a set of events. Water may be heated to boiling, steel balls may be made to run down inclined planes, oxygen liberated from a chemical reaction may be collected in an inverted vessel, and so on. The event is just as much a stimulus situation as is a display of objects by themselves. In many instances, the events that might otherwise be made to occur by the student's own activity in the laboratory can function to present the needed stimulus situation with equal effectiveness by way of a demonstration. In general, the functions of the demonstration in instruction are basically the same as those discussed for the display of objects.

ORAL COMMUNICATION BY THE TEACHER

There are many situations for which oral communication by a teacher can provide *all* the required instructional functions. But this is not true of every situation. It will be desirable to consider the possibilities provided to the instructional situation by this medium one by one, along with some important limitations.

1. *Presenting the stimulus.* In advanced forms of instruction, adequate presentation of stimuli can often be done verbally. The earth's orbit around the sun can be described, rather than being directly observed. The course of passage of a bill through the Congress can be verbally described. Appropriate conversation in a foreign language can be orally communicated. But there are real limitations to the use of oral communication for presenting stimuli. The science teacher would feel grossly handicapped if he had to depend solely on oral communication to describe wave motion. The description of a town meeting may not be as satisfactory a stimulus for learning as the direct observation of a town meeting, or a filmed record of one.

2. *Directing attention and learner activity.* Oral communication serves such a purpose very well. For the early years, it is difficult to find any medium that works as well. For later years of education, printed and pictorial materials may be able to equal the effectiveness of oral communication in performing this function.

3. *Providing a model for terminal performance.* For this purpose, oral communication appears to have no general advantage over other media. The terminal performance may sometimes be communicated more conveniently in printed or pictorial form. For example, if the objective is "computing the normality of chemical solutions," the printed example ".5N" is evidently a good model for the kind of performance required. Oral communication is needed, however, when the terminal performance is itself an oral one, as in constructing sentences in a foreign language, or in making a speech.

4. *Furnishing external prompts.* In performing this function, oral communication may be particularly effective in the early years. For example, the chains involved in the printing or writing of letters may be prompted by teachers' oral directions such as "First, a long line down," "Next, a line across near the top," and so on. Prompting can also be done well by printed means once

the student has learned to read, as is shown in many self-instructional programs (Klaus, 1965).

5. *Guiding the direction of thinking.* Asked to demonstrate the truth of the statement

$$8 \times 3 + 16 = 5 \times 8$$

the student's thinking may be guided by such questions as, "Can you think of another name for 16?"—and others as needed—to enable him to arrive at the expression

$$8 \times 5 = 8 \times 5$$

Again it is true that such guidance can also be given by printed means, and some self-instructional programs do this quite effectively.

6. *Inducing transfer of knowledge.* The questions that initiate this process can be presented orally. If students have learned the principles of distribution of powers among legislative, executive, and judiciary components of government, a question like the following can be asked: "What possible means could there be of legislative restraint on judicial powers?" A demonstration using actual objects or pictures is another possibility for setting the stage for knowledge transfer. In continuing the process, oral discussion is often employed.

7. *Assessing learning attainments.* The teacher often undertakes to carry out this function by means of oral questioning. But there are certainly limitations to this method. The attainment of concepts and principles can also be measured by means of printed statements, and often require the use of pictures or diagrams.

8. *Providing feedback.* This function can also be carried out by oral communication. For young children, a good deal of the teacher's conversation may consist of statements of "yes," "good!" "that's right," as the student or students attain successive goals of instruction. At later ages, the necessity for such "oral reinforcement" becomes greatly reduced, since the student is able to match his own performance with an external standard, or one that he himself supplies.

All of these functions, then, *can* be done by oral communication, and perhaps this is the reason why the model of the teacher and student talking to each other while seated on a log seems so appropriate for the instructional situation. But many of the functions can be done just as well by other means, as by the display of print and pictures. And certain subjects require something other than oral communication: much of science and mathematics cannot be taught without recourse to stimulation that includes actual objects and events.

PRINTED LANGUAGE MEDIA

Books, pamphlets, and leaflets are also a traditional part of the instructional situation. In the later periods of education, the amount of dependence on books as media of instruction is very high relative to dependence on other media. It is noteworthy, however, that oral discussion still has an instructional function at the level of postgraduate education. An experienced university scholar may derive most of his instruction from the printed media of books and learned journals; yet he finds it necessary to discuss with his colleagues the ideas he gets from books. At the other extreme of the educational scale, printed communication can accomplish very little; the presentation of actual objects accompanied by oral communication is the typical mode of instruction for children in the elementary grades. Accordingly, learning the skill of reading is the crucial event that determines the increasing dependence on printed media from the early grades of school onward.

Assuming that the student possesses the necessary prerequisite knowledge, instruction by means of a book is usually a remarkably rapid and efficient process. Although no figures are available, the amount of time required for oral communication must surely be three or four times as much as that needed for instruction by means of a book. For the vast range of subject matter that is taught following the primary school years, printed communication can certainly be the major medium of instruction, and often is. When pictures and diagrams are combined with printed text (as, for example, in a good high school physics text), the dangers of excessive verbalism can largely be overcome, and the book can impart a great deal of instruction in a relatively short time, when used by a suitably prepared student who can read. At this level of schooling, in fact, whatever ineffectiveness books possess as instructional media may often be attributed to difficulties that are not inherent in the medium itself: either the student has not acquired the necessary background knowledge or he has not learned how to read, or both.

There are, however, other limitations of the printed medium. These have to do with the ways in which the sentences on the printed page are functioning in the instructional situation. Many textbooks, after all, are poorly written from the standpoint of establishing the proper conditions for learning. For example, does the printed text introducing a topic direct attention to the proper stimuli? Does it inform the learner of the nature of the performance to be learned? Does it use prompts, where these are appropriate, or guide the direction of the student's thought? Does it assess the attainments of learning at frequent intervals, and provide for feedback to the learner? Many printed texts would score quite low on their performance of these necessary instructional functions. What happens, usually, is that the learner performs these functions himself by the time he has as much experience as a college student has. But it is perhaps too much to expect that a fifth-grader will have acquired this much sophistication about self-instruction through reading. The deficiencies of ordinary printed texts as instructional media often become markedly clear to people who try writing self-instructional programs.

The potentialities of printed texts for instruction are very high, and it is doubtful that they have been well exploited as yet. Designing a printed text that will efficiently instruct a ten-year-old is not simply a matter of matching his vocabulary. Primarily, it is a matter of *organizing* the statements in such a way that they will perform the instructional functions that have previously been described. Unless one is simply "telling a story" (which may be the case for some sorts of subject matter like history), it is doubtful that the proper sequence of printed statements is much like a story at all. Each sentence has a purpose, and sets of sentences are organized in such a way that learning will occur most readily. The reader will perhaps be able to identify the instructional functions of the following sequence of printed statements applicable to Figure 17.

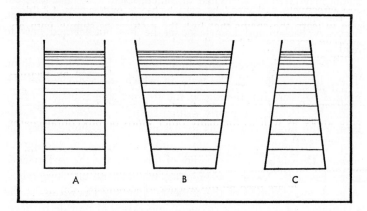

Fig. 17. Vessels of different shapes, each containing a liquid.

1. Look at the pictures.
2. How is the pressure at the bottom of a vessel full of liquid related to the shape of the vessel?
3. Remember that pressure is the ratio of a force to (what?).
4. In a vessel whose walls flare outward, where is the force of the central cylindrical portion of the water exerted? Where is the force of the water outside this central cylinder exerted?
5. The areas of the bottoms of the vessels are equal.
6. What can you say about the pressure at the bottom of the two vessels (A) and (B)?
7. State the relationship in general terms. (ANSWER: The pressure at the bottom of the vessel of liquid is not affected by the shape of vessel.)
8. Now look at the other vessel, with walls flaring inward (C).
9. Etc.

It will be apparent that not many textbooks are written with this kind of organization of instructional functions. As will be seen later, "instructional programs" often are. Both, of course, are examples of printed media.

PICTURES

As implied by the previous example, the most important function of pictures and diagrams as media of instruction is to display the stimulus situation. For the earliest years, this function may be most effectively performed by actual objects and events. Children have to learn the chains that link the pictures as stimuli with appropriate responses. Once these have been acquired, pictures greatly extend the range of stimulus situations that can be brought into the classroom. Another function well performed by pictures is that of prompting. For example, motion-picture sequences can be effectively used as a source of external stimuli for instruction in tying knots, as well as for many other kinds of procedural chains (Roshal, 1961).

Still pictures take many forms as media of instruction. They may appear on the pages of books, accompanying printed material. They frequently are used by the teacher to accompany oral instruction, in the form of enlarged prints, slides, filmstrips, or transparencies. The question as to whether one of these physical forms of still picture is "better" than another for instruction is surely not a sensible one, unless confined to the issue of whether one form can be seen better than another. A picture is a picture, and the educational question of interest is simply whether it can perform some particular instructional function better than something else, like printed statements. When the function is presenting a stimulus situation, there often is nothing feasible that can do the job a fraction as well as a picture.

Presenting the stimulus situation for problem solving, and thereby introducing group discussion, is a specialized function that often calls for a picture. Such is the case, for example, in presenting a science problem that is to be solved by the novel application of previously learned principles. Similarly, a picture may be used to pose a problem of creative description in a course in English. Over a tremendous range of educational subject matter, the uses of pictures are many, and it is not surprising that for some purposes a picture is worth an unlimited number of words.

The limitations of pictures in performing instructional functions are equally apparent. There are many occasions on which they

cannot be effectively used to inform the learner of the performance
to be expected as a result of learning. They cannot readily be used
by themselves to guide the learner's thinking, or to assess his performance, or to provide him with feedback. Although none of
these functions of pictures should be considered impossible, they
are much more frequently performed by some kind of verbal communication. There are, then, a number of instructional functions
that are better executed by words than by pictures.

MOTION PICTURES AND TELEVISION

Although these two media of instruction are often discussed
separately, there is no important reason for doing so. Logistically,
of course, different arrangements are required to employ them as
a part of instruction. But from the standpoint of instructional
functioning, they are the same. Each can display *events*, rather
than simply objects, and also *sequences of events*. "Moving pictures" is a good general name for the combined instructional
medium they represent.

The relation between moving pictures and still pictures is
analogous to that between demonstrations and objects. Demonstrations can present events as stimulus situations, rather than
simply the objects that participate in these events. The advantage
of moving pictures in performing this function is that they enor-
mously extend the range of stimulus situations that can be brought
into the classroom. Films and television can display not only balls
rolling down inclined planes, but many other kinds of events, both
real and imagined: the motions of planets around the sun, the flow
of blood through capillaries, the motion of molecules in a con-
tainer of gas, the actions of satellite particles surrounding an atomic
nucleus. They can show political and economic institutions in
operation, and re-create for the student the events of history. Their
potentialities as part of the conditions of instruction seem as yet
only partially realized.

Basically, what moving pictures do in a highly effective way
is to present the stimulus situation to the learner. For those instances in which commonly available objects are used in a demonstration, this may not seem a very valuable function. But there are

many demonstrations that require expensive equipment or space, and these can be well executed by means of films. (Examples can be found in the series of films produced by the Physical Sciences Study Committee for courses in high school physics.) For presenting problem situations whose solutions are not shown, but which are to be the subject of later class discussion, moving pictures are also excellent media. Their potential for this purpose currently remains largely unexploited, although such films have been made for use in courses in leadership and teacher training.

What other functions can be performed by moving pictures? They can provide the external prompting needed to learn chains and procedures (Lumsdaine, 1963). In certain instances, they are effective in communicating to the learner the kind of terminal performance expected; this is particularly true when a complex motor skill is to be learned. Sequences of pictures may also be used to provide feedback to the learner. If in the course of viewing a demonstration in physics, the learner predicts that one object will exert more force than another, a filmed sequence can then confirm that this is true (cf. Gropper, 1963).

Moving pictures are seldom used by themselves to perform instructional functions. A sound track is added. When this is done, the range of functions which can be performed is greatly increased, since all of the feats performed by oral communication supplement the stimulus-presentation function. In other words, the teacher is in effect put on the sound track. The oral communication thus provided is capable of directing the student's activities, describing the performance to be learned, guiding the thinking process, questioning for assessment purposes, and providing feedback. With such a combination of talents, the sound–motion picture should be a truly marvelous instrument for instruction! Unfortunately, the sound film that exploits these potentialities to their full extent is a great rarity. To a considerable degree, the reason may be that the content and sequencing of such films are governed by production considerations borrowed from the field of theatrical motion pictures (Lumsdaine, 1963). Except for highly specialized subjects (such as knot tying, micrometer reading), it is probably fair to say that a sound–motion-picture film that systematically uses the various instructional functions of moving pictures and oral communication in their proper places has yet to be made.

TEACHING MACHINES

Teaching machines do not represent a truly distinct medium for instruction, but rather a combination of media. Just as the sound–motion picture is considered a combination of moving pictures and oral communication, a teaching machine in its typical form combines printed communication with still pictures. This combination of media is also present in a good textbook, and it is in fact quite reasonable to compare a teaching machine to a book. One can consider a teaching machine as a "programmed" book, which is sometimes automated as well.

The "programmed" feature of the teaching machine, however, is likely to make it differ considerably from the usual textbook. In its simplest form, a teaching-machine program contains printed statements in "frames," each of which performs a *single* instructional function. When it is appropriate, the learner responds to a frame by answering a question asked therein, or by filling in a blank to complete a statement. In this way, assessment of the learner's progress is frequent, and the feedback to him is equally frequent. A good teaching-machine program is one that performs each instructional function meticulously, and in an order similar to that described in Chapter 8. There is every reason to suppose that good self-instructional programs are highly effective, as they have many times been shown to be (Glaser, 1965; Schramm, 1964).

To a limited degree, self-instructional programs can foster transfer of knowledge, or at least pave the way for it. Knowledge transfer can be "built into" a teaching-machine program, just as it can into a good textbook or sound film (Kersh, 1965). The technique of doing this is mainly one of presenting the student with a variety of problems requiring the application of principles after he has mastered these principles. Limitations to the variety of problems is in this instance imposed by the designer of the program, and accordingly is not determined by the student's own questions. Again in the case of this medium it is apparent that the well-conducted discussion performs a function that cannot quite be reached by a predesigned program, that is, of inducing the broad generalizing of a variety of individual ideas, and at the same time providing the critical means by which these generalizations can be refined and made more powerful.

SUMMARY OF MEDIA FUNCTIONS

The major varieties of media for instruction, as well as certain combinations of these varieties, have now been reviewed. It will be of some further interest, though, to compare their characteristics in a table. This summary is presented in Table 2.

The table indicates for each medium whether it can or cannot perform the instructional functions that have been described. In some cases, the word "limited" is used, to imply that the medium *can* be used for the instructional function referred to, but over a limited range of content. Examination of the first row, for example, provides the information that both oral and printed verbal communication are limited in usefulness for presenting stimuli. This is true because they can present only *verbal* stimuli, whereas actual objects and pictures are frequently needed. The action of a pendulum, for example, can surely be described in words, but no one would consider that an adequate stimulus for instruction on the topic of pendulums. Some of the major conclusions that may be drawn from comparisons within the table are as follows:

1. Oral communication is capable of most instructional functions, and is limited only in stimulus presentation. For this purpose objects or pictures are required. It should also be noted that many of the functions of oral instruction may often be accomplished *more rapidly* by printed media.

2. Various combinations of media (oral communication plus pictures, printed media plus pictures, and so on) acquire supplementary capabilities for instruction, and thus become much more useful than the individual media that compose them.

3. Sound movies and teaching machines can each perform a broad range of instructional functions because they combine the functions of more than one medium.

TABLE 2
Instructional Functions of Various Media

Function	Objects; Demonstration	Oral Communication	Printed Media	Still Pictures	Moving Pictures	Sound Movies	Teaching Machines
				Media			
Presenting the stimulus	Yes	Limited	Limited	Yes	Yes	Yes	Yes
Directing attention and other activity	No	Yes	Yes	No	No	Yes	Yes
Providing a model of expected performance	Limited	Yes	Yes	Limited	Limited	Yes	Yes
Furnishing external prompts	Limited	Yes	Yes	Limited	Limited	Yes	Yes
Guiding thinking	No	Yes	Yes	No	No	Yes	Yes
Inducing transfer	Limited	Yes	Limited	Limited	Limited	Limited	Limited
Assessing attainments	No	Yes	Yes	No	No	Yes	Yes
Providing feedback	Limited	Yes	Yes	No	Limited	Yes	Yes

4. The unique function of oral communication is judged to be that of inducing knowledge transfer. Of course, to perform this function properly, a suitable interaction between people ("oral communicators") must be designed, as in a discussion group or class. Oral communication *can* be deadening, as everyone knows. But it also has the potentiality of generating both breadth and incisiveness in previously acquired basic knowledge.

MODES OF INSTRUCTION

Environments for learning consist of the various communication media arranged so as to perform their several functions by interaction with the student. The particular *arrangements* these media may have in relation to the student are usually called the *modes of instruction*. Certain of these modes are traditional in education and have been used for many years, like the lecture and the demonstration. Others are much newer, but nevertheless are widely used, like televised instruction and sound-film presentations. It will be useful here to examine some of the most distinctive modes of instruction, in order to see if "what is going on" can be adequately described and understood in terms of instructional functions. Of course, there are many variations in the arrangements of media even within a given mode, and it will not be possible to describe all of these. Typical events must be considered in each case.

THE TUTORING SESSION

By a "tutoring session" is meant an interchange between a student and his "tutor," which has been preceded by reading by the student, and will be followed by more reading. This appears to be the fundamental character of the mode as practiced, for example, in English universities. However, this kind of tutoring session should not be confused with something that is often called a "cram" session, or even with a "special instruction" session, in which most of the time may be spent in oral communication by the teacher.

The tutoring session as here defined is not like the situation of the student and teacher on opposite ends of a log. Instead, the student has to a large extent done his own learning, primarily by reading books. The tutor's function is, first, to guide the student's thinking by answering the questions he has formulated on the basis of his reading. Second, the tutor conducts an assessment of the student's performance, attempting to judge what he has "gotten out of" his reading. Third, the tutor provides feedback to the learner on the basis of this assessment. And finally, he performs what is, strictly speaking, not an instructional function but a management function: he tells the student what he should read next. In other words, he recommends the direction of further learning that the student is to undertake. In this mode of instruction, then, it is apparent that most of the functions of instruction are performed by the student himself.

Americans should probably not be overly inclined to disparage such a system of instruction, which has, after all, worked very well for many generations. Instead, the important question might well be, What does it take to make such a mode effective? One answer appears to be, it takes a great deal of prerequisite, disciplined learning, including the capability of getting the most out of reading. It is difficult to argue that such a system is not a very good one for college instruction, and there appears to be no great amount of evidence to suggest that the typical system of American colleges and universities is any better. In fact, it may be that the American system of lectures and classes has arisen in part because students entering colleges have *not* acquired enough background knowledge and skill in reading to make it possible for such a system to work. Perhaps the more time-consuming stimulation of oral communication must be used because college students are not really well enough prepared to manage learning for themselves. At any rate, it is interesting to speculate about the extent to which the tutoring mode, accompanied by student reading, could be successfully used in American schools and colleges.

The limitations of the tutoring mode relate to the age at which it can be used, and to the amount of prerequisite knowledge and skill it requires of the student. Obviously, one would not employ this mode in the elementary grades, when students have not learned to read, much less to engage in self-directed study. But some sort of adaptation of the system might well be appropriate, even in the junior high years, if the materials assigned for study were self-instructionally designed, that is, if they were "programmed" for learning. Were such materials available, it would be possible for the teacher to expect the student to use them by himself, and then to follow such "self-study" periods by tutoring sessions devoted to questioning, discussion, assessment, and feedback to the learner.

Developments and tryouts of such combinations of instructional modes may be expected to occur in the near future.

THE LECTURE

The lecture, consisting of oral communication on the part of the teacher, is an extremely common mode of instruction in American schools. It is a very familiar mode to college teachers, and to a large extent also, to secondary school teachers. Junior high teachers might be surprised and even offended at the suggestion that their classroom behavior also includes a great deal of "lecturing," interspersed, naturally, with periods of assessment. Yet such is the case.

A lecture can accomplish, or try to accomplish, a number of different instructional objectives. Among these are the following:

1. It can establish and augment motivation to achieve. Everyone has heard lectures that inspire interest in the subject talked about, both in school and out. For the college and secondary school student particularly, a lecture that relates events of interest to the broader and larger objectives of an intellectual discipline can be of great educational value.

2. It can inform learners of the expected outcomes of learning. For example, part of a lecture on English writing might be devoted to the styles of good writers. But one probably would not expect a whole lecture to be concerned with such a function—at least not a whole series of lectures.

3. It can attempt to provide prompting and guidance to learning. But in most instances, the lecture does this very badly indeed. Some students do not have the prerequisite knowledge, others are inattentive, others may be bored. Most may be taking notes, which, so far as anyone knows, is an entirely useless activity quite unrelated to learning. The notion that one can import the essential oral communication functions from the teacher-log-student situation into the lecture hall is not very sensible. A certain number of verbal chains may be acquired in note taking, which can, to be sure, be recalled for examinations. But that is about all one can expect.

There are other limitations to the lecture as an instructional mode. Except for those instances in which the stimuli to be presented are verbal (as in certain subjects like English, philosophy, history), the lecturer must use media besides oral communication —objects, demonstrations, pictures. Assessment cannot be done in a lecture, nor can feedback be provided to the student. All in all, the use of the lecture might best be confined to the functions of motivating students and informing them of expected accomplishments. As a means of establishing conditions for learning, the lecture leaves much to be desired.

THE RECITATION CLASS

The recitation class is an instructional mode that has a long history in American schools. It has been depreciated by a generation of educational writers, probably for quite the wrong reasons. In the older tradition, the recitation class was a session in which the teacher "heard" the students perform what they had presumably learned through previous self-study, the latter being done either in the school or as homework. In other words, the recitation class is a mode devoted to assessment and feedback, and to very little else. It is true that the kind of assessment conducted, in classrooms of an earlier age, often consisted of the recitation of verbal sequences of varying lengths. But there needs to be a distinction made between *what* was being assessed, on the one hand, and *how* this function was carried out, on the other. It is recognized nowadays that the learning of verbal sequences is not always a desirable objective for instruction, and the criticism of "recitation exercises" on these grounds can be justified. But the conduct of "assessment exercises" to determine what the student has learned, and to provide him with a means of knowing what he has attained by learning, is an entirely reasonable mode for instruction.

The recitation class is another mode that depends for its effectiveness on self-instruction carried out by the student. Students in such a class are expected to be "prepared"; if a substantial proportion of them are not, the exercise has little value, since it simply has the effect of differentiating those who have mastered a learning assignment and those who have not. If previous learning has in fact been accomplished, then the questioning conducted by the teacher can have the effect of providing feedback to all the students, accomplishing a review at the same time.

The limitations of the recitation class arise not from the class exercise itself, but from the prerequisite learning that is left to the student. The purposes of instruction are not served simply by differentiating "bright" students who have found the learning assignment easy and "less bright" students who have not. If this mode is to function effectively, there must be some assurance that all members of the class can in fact learn the material assigned prior to the class meeting, within certain reasonable time limits. The recitation itself provides few clues as to the reasons why the required learning may be easy or difficult. Here is another situation in which teaching-machine programs, which are designed to be learnable by students of a wide range of abilities, may serve a particularly useful function. If the assigned learning takes the form of programmed instruction, whose content has been determined to be at the proper "level," then the succeeding recitation class can proceed readily with its valuable functions of assessment and feedback, with the assumption that all students are roughly equally well "prepared."

THE DISCUSSION CLASS

In the discussion class, the kinds of questions posed by the teacher are different from those of the recitation class. The questions assume that the knowledge required has been attained, and are designed instead to search out the nearest and the remotest implications of what has been learned. Very often, a discussion is begun by introducing a problem situation that has not been encountered during the preceding learning. If the class is in science, the question might be asked, "How would an astronaut go about determining the acceleration of a freely falling body on another planet?" Or if in English, a newly published poem of a young poet might be presented, and a discussion begun of its meaning or meanings. The oral communication that follows may originally occur between teacher and student, but for greatest effectiveness should probably progress to interactions between students. It should be emphasized particularly that the purpose of this communication is *not* to assess: differences in prerequisite knowledge among the participating students merely serves to detract from the value of the exercise. The purpose of the discussion is to make a public exploration of new ideas, of analogies, of similarities and differences among various branches of knowledge. Although novel ideas are to be encouraged, they should also be subjected to the discipline of public evaluation by other students.

The technique of conducting a successful discussion is a subtle art of the teacher, and it is not possible at the present time to specify in detail how it can best be done. This much should be said, however: the questions that are asked are not designed to elicit "facts" or "information," but rather to generate hypotheses within the students. During the course of the discussion, it is the leader's (teacher's) function to make frequent checks to see that this purpose is continually emphasized. The point of such discussion is not whether students "know the answers," but to a large extent whether they "ask the right questions."

Discussions cannot be successful unless the members of the group have previously acquired at least a certain minimum of prerequisite knowledge. A discussion of gravitational forces on distant planets cannot get off the ground unless the students know some fundamental principles about gravitational forces. A discussion of procedures of the United States Congress is similarly impossible unless the students have previously learned the principles of congressional powers and actions. Prerequisite learning *must be assumed*, regardless of how it may have been accomplished. Otherwise the discussion rapidly degenerates into an entirely inefficient attempt to have some students "catch up" with others. Again it is apparent that the prerequisite learning for any particular discussion may be done by self-instructional means, perhaps with the use of a teaching-machine program. At the high school and college level, of course, students may be able to manage their own self-instruction by means of conventional books.

A successful discussion class can be a great delight to both students and teacher. This is as it should be, since knowledge generalization is bound to be intellectual fun. Perhaps in part because of this fact, some educational writers have proposed that the discussion class (or something like it) ought to be the prototype for learning in the school. But an important limitation should be noted. As previous chapters have shown, the discussion class is *not* primarily concerned with learning at all, but with the transfer (generalizing) of what has already been learned. To make discussion the major kind of instructional exercise would therefore be deliberately to ignore the critical prior requirement of ensuring that learning occurs. To get learning to happen is still the basic problem. The conditions that bring learning about are not those of the discussion class. The major requirement of successful discussion, with its resultant effect on knowledge transfer, is certainly prior learning.

THE LABORATORY

In its most general sense, the laboratory is an instructional mode whose purpose is to present a stimulus situation that brings the student into contact with actual objects and events. Although familiarly associated with education in science, the laboratory in this broad meaning can equally well be a part of instruction in almost any subject. A laboratory period in a foreign language may present the stimuli of connected discourse in the language spoken by a native speaker. A laboratory in mathematics may begin with a complex problem requiring a variety of applications of mathematical principles for its solution. A laboratory in English writing can be designed to produce a description of some displayed object or event that is "tested" for its effectiveness in communicating. Sometimes the laboratory must be cast in the form of a field trip, as is often the case in geology and in social science. In contrast to other instructional modes, the laboratory uses actual objects and events for stimuli, rather than verbal communications about them. Of course, in language study, these events may themselves be verbal in form; but in this case they are stimuli to be responded to directly, rather than things to be "read about."

The laboratory has a fundamental importance in science instruction, as it does in other subjects. To learn Ohm's law as the verbal expression $E = IR$ into which certain numerical values can be substituted is an entirely inadequate objective for science instruction, as most science teachers are well aware. Ohm's law is a principle that combines certain concepts. Understanding of these concepts requires that they be tied in a stimulus sense to certain events in the learner's environment which can be directly observed. Accordingly, the laboratory is designed to make it possible for the student to observe and measure changes in voltage produced by changes in resistance (such as those associated with length of conducting wire). When the concepts *voltage, current,* and *resistance* are given objective meanings, Ohm's law likewise acquires a materiality that it would not otherwise have, and that is essential for further learning of other higher-level principles.

In addition, the laboratory can undoubtedly serve as a mode for teaching certain strategies and methods of science. Among these are the procedures of *formulating hypotheses, making operational definitions, controlling and manipulating variables, conducting experiments, designing "models,"* and *interpreting data.* To do all these things well naturally requires that exercises for the laboratory present the kinds of situations which will entail the use of previously acquired knowledge on the part of the student. They should have some novelty in them, so that they will not become simply exercises in "following a procedure," or in performing routines. The design of laboratory exercises having these functions is indeed a challenging task.

HOMEWORK

Most instruction in schools of today is likely to include "homework" as one mode on which considerable dependence is placed. Whereas homework assignments used to begin in about the ninth grade, the trend has been toward including them as a part of instruction well down into the elementary grades. Homework takes several forms, and may attempt to do several different things, with varying degrees of effectiveness:

1. Self-instruction on a prescribed topic, as a chapter in a textbook, the translation of a foreign language passage, the reading of a poem may constitute homework. The effectiveness of such assignments obviously depends on the feasibility of self-instruction

for the student. If the material employed makes self-instruction easy (as in the case of teaching-machine programs or programmed texts), such assignments may be quite effective even in the early grades. High school students have presumably acquired enough self-study capabilities so that reading a chapter of history, or a short story, may accomplish the required learning.

2. Practice in a variety of examples of previously learned principles is another common type of homework assignment. Examples at the end of chapters in mathematics and science texts are often used in this manner. Provided the principles have in fact been learned, such assignments can be quite effective. If the principles have not been mastered, the student may get "stuck" and be unable to instruct himself in the required principles. Should this happen frequently, one may expect homework to become a source of negative motivation for such a student.

3. Homework assignments sometimes take the form of "projects" in which the student is asked to organize a variety of activities for himself in such a way as to lead to the development of a product, like a report, a demonstration, or the description of an experiment. Some project assignments are reasonable and feasible, but some are obviously not. For example, asking a sixth-grade child to read a book and write a review of it is obviously reasonable if the book is written at a suitable vocabulary level, and such an exercise may result in some effective learning. But asking such a child to do a project requiring a scientific experiment is obviously unreasonable because the child does not have the requisite background knowledge to design and carry out such an experiment. It may even be doubted whether assignments of this latter sort are reasonable for ninth- and tenth-graders in today's schools, and for the same reason. Many "science" projects turn out to be concerned with trivial applications of well-known scientific principles. Although projects of this sort may have some motivational effects, their value as a part of science instruction appears highly doubtful at best.

On the whole, the most important function of homework would appear to be self-instruction in topics that can be presented by means of printed books, perhaps containing pictures and diagrams where necessary. This mode of instruction can perform a highly important and essential role when used in conjunction with other modes, such as the tutoring session, the recitation class, or the discussion class. Insofar as these latter modes require *prior learning*, the homework assignment is a means of providing it.

An additional implication is that homework needs to be carefully planned in two respects. First, its assignments should be integrated with preceding assessments to ensure that prerequisite knowledge has been attained, and with the subsequent conduct of classes which assume that homework learning has been effective. And second, homework assignments need to be of a nature that *all* students can readily master. Their purpose is not to distinguish between bright and dull students; rather, it is to ensure that all students have attained a specified set of prerequisite knowledges. These requirements of the homework assignment strongly suggest that the teaching-machine program or programmed self-instructional text should have outstanding usefulness for this purpose.

THE DESIGN OF INSTRUCTIONAL MODES

Modes of instruction are organizations of media to accomplish certain instructional purposes. The modes discussed here are simply those that are best known, or that have been longest in use. But many kinds of organization are possible, including some that use relatively new media, and it would not be correct to suppose that traditional ones are necessarily best. Tryouts of novel forms of media combination and organization may be expected to lead to improved exploitation of the principles governing the conditions of learning. Consider, for example, the potential effectiveness of the following sequence utilizing several media to teach the topic "Reflection and Refraction of Light":

Step 1: A *demonstration* is used, with accompanying oral communication, to teach definitions of concepts (angle of incidence, angle of reflection, angle of refraction, image, virtual image, and so on).

Step 2: A chapter of *programmed instruction* is assigned as the medium for learning the principles (the laws of reflection and refraction, images formed in a plane mirror, dispersion and deviation of light, and so on). Interspersed within the program are exercises designed to establish generalizability of the principles.

Step 3: An *assessment exercise* is conducted by the teacher, primarily to determine that the required principles have been attained. If students have not acquired these principles, they will not be able to undertake the next step.

Step 4: A brief *motion-picture sequence* is used to show a novel instance of reflection, or of refraction, or both. This introduces a *discussion* designed to answer the question "How would one go about investigating the problem shown in this film?"

Step 5: An *assessment of knowledge transfer* may now be carried out, by presenting (verbally or pictorially) to students additional "problems" of reflection and refraction.

Certain favorable characteristics may be predicted for such a combination of instructional media. The use of the demonstration serves to ensure that concepts will be soundly based upon observations of concrete objects and events. The acquisition of principles can occur in a manner that incorporates careful design of the conditions of learning, using the medium of programmed instruction, and therefore capable of individualizing the instruction. Assessment is used to ensure that all students have mastered the necessary prerequisites for a discussion, which can be introduced by means of pictures representing a real situation, avoiding the danger of excessive verbalization of the problem. Discussion can expand and refine the knowledge previously acquired, and ensure its transfer to novel problems. A final assessment can then verify the generalizability of what has been acquired.

Many other arrangements of media are possible for instruction; it is not proposed that this example would necessarily serve best for all purposes. The real point to be made is that the use of a variety of instructional modes is both feasible and potentially effective. The traditional modes are not necessarily either the best or the worst, for any given purpose. What is needed in each case is thoughtful design and management of the learning environment. This requires decisions that match the requirements of the conditions of learning, in each case, with the available media and their characteristics. If this approach is taken, it will be apparent that the technology of instruction has many modes available to meet many educational objectives.

GENERAL REFERENCES

Techniques of Instruction

De Cecco, J. P. *Human learning in the school.* New York: Holt, Rinehart and Winston, 1963.

Gage, N. L. (Ed.) *Handbook of research on teaching.* Chicago: Rand McNally, 1963.

Glaser, R. (Ed.) *Training research and education.* Pittsburgh: University of Pittsburgh Press, 1962.

Teaching Machines and Programmed Instruction

De Cecco, J. P. *Educational technology: readings in programmed instruction.* New York: Holt, Rinehart and Winston, 1964.

Glaser, R. (Ed.) *Teaching machines and programed learning, II: Data and directions.* Washington, D.C.: National Education Association, 1965.

Lumsdaine, A. A., and Glaser, R. (Eds.) *Teaching machines and programmed learning: a source book.* Washington, D.C.: National Education Association, 1960.

Schramm, W. *The research on programed instruction.* Washington, D.C.: U.S. Department of Health, Education, and Welfare, 1964. (OE-34034)

Stolurow, L. M. *Teaching by machine.* Washington, D.C.: U.S. Department of Health, Education, and Welfare, 1961. (Cooperative Research Monograph No. 6, OE34010.)

Motion Pictures and Television in Instruction

Gropper, G. L. Why is a picture worth a thousand words? *A V Communic. Rev.*, 1963, *11*, 75–95.

Lumsdaine, A. A. Instruments and media of instruction. In

N. L. Gage (Ed.), *Handbook of research on teaching.* Chicago: Rand McNally, 1963. Pp. 583–682.

May, M. A., and Lumsdaine, A. A. *Learning from films.* New Haven, Conn.: Yale University Press, 1958.

Roshal, S. M. The instructional film. In G. Finch (Ed.), *Educational and training media: a symposium.* Washington, D.C.: National Academy of Sciences-National Research Council, 1960. Pp. 114–121.

REFERENCES

Numerals in brackets indicate page numbers where reference is cited.

AUSUBEL, D. P. *The psychology of meaningful verbal learning.* New York: Grune & Stratton, 1963. [15, 53, 61, 156, 164, 171, 203, 214, 235]

AUSUBEL, D. P. The use of advance organizers in the learning and retention of meaningful verbal material. *J. educ. Psychol.,* 1960, *51,* 267–272. [221]

BARNES, J. M., and UNDERWOOD, B. J. "Fate" of first-list associations in transfer theory. *J. exp. Psychol.,* 1959, *58,* 97–105. [107]

BLOOM, B. S. (Ed.), ENGELHART, M. D., FURST, E. J., HILL, W. H., and KRATHWOHL, D. R. *Taxonomy of educational objectives. Handbook 1: Cognitive domain.* New York: McKay, 1956. [261, 262, 266]

BRIGGS, L. J., and REED, H. B. The curve of retention for substance material. *J. exp. Psychol.,* 1943, *32,* 513–517. [156]

BROOKS, N. *Language and language learning: theory and practice.* New York: Harcourt, Brace & World, 1959. [203]

BROWN, J. S. *The motivation of behavior.* New York: McGraw-Hill, 1961. [207, 235]

BRUNER, J. S. The act of discovery. *Harvard Educ. Rev.,* 1961, *31,* 21–32. [256]

BRUNER, J. S., GOODNOW, J. J., and AUSTIN, G. A. *A study of thinking.* New York: Wiley, 1956. [169, 171]

CARR, H. Teaching and learning. *J. genet. Psychol.*, 1930, 37, 189–219.   [216]

COFER, C. N. (Ed.) *Verbal learning and verbal behavior.* New York: McGraw-Hill, 1961.   [61, 99, 112]

COMMISSION ON SCIENCE EDUCATION. *Science: a process approach.* Part 4. Washington, D.C.: American Association for the Advancement of Science, 1963.   [185, 187, 229]

COMMISSION ON SCIENCE EDUCATION. *Science: a process approach. Teachers guide.* Washington, D.C.: American Association for the Advancement of Science, 1963.   [203]

CONGDON, A. R. *Training in high school mathematics essential for success in certain college subjects.* New York: Teachers College, Columbia University, 1930.   [203]

DE CECCO, J. P. *Human learning in the school.* New York: Holt, Rinehart and Winston, 1963.   [236, 296]

DE CECCO, J. P. *Educational technology.* New York: Holt, Rinehart and Winston, 1964.   [252, 266, 296]

DEESE, J. From the isolated verbal unit to connected discourse. In C. N. COFER (Ed.), *Verbal learning and verbal behavior.* New York: McGraw-Hill, 1961.   [121]

DEESE, J. *The psychology of learning.* (2nd ed.) New York: McGraw-Hill, 1958.   [112]

DRESSEL, P. L. (Ed.) *Evaluation in general education.* Dubuque, Iowa: Brown, 1954.   [262, 266]

DURRELL, D. D. *Improving reading instruction.* New York: Harcourt, Brace & World, 1956.   [204]

EBBINGHAUS, H. *Memory: A contribution to experimental psychology.* (Transl. by H. A. Ruger.) New York: Teachers College, Columbia University, 1913.   [14]

ESTES, W. K. The statistical approach to learning theory. In S. Koch (Ed.), *Psychology: A study of a science; Vol. 2. General systematic formulations, learning, and special processes.* New York: McGraw-Hill, 1959.   [76]

FAGERSTROM, W. H. *Mathematical facts and processes prerequisite to the study of the calculus.* New York: Teachers College, Columbia University, 1933.   [204]

FERSTER, C. B., and SKINNER, B. F. *Schedules of reinforcement.* New York: Appleton-Century-Crofts, 1957. [36, 78]

FLAVELL, J. H. *The developmental psychology of Jean Piaget.* Princeton, N.J.: Van Nostrand, 1963. [140]

FRENCH, W. *Behavioral goals of general education in high school.* New York: Russell Sage, 1957. [242, 266]

FRIES, C. C. *Linguistics and reading.* New York: Holt, Rinehart and Winston, 1963. [196, 197, 198, 204]

GAGE, N. L. (Ed.) *Handbook of research on teaching.* Chicago: Rand McNally, 1963. [296]

GAGNÉ, R. M. The acquisition of knowledge. *Psychol. Rev.*, 1962, *69*, 355–365. [153]

GAGNÉ, R. M. The learning requirements for enquiry. *J. Res. Science Teaching*, 1963, *1*, 144–153(b). [256]

GAGNÉ, R. M. Learning and proficiency in mathematics. *Math. Teacher*, 1963, *56*, 620–626(a). [149, 245, 253]

GAGNÉ, R. M. Problem solving. In A. W. MELTON (Ed.), *Categories of human learning.* New York: Academic Press, 1964(a). [134, 145, 161, 171, 203]

GAGNÉ, R. M. The implications of instructional objectives for learning. In C. M. Lindvall (Ed.), *Defining educational objectives.* Pittsburgh: University of Pittsburgh Press, 1964(b). [203, 242]

GAGNÉ, R. M., and BASSLER, O. C. Study of retention of some topics of elementary non-metric geometry. *J. educ. Psychol.*, 1963, *54*, 123–131. [148, 151, 165]

GAGNÉ, R. M., and BOLLES, R. C. A review of factors in learning efficiency. In E. GALANTER (Ed.), *Automatic teaching: the state of the art.* New York: Wiley, 1959. [205]

GAGNÉ, R. M., and BROWN, L. T. Some factors in the programming of conceptual learning. *J. exp. Psychol.*, 1961, *62*, 313–321. [224]

GAGNÉ, R. M., MAYOR, J. R., GARSTENS, H. L., and PARADISE, N. E. Factors in acquiring knowledge of a mathematical task. *Psychol. Monogr.*, 1962, *76*, No. 7 (Whole No. 526). [153, 224, 233, 258]

GAGNÉ, R. M., and PARADISE, N. E. Abilities and learning sets in knowledge acquisition. *Psychol. Monogr.*, 1961, 75, No. 14 (Whole No. 518). [153]

GAGNÉ, R. M., and STAFF, Univ. of Md. Math. Project. Some factors in learning non-metric geometry. *Monogr. Soc. Res. Child Develpm.*, 1965 (in press). [152, 153]

GALANTER, E. H. (Ed.) *Automatic teaching: the state of the art.* New York: Wiley, 1959. [266]

GARDNER, J. W. *Excellence.* New York: Harper & Row, 1961. [266]

GIBSON, E. J. A systematic application of the concepts of generalization and differentiation to verbal learning. *Psychol. Rev.*, 1940, 47, 196–229. [124]

GIBSON, E. J. Retroactive inhibition as a function of degree of generalization between tasks. *J. exp. Psychol.*, 1941, 28, 93–115. [119]

GIBSON, E. J. Intra-list generalization as a factor in verbal learning. *J. exp. Psychol.*, 1942, 30, 185–200. [118]

GILBERT, T. F. Mathetics: the technology of education. *J. Mathetics*, 1962, 1, 7–73. [58, 91, 93, 112, 139, 269]

GLASER, R. (Ed.) *Training research and education.* Pittsburgh: University of Pittsburgh Press, 1962. [296]

GLASER, R. (Ed.) *Teaching machines and programed learning, II: Data and directions.* Washington, D.C.: National Education Association, 1965. [266, 282, 296]

GLASER, R., and KLAUS, D. J. Proficiency measurement: Assessing human performance. In R. M. GAGNÉ (Ed.), *Psychological principles in system development.* New York: Holt, Rinehart, and Winston, 1962. [258]

GOODNOW, J. J. Determinants of choice-distribution in two choice situations. *Am. J. Psychol.*, 1955, 68, 106–116. [169]

GOSS, A. E. Comments on Professor Noble's paper. In C. N. COFER and B. S. MUSGRAVE (Eds.), *Verbal behavior and learning* New York: McGraw-Hill, 1963. [99]

GROPPER, G. L. Why is a picture worth a thousand words? *A V Communic. Rev.*, 1963, 11, 75–95. [281, 296]

GROSE, R. F., and BIRNEY, R. C. (Eds.) *Transfer of learning* Princeton, N.J.: Van Nostrand, 1963. [236]

GUTHRIE, E. R. *The psychology of learning.* New York: Harper & Row, 1935.   [12, 33, 77, 88]

GUTTMAN, N., and KALISH, H. I. Discriminability and stimulus generalization. *J. exp. Psychol.,* 1956, *51,* 79–88.   [79, 80]

HALL, J. F. *Psychology of motivation.* Philadelphia: Lippincott, 1961.   [207, 236]

HARLOW, H. F. The formation of learning sets. *Psychol. Rev.,* 1949, *56,* 51–65.   [16, 129]

HARLOW, H. F. The development of learning in the rhesus monkey. *Amer. Scientist,* 1959, *47,* 459–479.   [59]

HARLOW, H. F., and HARLOW, M. K. Learning to think. *Scient. Amer.,* 1949, *181,* 36–39.   [140]

HILGARD, E. R. *Theories of learning.* (2nd ed.) New York: Appleton-Century-Crofts, 1956.   [29]

HILGARD, E. R. (Ed.) *Theories of learning and instruction, 1964. Sixty-third yearb.* Chicago: National Society for the Study of Education, 1964, Part I.   [235]

HILGARD, E. R., and HUMPHREYS, L. G. The retention of conditioned discrimination in man. *J. gen. Psychol.,* 1938, *19,* 111–125.   [71]

HILL, W. F. *Learning: a survey of psychological interpretations.* San Francisco: Chandler, 1963.   [29, 86]

HOVLAND, C. I. "Inhibition of reinforcement" and phenomena of experimental extinction. *Proc. Nat. Acad. Sci.,* 1936, *22,* 430–433.   [68]

HOVLAND, C. I. The generalization of conditioned responses. I. The sensory generalization of conditioned responses with varying frequencies of tone. *J. gen. Psychol.,* 1937, *17,* 125–148.   [69, 70]

HULL, C. L. The concept of the habit-family hierarchy and maze learning. *Psychol. Rev.,* 1934, *41,* 33–54, 134–152.   [59]

HULL, C. L. *Principles of behavior.* New York: Appleton-Century-Crofts, 1943.   [12, 29, 59]

HUNT, J. McV. *Intelligence and experience.* New York: Ronald, 1961.   [236]

JAMES, W. *Principles of psychology.* New York: Holt, Rinehart and Winston, 1890.   [90]

JENKINS, H. M., and HARRISON, R. H. Effect of discrimination training on auditory generalization. *J. exp. Psychol.*, 1960, 59, 246–253. [80]

JENKINS, J. J. Mediated associations: paradigms and situations. In C. N. Cofer and B. S. Musgrave (Eds.), *Verbal behavior and learning.* New York: McGraw-Hill, 1963. [99]

JENSEN, A. R. An empirical theory of the serial-position effect. *J. Psychol.*, 1962, 53, 127–142. [101]

JOHNSON, D. M. *The psychology of thought and judgment.* New York: Harper & Row, 1955. [171]

KARPLUS, R. Beginning a study in elementary school science. *Amer. J. Physics*, 1962, 30, 1–9. [186]

KATONA, G. *Organizing and memorizing.* New York: Columbia University Press, 1940. [16, 156, 158, 159, 164, 171]

KEARNEY, N. C. *Elementary school objectives.* New York: Russell Sage, 1953. [242, 266]

KELLER, F. A., and SCHOENFELD, W. N. *Principles of psychology.* New York: Appleton-Century-Crofts, 1950. [29, 86, 112]

KENDLER, H. H. The concept of the concept. In A. W. Melton (Ed.), *Categories of human learning.* New York: Academic Press, 1964. [58, 145]

KENDLER, H. H., and KENDLER, T. S. Effect of verbalization on reversal shifts in children. *Science*, 1961, 141, 1619–1620. [133]

KERSH, B. Y. Programing classroom instruction. In R. Glaser (Ed.), *Teaching machines and programed learning, II: Data and directions.* Washington, D.C.: National Education Association, 1965. [282]

KIMBLE, G. A. *Hilgard and Marquis' "Conditioning and learning."* New York: Appleton-Century-Crofts, 1961. [13, 29, 35, 36, 58, 68, 71, 76, 86, 225]

KLAUS, D. Programing techniques. In R. Glaser (Ed.), *Teaching machines and programed learning, II: Data and directions.* Washington, D.C.: National Education Association, 1965. [275]

KNIGHT, F. B. Some considerations of method. In G. M. Whipple (Ed.), *National Society for the Study of Education, Twenty-*

ninth yearbook. Report of the society's committee on arithmetic. Bloomington, Ill.: Public School, 1930, Chap. 4. [203]

KOFFKA, K. *The growth of the mind.* (2nd ed.) New York: Harcourt, Brace & World, 1929.   [15]

KÖHLER, W. *The mentality of apes.* New York: Harcourt, Brace & World, 1927.   [15]

KÖHLER, W. *Gestalt psychology.* New York: Liveright, 1929. [15]

KRUEGER, W. C. F. Rate of progress as related to difficulty of assignment. *J. educ. Psychol.,* 1946, 37, 247–249.   [102]

LEAVITT, H. J., and SCHLOSBERG, H. The retention of verbal and of motor skills. *J. exp. Psychol.,* 1944, 34, 404–417.   [81]

LINDQUIST, E. F. (Ed.) *Educational measurement.* Washington, D.C.: American Council on Education, 1950.   [266]

LINDVALL, C. M. (Ed.) *Defining educational objectives.* Pittsburgh: University of Pittsburgh Press, 1964.   [242, 266]

LORGE, I., TUCKMAN, J., AIKMAN, L., SPIEGEL, J., and Moss, G. Problem solving by teams and by individuals in a field setting. *J. educ. Psychol.,* 1955, 46, 160–166.   [257]

LOVELL, K. *The growth of basic mathematical and scientific concepts in children.* New York: Philosophical Library, 1961. [140]

LUMSDAINE, A. A. Instruments and media of instruction. In N. L. Gage (Ed.), *Handbook of research on teaching.* Chicago: Rand McNally, 1963. Pp. 583–682.   [281, 296]

LUMSDAINE, A. A., and GLASER, R. (Eds.) *Teaching machines and programmed learning: a source book.* Washington, D.C.: National Education Association, 1960.   [266, 296]

McCLELLAND, D. C., ATKINSON, J. W., CLARK, R. A., and LOWELL, E. L. *The achievement motive.* New York: Appleton-Century-Crofts, 1953.   [207, 236]

McGEOCH, J. A. *The psychology of human learning.* New York: McKay, 1942.   [14]

McGEOCH, J. A., and IRION, A. L. *The psychology of human learning.* New York: McKay, 1952.   [29, 102, 112, 118]

MAGER, R. F. *Preparing objectives for programmed instruction.* San Francisco: Fearon, 1962.   [242]

MAIER, N. R. F. Reasoning in humans: I. On direction. *J. comp. Psychol.*, 1930, *10*, 115–143.   [160, 221]

MAY, M. A., and LUMSDAINE, A. A. *Learning from films.* New Haven, Conn.: Yale University Press, 1958.   [297]

MELTON, A. W. Learning. In W. S. Monroe (Ed.), *Encyclopedia of educational research.* New York: Macmillan, 1940.   [14]

MELTON, A. W. The taxonomy of human learning: overview. In A. W. Melton (Ed.), *Categories of human learning.* New York: Academic Press, 1964.   [14]

MELTON, A. W. (Ed.) *Categories of human learning.* New York: Academic Press, 1964.   [29, 61]

MILL, J. *Analysis of the phenomena of the human mind.* (Ed. by A. Bain, A. Findlater, and G. Grote; ed. with additional notes by J. S. Mill.) London: Longmans, 1869.   [9]

MILLER, G. A. *Language and communication.* New York: McGraw-Hill, 1951.   [103, 171, 200]

MILLER, G. A. The magical number seven; plus or minus two: some limits on our capacity for processing information. *Psychol. Rev.*, 1956, *63*, 81–97.   [101]

MOWRER, O. H. *Learning theory and behavior.* New York: Wiley, 1960 (a).   [34, 35, 37, 60, 61, 85, 86]

MOWRER, O. H. *Learning theory and the symbolic processes.* New York: Wiley, 1960 (b).   [59, 61, 171]

MURDOCK, B. B., JR. The retention of individual items. *J. exp. Psychol.*, 1961, *62*, 618–625.   [106]

NATIONAL COUNCIL OF TEACHERS OF ENGLISH, COMMISSION ON THE ENGLISH CURRICULUM. *The English language arts for today's children.* New York: Appleton-Century-Crofts, 1954. [204]

NATIONAL COUNCIL OF TEACHERS OF ENGLISH, COMMISSION ON THE ENGLISH CURRICULUM. *The English language arts in the secondary school.* New York: Appleton-Century-Crofts, 1956. [204]

NATIONAL COUNCIL OF TEACHERS OF MATHEMATICS. *The learning of mathematics: its theory and practice.* 21st Yearbook. Washington, D.C.: The Council, 1953.   [204]

NOBLE, C. E. Meaningfulness and familiarity. In C. N. Cofer

and B. S. Musgrave (Eds.), *Verbal behavior and learning.*
New York: McGraw-Hill, 1963.   [103]

NORTHROP, F. S. C. *The logic of the sciences and the humanities.*
New York: Macmillan, 1947.   [32]

PATRICK, C. *What is creative thinking?* New York: Philosophical
Library, 1955.   [171]

PAVLOV, I. P. *Conditioned reflexes.* (Transl. by G. V. Anrep.)
London: Oxford University Press, 1927. (Also available in
paperback; New York: Dover.)   [12, 29, 58, 86]

PIAGET, J. *Construction of reality in the child.* New York: Basic
Books, 1954.   [140]

POSTMAN, L. The present status of interference theory. In C. N.
Cofer (Ed.), *Verbal learning and verbal behavior.* New York:
McGraw-Hill, 1961.   [58, 139]

POSTMAN, L. Short-term memory and incidental learning. In A. W.
Melton (Ed.), *Categories of human learning.* New York:
Academic Press, 1964.   [14, 209]

RIESSMAN, F. *The culturally deprived child.* New York: Harper
& Row, 1962.   [208]

ROBINSON, E. S. *Association theory today.* New York: Appleton-
Century-Crofts, 1932.   [14]

ROSHAL, S. M. The instructional film. In G. Finch (Ed.), *Educational and training media: a symposium.* Washington, D.C.:
National Academy of Sciences–National Research Council,
1960. Pp. 114–121.   [297]

ROSHAL, S. M. Film-mediated learning with varying representation
of the task: viewing angle, portrayal of demonstration, motion,
and student participation. In A. A. Lumsdaine (Ed.), *Student
response in programmed instruction.* Washington, D.C.: National Academy of Sciences–National Research Council, 1961.
[279]

RUSSELL, D. H. *Children's thinking.* Boston: Ginn, 1956.   [140]

SALTZ, E. Response pretraining: differentiation or availability?
J. exp. Psychol., 1961, 62, 583–587.   [123]

SCHRAMM, W. *The research on programed instruction.* Washington, D.C.: U.S. Department of Health, Education, and Welfare, 1964 (OE-34034).   [282, 296]

SCHWAB, J. J. The teaching of science as enquiry. In *The teaching of science*. Cambridge, Mass.: Harvard University Press, 1962. [214]

SHAW, G. B. *Adventures of the black girl in her search for God*. New York: Putnam, 1959. [62]

SKINNER, B. F. *The behavior of organisms; an experimental analysis*. New York: Appleton-Century-Crofts, 1938. [11, 12, 29, 38, 58, 59, 71, 86]

SKINNER, B. F. *Walden Two*. New York: Macmillan, 1948. [86]

SKINNER, B. F. Are theories of learning necessary? *Psychol. Rev.*, 1950, 57, 193–216. [81]

SKINNER, B. F. *Science and human behavior*. New York: Macmillan, 1953. [86]

SKINNER, B. F. *Verbal behavior*. New York: Appleton-Century-Crofts, 1957. [112]

SPENCE, K. W. *Behavior theory and conditioning*. New Haven, Conn.: Yale University Press, 1956. [64]

STEPHENS, J. M. Transfer of learning. In C. W. Harris (Ed.), *Encyclopedia of educational research*. New York: Macmillan, 1960. [236]

STOLUROW, L. M. *Teaching by machine*. Washington, D.C.: U.S. Department of Health, Education, and Welfare, 1961. (Cooperative Research Monograph No. 6, OE34010.) [296]

TAYLOR, D. W., BERRY, P. C., and BLOCK, C. H. Does group participation when using brainstorming facilitate or inhibit creative thinking? *Tech. Rept. No. 1, NR 150–166*, Department of Industrial Administration and Department of Psychology, Yale University, 1957. [257]

TAYLOR, J. A. The relationship of anxiety to the conditioned eyelid response. *J. exp. Psychol.*, 1951, 41, 81–92. [65]

THORNDIKE, E. L. Animal intelligence: An experimental study of the associative processes in animals. *Psychol. Rev. Monogr. Suppl.*, 1898, 2, No. 4 (Whole No. 8). [10, 58, 74]

THORNDIKE, E. L. *Animal intelligence*. New York: Macmillan, 1911. [29, 86]

THORNDIKE, E. L. *Human learning*. New York: Appleton-Century-Crofts, 1931. [30, 59]

TOLMAN, E. C. *Purposive behavior in animals and men.* New York: Appleton-Century-Crofts, 1932.   [12, 30]

TOLMAN, E. C. There is more than one kind of learning. *Psychol. Rev.,* 1949, *56,* 144–155.   [59]

TRAVERS, R. M. W. *Essentials of learning.* New York: Macmillan, 1963. Chap. 6.   [236]

TYLER, R. W. Achievement testing and curriculum construction. In E. G. Williamson (Ed.), *Trends in student personnel work.* Minneapolis: University of Minnesota Press, 1949. Pp. 391–407.   [242, 266]

UNDERWOOD, B. J. Studies of distributed practice: IX. Learning and retention of paired adjectives as a function of intralist similarity. *J. exp. Psychol.,* 1953, *45,* 143–149.   [120]

UNDERWOOD, B. J. An evaluation of the Gibson theory of verbal learning. In C. N. Cofer (Ed.), *Verbal learning and verbal behavior.* New York: McGraw-Hill, 1961.   [140]

UNDERWOOD, B. J. Laboratory studies of verbal learning. In E. R. Hilgard (Ed.), *Theories of learning and instruction.* Sixty-third Yearb. Chicago: National Society for the Study of Education. Part I, 1964 (a).   [105]

UNDERWOOD, B. J. The representativeness of rote verbal learning. In A. W. Melton (Ed.), *Categories of human learning.* New York: Academic Press, 1964 (b).   [14, 58]

UNDERWOOD, B. J., and SHULZ, R. W. *Meaningfulness and verbal learning.* Philadelphia: Lippincott, 1960.   [99, 103, 112]

UNESCO. *The teaching of modern languages.* New York: Columbia University Press, 1955.   [204]

WATSON, J. B. *Psychology from the standpoint of a behaviorist.* Philadelphia: Lippincott, 1919.   [12]

WATSON, J. B., and RAYNER, R. Conditioned emotional reactions. *J. exp. Psychol.,* 1920, *3,* 1–14.   [65]

WERTHEIMER, M. *Productive thinking.* New York: Harper & Row, 1945.   [15, 16, 30, 171]

WILSON, A. B. Class segregation and aspirations of youth. *Amer. Sociol. Rev.,* 1959, *24,* 836–845.   [208]

WOODWORTH, R. S. *Dynamics of behavior.* New York: Holt, Rinehart and Winston, 1958.   [59, 61, 140, 171]